THUNDERBOLT! is the story of a man, a plane and a fighter group in the deadly air war over Europe in World War II.

When Robert S. Johnson returned from the European Theatre in 1944 he was the highest-scoring American ace of the war, with 28 confirmed kills against the fighter pilots of the Luftwaffe.

The plan he flew was the Republic P-47C Thunderbolt, a rugged 2,000 horsepower fighter that weighed seven tons. British pilots told Johnson that the "Jug" wouldn't stand a chance against the maneuverable German ME-109 and the Focke Wulf 190!

But in the hands of aces like Johnson and Gabreski the Thunderbolt proved itself the most deadly fighter plane of the war. At the end of hostilities, Johnson and his comrades of the 56th Fighter Group had shot down more German planes than any fighter group in the E.T.O. During two years of fighting they lost 128 Thunderbolts in combat, but they destroyed 1,006 German aircraft—a ratio of eight to one against the toughest opposition American pilots have ever met!

Air Force Photo

Captain Robert S. Johnson

An Extraordinary Story of a
World War II Ace

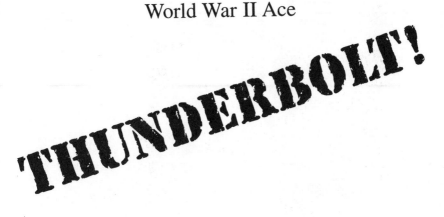

By Robert S. Johnson

THE HONORIBUS PRESS
Spartanburg, South Carolina

ISBN 1-885354-05-3

This edition published by arrangement with Honoribus Press.

First Printing: July, 1959
Second Printing: May, 1961
Third Printing: September, 1963
Fourth Printing: July, 1970
Fifth Printing: July, 1971
Sixth Printing: January, 1973
Seventh Printing: September, 1997
Eighth Printing: February, 1999

Printed in the United States of America
Altman Printing Co., Inc.
Spartanburg, SC

Cover Painting by Harley Copic

DEDICATION

. . . to all those men within whom burns the spirit of the fighter pilot; the men who fought as aces; the others to whom fate was unkind and who fell in battle; to the countless others who sought eagerly to fly the fighters, but who fought a war equally vital and deadly—in the bombers and transports, the tiny liaison planes and the swift reconnaissance ships; to all these men, and to the youths of today who have yet to share with us the wonder and the spirit of our world on high; to all of you, I respectfully dedicate this book.

Robert S. Johnson

Air Force Photo

When the massive Republic P-47C Thunderbolt fighters first arrived in England, veteran Royal Air Force pilots told Johnson and his friends from the 56th Fighter Group that the "Jug" wouldn't stand a chance against the maneuverable German planes. Disregarding these dire forecasts, the 56th Fighter Group turned the P-47, the most rugged fighter of the war, into one of the deadliest fighters in history.

Streaming heavy contrails, a swarm of Fortresses roars toward German targets. One of the Thunderbolt's prime mission assignments was to provide close escort for these "Big Friends."

FINAL MISSION

Captain Robert S. Johnson   56th Fighter Group

1

There were three of them. Each with double wings and a whirling propeller flashing in the bright Oklahoma sun. I first saw them as they rolled on their backs, arcing over to inverted flight to begin a plunge for the earth. The ground seemed terrifyingly close to the descending trio. For a moment the sun gleaming off their whirling propellers made three simultaneous flashes of light in the sky. The beautiful winged machines increased rapidly in size, slicing downward from the blue as a single entity.

I did not know it then, and I would not appreciate for years to come the rare spectacle of precision piloting which

I observed. I could only stare, utterly fascinated, as the three little pursuits seemed to rush headlong to oblivion, about to dash themselves into the ground.

Then I heard their cry. A shrill and weird sound; the painful whine of the engines, whirling propellers faster and faster as they flung the little planes through the air.

The three pursuits were almost into the ground, when the planes were wrenched from their dives. Three hands, operating as one, gripping control sticks in three different cockpits, flawlessly timed, hauling back. The trio snapped up into the sky. I followed every motion, struck dumb, staring, as the pursuits zoomed up and over, twisted and turned intricately as if a single hand were maneuvering them, then floated mysteriously in an invisible balance of their wings and of gravity.

In later years, I have been able to look back and recognize this scene as *the* moment: the very first time I had ever *seen* an airplane. The fascination of these three snappy pursuits, orange wings bright in the sun, alive, incredibly agile, held for the eight-year-old boy I then was the barest promise that would one day be fulfilled in a way not even the dreams of youth could imagine.

That was on a morning in the summer of 1928, in the town of Lawton, Oklahoma. My dad shouted for the kids to pile into the car. That meant myself and my two older sisters, Dorothy and Margaret. And Pat, of course, my little white Spitz.

A ride with Dad was always a special event. The Johnson family owned a 1926 Essex, which likely was the most reliable auto in the town of Lawton. Since he had been twelve years old, Dad had been an automobile mechanic, and worked at a garage in Lawton. The wonderful thing about our Essex was that Dad had fitted the muffler with a cutout. I could reach down to grasp a hidden wire and bypass the muffler. At once a horrible roaring noise was produced. Sometimes Dad took a dim view of my actions. I would wait until we were in the center of Lawton and everything was peaceful and quiet. Then I'd jerk up on the wire and the Essex would boom lustily.

On this particular morning we left the house and, four miles later, turned onto the old military road, Fort Sill Boulevard. Time, aided by the passing of many military convoys, and the assorted tanks, trucks and wagons, had cracked and split the concrete. The Essex bumped its way merrily down the Boulevard, and, as we drove, Dad mentioned something about an air show at the Army's Post Field. I didn't know what he was talking about. I'd never heard of an "air show," and since I'd never seen an airplane, I didn't even care.

Frankly, I wished I didn't have to be in the car. I was supposed to go fishing that afternoon, and what could be more fun than fishing? It wasn't too bad, though. I knew we would visit Mr. Rogers at the big Rogers Dairy, and that helped to make up for losing out on the fishing. Mr. Rogers had a large dairy herd, mules, and other animals in large numbers. Best of all, he had riding horses, and Dad said that likely I would be able to get a ride. That made everything okay.

We were almost to the dairy; the Essex was grinding its way up the long sloping hill which lay just before Mr. Rogers's place. I stood up to get a better view. I could see the barns and the silo, and I tried to see if any of the riding horses were out. The dairy was on the left side of Fort Sill Boulevard, and Post Field to the right.

I'd seen the airfield many times before, but it was only a big empty space with high and thick buffalo grass covering the field. There were plenty of those in Oklahoma, and Post Field was nothing special. But something was going on; hun-

dreds of people milled around the field. And so many cars!
They were parked, it seemed, by the hundreds. Wagons and
horses were also on the field, making the whole place look
like a county-fair ground. Clouds of dust boiled up and . . .

There—in the sky! Three tiny airplanes. . . . I stared as
they plunged earthward. The rest of the Johnson family
stared right with me. Dad jammed on the brakes and the
Essex banged to a stop. The pursuits rushed closer and closer
to the ground, until the scream of their engines drowned out
even my sisters' excited shrieks.

And then they swooped out of their dives, leaped again
for the sky in their twisting maneuvers.

Dad started up the Essex and continued on to the dairy.
My eyes never left the field. There were so many planes on
the ground! I saw giant bombers with great fabric wings and
big wooden propellers. I didn't know what they were, just
tremendous airplanes, but Dad told me they were bombers,
and explained what they were supposed to do. Later that
day he took me to the field and showed me the big machine
guns, and the bombs fastened to the fuselage and the wings.

Dad stopped the car just inside the gate, where Mr. Rogers
was waiting for us. Any other time I would have dashed inside to where the horses were tied or fenced, but not today.
I was jumping up and down on the seat, frantic to see what
was happening at the field.

Dad grinned. He swung me up on his shoulders so that I
could straddle his neck. The view was perfect. The three
little pursuits were back again. Dad told me they were very
fast and maneuverable, and that the Air Service used them
for air fighting. Then I didn't even listen any more, just
watched.

They were so low most of the time! They didn't always

stay in their tight formation. Sometimes they would swoop upwards, and the three planes would seem to explode outward in different directions, the pilots looping up and around, to come together again in a breath-taking dive.

Dad told me they were Army pilots known as the Three Musketeers, and that they were some of the best fliers in the world. I certainly believed that! He explained some of the maneuvers to me, and I still remember the descriptions —spoken as the pursuits went through their paces—as they slow-rolled and barrel-rolled. They split-S'd, looped, chandelled. They whirled through Immelmanns, did vertical reverses, skidded wildly, flew inverted across the field. Every now and then they would dive for the ground, upside down. At the last moment the pilots would roll out neatly and burst across the field, their wheels almost skimming the buffalo grass.

The hours fled; we watched the last plane in the air land. The pilot taxied over to the long line of pursuits and bombers, and the big propeller came to a halt.

I watched, still on Dad's shoulders, until the people began climbing into their cars to drive away. The dust began to rise in thick clouds, and soon most of the field was obscured. I protested as Dad turned around and walked to the farmhouse; I wanted to see more. That was all; Dad gave me a playful whack on the behind and sent me to fetch a can of milk. I don't think I even looked at the farm animals. Who wanted to ride a horse *now!* All the way home I was quiet, thinking only of the airplanes. That night Mom complained because I hardly touched my food.

I was dreaming. Every eight-year-old boy *knows* what he's going to be when he grows up. Me—I had wanted the life of the cowboy. I'd ride beautiful horses and live in the open. Or, maybe, I'd even be a fireman! Then, sometimes, there was nothing more wonderful than to be a locomotive engineer.

But now—who wanted to do *any* of these things! *I* was going to fly. I just knew that I would! I wanted to be, I was going to be, an Army pilot, the *best* Army pilot in the world. I would fly a snappy pursuit like one of those three little biplanes I'd seen. I'd fly just like the Three Musketeers.

2

It was a beautiful sunny day. No time to pay strict attention to English lessons. Besides, I was daydreaming about airplanes, a disease to which I had recently succumbed. I found far more interest in the sight of two Army blimps floating lazily over Fort Sill than I did in the technicalities of splitting infinitives. The two blimps swung gently in the breeze at five hundred feet, held captive by their cables anchored close together near the balloon hangar on the Fort.

A vivid streak of flame burst suddenly into existence. Not a sound reached me, just that startling, silent flash of fire, then deep red flame mushrooming into the sky.

I stared, unbelieving. Several tiny figures tumbled through the air, twitching and jerking, as if in a frenzy. The flames engulfed both the blimps, the cables sagged, and in moments only a pall of dirty black smoke was left, drifting idly out of sight.

The next day the reality of what I had seen struck home. The hydrogen gas within one of the observation blimps had, without warning, exploded. Searing flame burst into the sky above, curled downward, licked into the personnel basket. Three men at least, perhaps four, caressed by that terrible flick of fire, had leaped in agony into space, and died.

Fort Sill was a Field Artillery School, one of the largest in the country. Often hundreds of troops would be out on the firing range, blasting with their artillery, over which hovered the big observation balloons and the blimps from which observers directed fire. At Post Field—the object of my attention since the unexpected appearance of the Three Musketeers—were based the observation planes and the pursuits which worked as advance units for the artillery.

Fort Sill lies in a valley, bordered by the foothills of the Wichita Mountains, which rise to the northwest. To the east stretch the seemingly endless rolling and flat plains, balanced by granite mountains jutting into the sky.

One of these peaks, Signal Mountain, rose to its full height within the Army's artillery range. From Signal Mountain we enjoyed a marvelous view of Fort Sill and the country where I was spending, I would come to realize, perhaps the finest years of my life. Far below us Fort Sill lay sprawled in the valley, sprinkled heavily with trees. At the right time of day the sun transformed Medicine Creek into flashing reflections, where the stream wound its way through the fort.

We could see the old Indian stockade, and the rock jail nearby. The earth and air all about me were rich in history. The basement of that very same jail had once held prisoner no less fearsome a figure than the Apache warrior, Geronimo, and it was within those walls that he had finally perished. Often, I visited this last encampment of the Indian, and wondered about his time.

The valley was abundant with oaks, maples, cottonwoods. At the eastern end of Fort Sill squatted the stockade, a massive and unlovely structure with walls of white rock, three feet thick. Here, being weathered slowly by the years, were the plaques on which I could read of Lieutenants Robert E. Lee, Ulysses S. Grant, William T. Sherman . . . commemorating the days when they had passed through in the mid-1840's, in the midst of the Indian Wars.

With several friends I would climb Signal Mountain, or imitate a mountain goat in scaling the steep bluffs which lay between the Signal Mountain peak and the fort where troops fired blazing shells from their big guns. Most of the time the artillery fired the big guns at night, and sometimes they used tracers. Even when they didn't, the shells were so hot we could see the incandescent steel arcing its path through the air.

Each exploding shell was another brilliant white flash. A soundless detonation in the dark. Sometimes a battery of guns would fire, the red phantoms would streak in a jumbled group up and over and down, and then the sound, ragged blasts and crumps, would reach us. More silent releases of light, and again a mass of exploding sound snatching at our ears as we watched from the bluffs.

If we looked upward with care, and concentrated, we could see the ragged blue exhausts of the observation planes, circling like droning ghosts in the night sky. This was the best part of the night firings. The Oklahoma night under a full moon was a landscape painted in faint blue and unearthly light. If there were high clouds, then the valley and the mountains beyond would become shrouded in blackness. Nothing was so startling during these times as an observation plane grumbling its way overhead, and then exploding the darkness with a release of flares.

Ever since watching the Three Musketeers perform in the aerial display by the Army's Air Service, I had special reason for visiting the Rogers Dairy or Fort Sill so that I might watch the planes at Post Field. Before long I came to know by heart the details of every one of the different types of planes at the field.

I identified each of the observation planes and the bombers, and came to recognize the various trainers which visited the grass field. My favorites were still the fighters, especially the wicked-looking little Boeing P-12 biplanes and the sleek, low-wing Boeing P-26, which, we were told, was the deadliest thing in the air. Whenever one of these airplanes passed overhead, I would look up and, at a single glance, identify the type as it sped by.

There were, however, many other things in life besides watching blazing artillery at night or airplanes at Post Field! Between Fort Sill and the mountain stretched a vast reservation where the U. S. Army let their many horses run free, animals from the cavalry and artillery, as well as beautiful polo ponies. The field was about six miles from the Johnson home, in the residential section of Lawton. My friends and I would go in a group to the field; by stretching our legs and trotting we could make it in just over an hour. Before us on the vast plain roamed several hundred horses.

We wanted to ride. At first the animals didn't share our

enthusiasm, and shied from us. This meant we had to catch them, which was easier said than done. We tried everything, including the foolish attempt to catch the horses by *running* after them. Exhaustion soon proved the futility of this venture.

Experience taught us never to alarm the horses, but to move in quietly and slowly while they surveyed our approach. In time we developed a sure touch. We'd pat an animal gently on his neck and talk soothingly. Then one of us held the horse by his head while another fellow climbed onto his back. When alone, I'd put an arm over the horse's neck and swing up.

And then—bareback—away we went! We rode Indian style, no ropes, no saddles, just the horse and a boy on top. We would race for miles down the vast pasture land, each of us exhorting his own animal to outspeed the other mounts. We'd ride the horses just as swiftly as they could run, shouting and crying out joyously, racing like the wind, all for the sheer joy of riding.

We each had our favorite mounts, but then the urge to try something new would lead us to other animals. I became good friends with a hitch horse named Baldy, a sorrel with an all-white blaze face. Our mutual good will lasted only so long as I stayed off Baldy's back. He objected strenuously to being ridden, and when I tried, his friendliness disappeared like a shot out of a gun.

Baldy went wild. He pitched, bucked, reared, and flung himself about in wild gyrations. He did everything that a horse can possibly do to throw me off. Baldy and I had some fine rides together, for every time that I swung to his back he seemed to go crazy. Finally, when he discovered that he couldn't get me off, he simply ignored me. I was no more to him than a big, annoying fly he couldn't shake. He'd calm down and trot off wherever he wanted to go, wholly ignoring Bobby Johnson on his back.

That is, until I dug my heels into his flank. That was it! Baldy went wild again, working frantically and desperately to shake me. Away we'd go, pitching and bucking our way across the fields. I'd shout at the horse, and Baldy would only renew his frenzied efforts to rid himself of me. He never did throw me, and I think that creature finally resigned himself to his fate. He seemed to give up, and I was able to ride him whenever I wanted.

When our day's racing was over, I'd ride my horse back to the edge of the reservation and slide off slowly. Now it was time to rub or to give him a gentle pat on his neck, to thank him for the day's fun. Each time I finished riding I was all sweated up from the horse, and my body smell wasn't one iota different from that of the animal—as Mom and my sisters often told me.

At the fence I'd leave my friends and strike out for home. A good mile and a half lay between the Army reservation and the highway. After a while I think I came to know every prairie-dog hole and every rattler in the fields.

From the highway a side road stretched another four or five miles. I could have walked this way, I suppose, but to make the trip shorter I'd cut across fields, through back yards and over fences. After one of those days of riding, I just never had any trouble falling asleep. Dad said that no sooner did my head hit the pillow than I was a goner.

Two miles west of our house was a little stream, shallow, rock-filled and muddy. It wasn't anything to look at or to get excited about, but it was a favorite meeting place where I'd get together with my friends.

The lure of the stream were the crayfish, more commonly known to us as crawdads. We'd wade barefooted into the muddy water and move our feet about slowly. Soon the crawdads would become curious and nibble with their pincers at our toes. We reached down and scooped them out. Sometimes we would "fish" for the crawdads. Bacon rind or pork on a string was a perfect bait. The crawdads would snap onto the food and we'd lift them out. We didn't need any hooks for that!

With a good catch by our sides, we gathered wood and built a small fire. While the wood was started burning, two of the boys cleaned the crawdads and stuck the tails on a stick. Those impromptu meals of crawdad tails, on the bank of the stream, all by ourselves, were fit for a king.

In the country around Lawton we never lacked for things to do. If our taste wanted for something different, we'd all meet at our favorite fishing hole. Farther down the stream from where we fished for crawdads, the banks widened and the water deepened, swirling gently as it flowed over the rocks and rough bottom.

Here we sought what I can only describe, to this day, as some of the most succulent catfish that ever swam in *any* stream. No fancy fishing tackle for us. If we didn't have the few cents for the store-bought fishhooks, we'd bend pins into the necessary shape. When each of us had a string of catfish, each plump and running from six to ten inches, we'd hie for home for a family feast.

Many a time our group supplied game meat for the family table. Not of necessity, but from the joy of hunting and the flavor of the wild animals. Rabbits were my favorite to bring home. When I was eleven years old I had a Montgomery Ward six-shot .22 rifle (which hangs on the wall of my den today).

The rabbits weren't our only prey. Moving through the fields and brush, I bagged a plentiful supply of squirrels and doves. There were snakes and prairie dogs to hunt, and some fast and fancy shooting with the .22 would bring down even the skulking coyotes. To say nothing of an uncountable quantity of fence posts and tin cans which we peppered.

While these days of hunting were wonderful, we wanted to really camp out by ourselves, without coming home every night, or sleeping in a bed. We wanted to go out in the woods, just a group of us, on our own, answering only to ourselves. This boyhood dream, by the good graces of membership in the Boy Scouts and understanding parents, was made to come true. Our folks would drive four or five of us out to the Wichita Mountains, and dump us off. For the next ten days to two weeks we were all to ourselves— Tom Sawyer and Huck Finn had nothing on us!

We lived in swimming trunks and tennis shoes, and much of the time even the shoes rested empty by our campsite. Each night we slept in the open, nothing more than the blankets we'd brought providing cover. It never seemed to rain; as well as I can remember, at least, never on any of these camping expeditions.

Two of my closest friends in Lawton, Joe Reed and Wayne King, were classmates with whom I'd grown up. Both their fathers owned airplanes, and ran a little flight school in the town's "municipal airport" which straddled the edge of Lawton. The "airport" was a grass strip within a mile square of grassland. It boasted one old tin hangar of corrugated metal, and ten to fifteen planes of sundry type and questionable origin.

Joe Reed, Sr., was an old Army pilot who had flown and fought in World War I, and who still maintained active status in the Army Reserve. He was the town postmaster for Lawton, a full-sized job for the population of some twenty thousand people. Reed owned the school—the Joe Reed School of Flying—and Klais King was his manager. Every now and then Joe, Wayne and myself would hike down to the school to watch the airplanes taking off, going through their maneuvers in the air, and practicing landings.

Those were moments filled with both wonder and pleasure as I watched all those planes in the air—and with no small heartache. Once in a while Joe and Wayne would be taken up for rides by their fathers. But not Bobby Johnson! I'd sit on the ground, aching with envy, and bemoan my fate as my friends soared through the air.

You could never have proved it to me then, but being "stuck on the ground" perhaps did me far more good than taking those brief hops would have done. Waiting for my friends, I visited the operations shack, and spent my time talking to pilots, reading pamphlets and instruction booklets, and actually soaking up an invaluable background in aviation and in flying.

But how I wanted to fly! I ached in every bone with the desire to be borne aloft on wings. I hung around the airport, with enormous calf eyes pleading for a flight. I offered to wash airplanes, scrub floors, paint, carry out garbage, dig ditches—*anything* just to get a ride. Somehow, the offer was never accepted, and I remained forlorn—on the ground.

I saw an opportunity to fly through the Boy Scouts—Troop 39, to which I belonged. We weren't the number one troop, perhaps, in Merit Badges for cooking and campfires, but we sure were the top group in sports. We led all the scouts in boxing and wrestling, and I was the Troop 39 champ in both these two sports.

Troop 39 didn't pass up any opportunities for special events, either. On several occasions barnstormers came to town to put on flying shows. They landed on large open fields near Cameron College, bringing in all different kinds of two-seat and three-seat open-cockpit biplanes. Our entire troop would go out to the fields to help the barnstormer pilots. In addition to their daredevil acts, the pilots took passengers up for rides. We helped people to and from the planes, and aided the barnstorming group in controlling the crowds.

All this for the promise that we would each get a ride in a plane before the day was over. The promise was worth it; especially to me! Not even the hot, dusty, and crowded fields dampened my enthusiasm, or passing the day without food, or carrying water buckets, or dashing about madly to deliver messages. *Anything* was worth it—just so long as I'd get my chance to fly.

At the close of each day several scouts would, indeed, get a ride. But somehow, whenever it came my turn to fly, the day would be over. The pilot would grin in a friendly way and say, "Sorry, kid. Got a schedule to keep; I've gotta leave. Maybe next time." And away he would go.

I was twelve years old when the Great Day arrived. I should say the Great Night. It couldn't have come as a bigger surprise.

A giant (it was a giant in those days) Ford Tri-Motor transport—corrugated skin, three roaring engines, and blazing with all manner of lights—landed at the municipal airport. That pilot sure knew his business.

The Tri-Motor was lit up like a county fair grounds. Lights had been fastened to the wings and the fuselage until it looked like a big carnival show floating through the night skies.

Dad took the entire family down to watch the Ford taking off and landing at the airport with passengers, for short flights over Lawton, to let the townspeople see what the place looked like at night. It was an eerie sight, and I think perhaps that pilot had once worked at a circus. As the plane flew over the edge of town the pilot released a string of Roman candles. Immediately the sky blossomed forth with a procession of fireballs, brilliant and multicolored, illuminating the entire valley. This pyrotechnic display, of course, caught the interest of people in the town, who flocked by the hundreds to the airport just to see what was going on.

And then, out of the blue Dad asked *the* question.

"Son, would you like to go up?"

Would I!

I climbed aboard. The interior of the Tri-Motor was dark. The smell of gasoline and oil came to me; I was aware of the feel of the metal. Wonderful sensations all; I drank in every moment.

I was tense and breathless as the pilot hit the switches. The engines ground over slowly and abruptly burst into a shattering roar. The airplane shook and vibrated as it rumbled over the ground, taxiing across the field and swinging into position for takeoff. From the window I could see the wing outlined dimly against the night sky, and an engine with blue exhaust flames ghosting out from it.

The moment arrived. The roar deepened, increased in volume as the pilot fed power to the engines. I felt a sensation of sudden and rapid movement . . . a rumbling as the airplane accelerated in its dash over the ground.

I expected—a sudden upward rush, I suppose, a feeling of soaring. There was none of this. Without prelude, the vibration and the bouncing just stopped. The engines roared sweetly, a new note, a throbbing, in their voice.

I could hardly believe it—I was flying! Nose glued to the

window, eyes wide open and hungry, I stared out and down at the lights so far below us. I could see for miles and miles. Far off in the distance lights gleamed through the night. I had a feeling of enormous depth, of a vast and endless plain stretching before me.

All too soon, the motion of the airplane changed. We were returning to earth. Wind whistled past the wings and the engines descended in volume to a friendly sigh. A rumble, ever so slight a jar as the wheels touched. Then the vibration and bouncing on the grass as the pilot taxied back to the operations shack.

We had been aloft for fifteen minutes—the best quarter hour of my life!

3

I have known pilots who professed to believe only in the material world. To them the search for reality in their own minds, a seeking and finding of God, was a drastic change in life brought about by the proximity of enemy guns, and the clutch of Death's hand tightly about a windpipe. Not until then, perhaps, had they found cause or need sufficiently imperative to seek sustenance beyond themselves.

Like the majority of men with whom I fought the enemy, I did not find it necessary to make any such hasty search. My boyhood had been full, indeed; rich, both in material things and the religious beliefs of my family and our church.

I learned soon enough that a belief in God is not something to be snatched at in moments of fear, as the straw clutched in desperation by the drowning man. It is something that lies deep within a man as an inner source of strength.

Faith to me is indispensable, yet I came to realize quickly enough that there is no substitute for facing up to the realities of life and sudden death. A man fights with his weapons of skill and courage, and belief; skill and courage are not to be found so suddenly as belief; they must be nurtured over the years.

The man who enters combat encased in solid armor plate, but lacking the essential of self-confidence, is far more exposed and naked to death than the individual who subjects himself to battle shorn of any protection but his own skill, his own belief in himself and in his wingmen. Righteousness is necessary for one's peace of mind, perhaps, but it is a poor substitute for agility with a Thunderbolt and a resolution to meet the enemy under any conditions and against any odds.

Perhaps if I had never kept burning fiercely the desire to fly, to become a fighter pilot, I might not have learned these truths. Certainly I would never have one day found myself sitting within seven tons of deadly fighter plane, with tremendous killing power at my finger tips, as I hurtled through the enemy skies of Germany. The hours I spent more than thirty thousand feet in the bitterly cold air over that alien land were most productive of self-study. Nothing makes a man more aware of his capabilities and of his intrinsic limitations than those moments when he must push aside all the familiar defenses of ego and vanity, and accept reality by staring, with the fear that is normal to a man in combat, into the face of Death.

My reflections on my own conduct and skill in battle

enabled me to appreciate the things I had done as a young-ster which affected most strongly my future in the Army Air Forces, and my abilities as a pilot and a gunner.

Three specific things shaped my life in these respects. The first was my frequent shooting with my .22 rifle. As a boy I never tired of practicing with the .22, and I expended literally hundreds of rounds shooting at daisies waving in the fields. I hammered away with the small bullets at racing rabbits and scampering woodchucks, small game that blended so well with the matching landscape that my eyes became expert at following the most difficult of moving targets.

Shooting at the crows and swift hawks in Oklahoma did more than anything else to develop a sure gunner's eye. I learned for myself through constant practice and experience the need for leading a moving target, about bullet drop with distance, compensation for wind effect, and other in-cidentals of aiming properly. These were the factors which were to become so indispensable, high over Germany, when a well-aimed burst constituted all the difference be-tween defeat and victory, between life and death.

The second lesson came from my boxing experience. Noth-ing taught me so well the meaning of fear, and what it re-quired to control, or to overcome, that fear. Whenever I was in the ring, I was affected with a strong feeling of anticipation of what might come next that amounted al-most to a sense of wonder. I was always tense, literally quivering with excitement when I was to mix it up. I never could tell who, or even what, I might encounter. The not knowing kept me keyed up, ready for and anticipating any-thing.

Perhaps my friends never realized it, but I used to crawl into the ring. At least, it was to me a reluctant entrance. I never liked to fight. I was *afraid* to fight! But fear had to be faced. Was there a better way of hiding my distaste, of overcoming this fear, than to stand up to it, and fight? This need was imponderable then, but it made sense later, and it still does now. After all, when the news got around that a boy didn't want to fight, that he was afraid to fight, he had damned well better be prepared to defend himself against all comers!

I never lost this sticky sensation of fear until the dreaded moment actually arrived, when I started across the ring to size up my opponent. Invariably it was someone bigger than I was, someone who looked tough, and was tough.

Then I was no longer afraid. I was scared silly. I was so tense that I'd quiver right down to my sneakers.

Finally, the bell. Moving out into the ring; the first hard punch. Then something happened. I didn't know what it was; I cared even less. When leather smacked me hard in the face, it seemed to knock all the fear right out of me. I no longer cared how big and tough or mean the other guy was. He was hitting me. Hitting *me*. Things changed. I don't know how, but I'd come to realize that I wasn't just standing there, or backing up, or covering the punches. I'd swarm all over my opponent, arms flailing like pistons, fists flying, banging away with all my strength. Somehow I'd weather all the punches thrown at me, even those that struck home, and constantly I'd be slamming my own right into the target.

I always had the feeling that I must fight my best, that I had to put everything I could into the battle. If my opponent was easy, then this grim determination usually ended the fight in a hurry, with the other boxer flat on his back. But if he was as tough as I always feared he would be, then he was going to have to earn every minute in the ring with me. Because I was so busy swinging that I forgot to be scared!

I was sixteen when I was paired off at the local athletic club against a boy who had done a lot of fighting. He was mean in the ring, and with the kind of reputation for cutting up other fighters that scared me half to death. He was in his early twenties, an old man to me at a bare sixteen. And I was an amateur. *He* wasn't. His nose had been broken, he had grotesque cauliflower ears. His cheeks and the area around his eyes had been badly scarred from innumerable ring battles. The only thing that seemed fair about the fight was my weight; at 118 pounds I was within a few pounds of him.

I didn't know who my opponent would be until I was actually in the ring. For a while I had the floodlights all to myself; no one else appeared. Then along came this character, who vaulted the top rope, like a spring, all determined and cocky, and absolutely ready to beat in my brains. When I saw this pug, I fair to jumped out the other side of the ring.

A close friend, Fred Gray (I worked for him at his cabinet shop), jumped to his feet and yelled that I wasn't going to fight *this* pro. Fred raised all kinds of hell, and his voice kept rising. He gesticulated wildly with his hands, and ended up screaming at "Speedy" Sparks, the manager of the athletic club, about the slaughter that would ensue. The slaughter—everyone (including myself) was convinced—of Bobby Johnson.

The crowd in the theater felt equally outraged. Pretty soon the place was bedlam, the people stamping their feet and picking up the chant to prevent the fight.

Hell, I couldn't walk out then! The way the theater crowd was shouting and stamping, you'd think I was a helpless cripple about to be thrown into a pit of starving lions. Maybe the situation was bad, but I couldn't let things stay this way—the whole theater was trying to save poor little Johnson. The other guys would razz me for months.

I asked the referee to give us our instructions. I stood quietly while this other bird jumped around like a lunatic, shadow boxing, weaving in and out, and putting on what he considered to be a grand and fearsome spectacle.

We both came out with the bell. He danced quickly from his corner; I moved out cautiously in a crouch. As he came in, I aimed for his stomach and with all my strength threw a right. I missed. My fist thudded flush against his heart, a cruel blow that sent him reeling across the ring, where he came off the ropes and collapsed to the canvas. And he stayed down for the count of ten!

Then he jumped to his feet and screamed hysterically that he hadn't heard the count; he berated the referee in an amazing scene of outraged innocence. The referee was so confused he didn't know what to do; he turned to me.

"Let him come on!" I shouted. Only one punch had been thrown; this wasn't the way to stop a fight.

This time my opponent was more cautious. His feet sped across the canvas as he tried to spar with me. He was the real Fancy Dan type, long left hand flicking in and out. But he hadn't hit me yet, and I figured that he'd never suspect me of going after his heart again.

I ducked to let a jab slip over my shoulder. He was wide open, and I whaled another right that smashed against his heart. His eyes opened wide and his jaw sagged. A sickly, dazed expression spread over his face as he crumpled to the canvas.

This time the referee counted to ten *loudly*. But when he

threw his arms up, the other fighter didn't move. I was scared again—in a different way. He *couldn't* move.

Doctors rushed into the ring, and half dragged and half carried him into the dressing room. I learned later that this man never again climbed through the ring ropes to fight.

That match taught me something important. I learned right then and there that just because a man looks mean and ugly, it doesn't mean that he's tough. It just means that somebody might have used his face for a punching bag.

The third thing that in later years came to my assistance was my football experience. I played three years in high school and again in college. I was anything but a fearsome or an imposing figure on the gridiron. In college I weighed an unimpressive 145 pounds. The tackle on my left sagged the scales at 260 pounds, the man on my right was 225 pounds, and the center—the lightest of all—was seventy pounds heavier than I!

In high school I started out on the field as a back. It didn't take long before I twisted my ankles; the coach shifted me to guard. Mostly I held this position, though sometimes I was used as blocking back, and occasionally moved to center.

Our quarterback at Cameron Junior College was Orban "Spec" Sanders, a man who was a beautiful machine on the gridiron. I played with him often, and his skill on the field was a marvel to behold. The coach forecast that Spec would go a long way. Later, with the football Yankees, he upheld the coach's prophecy by setting a string of records for the game.

When I was put in leading guard position, I led the team plays. I couldn't run very fast, but I was shifty on my feet and could dodge about like a greased porker. With my weight and my ability to twist and evade other players, I didn't get hit very often. But when I did—oh, brother!

Our coach was Jess Thompson, a rugged character who had played center in his own college days. He weighed about 230 pounds and stood five feet eleven inches—every bit of it muscle. He had a neck like a bull, and he not only looked and acted the part, but his bellowing made him sound like an enraged steer.

To condition us Jess didn't waste time with the recommendations of the state athletic manuals. He'd drag the team out to plowed fields where the furrows were long and deep. Then he'd stand on the side and roar at us to run. It was a most revealing training system. It either broke your legs or made you into a hell of a ballplayer. With all our gear on, and leaping like frenzied stags across those furrows in that Oklahoma sun of 117 degrees, we felt as if we were sweating bullets.

Thompson never accepted excuses. He wanted the best team there was, and to play under him you just had to be good. One of our backs moved like a bolt of lightning. He was too fast to be caught by anyone on the team. The only way to stop him was to intercept him as he tore down the field.

His speed made him a terrific weapon in a closely fought game. Thompson never relented in training that boy to develop more and more speed. We'd sit on the side of the field as the coach sent our star runner dashing down the furrows. He'd roar at him, "*Run,* boy! There's an old lady leading a cow wants to git by! Good Lord, what for you want to rest? C'mon, boy, RUN!"

While Jess Thompson gave free rein to his thundering voice and his scathing denunciations of the team as a pack of half-witted, fumble-fingered, crippled morons, every one of us came to recognize the true friend that our coach could be—and was.

Jess gave me one bit of advice which stuck hard with me for years and, if nothing else, proved a boon to me psychologically. Since I was the squirt on the team, he'd pull me aside before a particularly rough game, look me in the eyes, and say, "Now go out there and get 'em. Don't forget that they get into their pants one leg at a time, just like you do. . . ."

I never forgot those words. They often came back to me in combat when the stakes weren't touchdowns, but death.

I'd be boring in on a head-on pass with a Jerry. It was a sight to unnerve the strongest of men. I'd stare at the German fighter as it rushed at me, wings and nose ablaze with its firing guns and cannon.

I was just plain scared! Then, so many times, I told myself, "Johnson—that's no superman out there. He gets into his pants one leg at a time, just like you do."

And it never failed me. I'd bore right in, that Thunderbolt of mine and its eight flaming guns a hell of a lot more murderous-looking than the Kraut fighter. I used to wonder just how scared that Jerry was. . . .

4

The Lawton Cabinet Shop, where I worked for Fred Gray (who had defended me so vigorously at a certain boxing match) proved the source of the money to buy flying lessons and a builder of muscle. I first took a job with Gray when I was eleven years old, and for several years afterward was his general assistant. That meant a great deal more than being a flunky who swept the floor and ran errands. In those days, an eleven-year-old boy who accepted a man's job was expected to do a man's work.

During the winter—working after school until as late as ten or eleven o'clock and twelve to sixteen hours on Saturday—I made four dollars a week. When summer came, I was at the cabinet shop six full days, working anywhere from eight to sixteen hours a day. Unhappily, my pay remained the same—the unchangeable four dollars a week. I earned every penny. One distasteful chore was lifting heavy three-by-twelve beams, twenty feet in length, and helping to push them through spinning saws. To do this I had to walk backward, holding the boards. This probably did more to develop my stomach, shoulder and arm muscles than anything else I did. The effort had an unusual result: when I sweated at my work, the sawdust flying about in the air covered my body until I looked like a strange, furry creature.

The labor in the carpentry shop produced wages that held a value entirely out of proportion to the four-dollar face value. It cost money to fly, and woodworking earned money for me.

With this heartening fact buzzing in my head, I went to see Merle Donnley, who was then managing the little municipal airport for Joe Reed. His words were music. I received the wonderful news that I could purchase fifteen minutes of flying instruction for a dollar and a half. Why—for six bucks, I could fly with an instructor, for a whole hour! We shook hands on our business agreement. Bright and early every Sunday morning I'd be at the field for my flight lessons.

Merle was my instructor. When I arrived at the airfield for my first lesson, he pointed out a little Wiley Post trainer. The biplane was neat and trim, with side-by-side seating in an open cockpit. I felt wonderful! Here I was taking the second airplane ride of my life, and I was a student. Merle fired up the little ship, banged home the throttle, and horsed her into the air. Barely off the ground he held his hands in front of him and said, "You've got it; she's yours."

I was *flying* the plane! And—wouldn't you know it?—I was smack in a crosswind on takeoff. I had about three or four seconds of the thrill of holding the controls when a sharp gust slapped the little Post right under the wing and threw the plane hard over on her side. The ground flipped to a crazy angle. By sheer instinct I leaned windward and worked opposite stick and rudder—not realizing that I had moved the controls exactly as I was supposed to do. Merle was surprised, and even more pleased.

At the end of my second lesson, with the grand total of thirty minutes noted in my logbook, I was eager to try something new. Among the planes at the Reed school was a Travelair biplane, more powerful and larger than the Wiley Post.

"If that's what you want, Bobby," Merle shrugged, "we'll give it a whirl."

I didn't get the impression that he thought it was the best idea in the world, but it was my money.

The new ship had a deep song of power. I was fairly bursting with joy and pride in myself when we eased back on the stick and climbed her off the grass. Pride, however— especially born of only thirty minutes' experience—is no substitute for hours spent in training. I attempted to glide toward the ground, and to land the big biplane exactly as I had done with the Wiley Post. I learned soon enough, as I consistently overshot the field, that this didn't work. So Merle would push home the throttle and go around. The next time I was cagey. I started my landing approach from farther out, intending to glide right into the field.

Merle just sat there, looking at me with no little distaste. Several times I really fouled up. I came in too high, or too fast, or allowed the wind to drift me away from the runway. The crusher came when, in the interests of survival,

Merle wrested the controls from my hands to slip the biplane in beautifully to the ground.

As far as I was concerned, this was for the birds, and a hell of a way to spend my few hard-earned dollars. Wisely I turned my back on the bigger airplane, determined to return to it later. I marched back to the Wiley Post, which now assumed all the characteristics of a true and faithful friend.

Either for pressing business reasons or in the hope of some relaxation, Merle Donnley soon returned to the airport office, and assigned Klais King (the former manager) as my instructor. From here on flying was all the fun and wonder I felt it should be.

We went through the training routine so familiar to all who have experienced the grind of mastering the air. Straight-and-level flight, a unique trick in itself, when an airplane wants to follow the whims of the wind. Gentle turns to the right and left, then steep turns. Climbs and glides, and climbing and gliding turns. Stalls without power, stalls with the engine straining like a sewing machine, with the nose hanging in the sky. Slips and skids and spins and— never to be forgotten—the relentless co-ordination exercises. Turns around pylons, and turns on a point. S-turns to develop proficiency in compensating for the effect of wind. Taking off and landing, a strange sort of swooping activity in which I'd land, hear the muttered words of "Take 'er around again," and bang home on the throttle to lift into the air.

Six hours and forty-five minutes after starting my first lesson, King decided that I was ready to be kicked out of the nest. To me the prospect of achieving my first solo flight lay years in the future. That morning my landings had gone to hell. I couldn't hold a proper approach. I came in too high or too low. I was skidding and slipping. I couldn't flare out properly above the ground. I flew like a stumblebum, bouncing and slamming the ship around with what appeared to onlookers to be absolute abandon.

Since my rejection of the powerful biplane and my return to the Wiley Post, I had thought of myself as pretty much of a hot rock. I flew well, I gained skill with every flight, and I was doing things the way the book and my instructor wanted me to. On this morning, however, my flying was so incredibly poor in the first minutes I spent in the air that I despaired ever of reaching that time of solo. My ego, which had soared so loftily, was badly punctured. Self-confidence had been replaced by a wavering question of whether I would ever learn to fly.

I made another landing, a staggering bounce that proved a fitting end to a sloppy approach. Once the airplane managed to hug the ground without further antics, Klais grunted, "I've got it." He took over the controls and taxied to the operations hut.

I feared that I had frightened even my instructor, for Klais silently unfastened his safety belt and crawled out. But why had he left the motor running? A cardinal safety rule when leaving an airplane was to be sure the engine was dead. He turned and looked at me. "Bob—do you think you can take it around by yourself?"

I was still somewhat in a daze. Without hesitating I said, "Sure." That's all. I didn't even realize what I was saying. Someone had asked me if I could do something, so naturally I said, "Sure."

I taxied to the edge of the field, kicked rudder and swung the Wiley Post into the wind. In position, I looked straight ahead and opened the throttle. The little airplane surged ahead, and I flew as I always had before with Klais at my side. As my speed increased, I eased the stick forward to lift the tail off the grass. More speed, the ground rushing by, the sound of wind becoming louder. Almost by feel I applied gentle back pressure. The Wiley was a sensitive creature; her wings grabbed air and in a wonderful floating motion the ground fell away beneath the wheels.

I climbed straight out. Three hundred feet above the earth I turned to ask Klais a question. The first word died in my throat, and even as I saw just how empty the instructor's seat was, I broke into a grin. Then I was laughing, a joyous sound that seemed to be the jubilation of a stranger. In half wonder I shouted to myself, "Johnson—can you get this thing on the ground?"

Only then, at that moment, did the realization sink in that I was truly on my own. If I became frightened, or failed to fly properly, or made a disastrous error near the ground —no one could snatch me from my difficulty. This was it— the moment for which all fledglings wait and yearn so desperately. I understood then why the instructors referred to a student's first solo flight as being "kicked out of the nest." It was simple. You either flew to earth gently, or you met the ground with a sickening crash.

For me, however, there was only that single instant of reflection about my ability. The rest was wonder, a joy compounded of exhilaration, a limitless sense of freedom and reach to the very limits of the sky. How many pilots have shared this sensation which defies of adequate description! The instant of knowing that the skies truly are yours in which to fly and soar, to glide and swoop, is truly a moment of sweetness incomparable to any other. It is more a feeling, a sensing, than it is sober realization. All at once the world is brighter.

It is a wonderful thing to nudge gently with your foot

at the rudder bar, to ease the stick in your hand slightly to the side, and by that insignificant effort to move the entire world before you to a steep angle from the familiar horizontal. The world is then your toy, a plaything, the fields and mountains and lakes to be whirled about at your whims.

All these things are understood, not by all students who embark on their first solo flight, but by that fledgling pilot who has been in love with the air and with flying—even when the wonder of actual flight could be no more than the merest dream. All this becomes known to him in a sensing of flight that at once becomes an inseparable part of him. The moment does not come often, but once found, it is sought eagerly forever more.

There was still an urgent matter at hand, I realized. The sensations experienced in half wonder were not all. I still had to land the airplane, to return it to earth in a semblance of a normal landing, to set it down in one piece.

Now came concentration. A job to do. I circled the postage stamp of the grass field. I was going to fly the way I had been taught to fly; and I ignored the fact that the instructor wasn't there beside me. Intent on what I was doing, I kept up a running chain of orders to myself.

Look straight ahead. That's it, Johnson. Wings straight and level. Now, left turn. Co-ordinate those controls. Left rudder, stick over for aileron. Roll her into the turn. Now— gently—apply opposite pressure. Ease her out. You're on your downwind leg. Check that wind. Be sure drift doesn't throw you off. There's the runway. Good, you're parallel. Now you're passing the end of the runway. Clear the air around you. No one on a long final approach.

Again left rudder, left aileron. Roll her into the turn, opposite pressure. Wings straight and level, nose down slightly to lose height. There—pick your spot to land. Got it fixed in your mind? This is it, then.

Chop the throttle. The little biplane slows perceptibly in the air. The engine roar fades to a murmur; now the wind is louder, a stream running through the wings and wires, past your cockpit. Nose down to maintain flying speed. Roll into the turn; good, you're on your final now, floating earthward. The ground moves up to meet you. Not too quickly, at just the right speed.

Keep your eye glued to that spot for touchdown. Bring her down as if she's on a guy wire. Gauge your distance, carefully now. Got to lose some more speed. Stick back; let the nose come up some more. Stronger control movements now; she answers a bit sluggishly, near stalling speed. Back with that stick . . . easy . . . hold her off. Now, stick all the way back! I made one of the prettiest landings I had ever made, or was to make, in my life! Right smack on the spot I'd been aiming for.

I taxied up to the hangar. Only then did I sneak a look at that empty right seat. Klais was waiting for me, a wide grin on his face as I cut the engine and climbed out. I think my face was about to split from the smile I couldn't hold back. Klais pumped my hand and congratulated me. Right then and there I was cock of the walk. I felt sure I was just about the hottest pilot there was. At fourteen years of age, I imagine I could be forgiven those wonderful moments of grandeur.

An older friend, Tedo Swain, proved a minor miracle. Tedo was an experienced pilot with an instructor's rating, who owned several airplanes. Flying was his business, and often I was able to fly with Tedo on trips, or just for the fun of it. Sometimes he'd give me the controls and I piled up more time and experience.

By the time I was sixteen I had accumulated the magnificent total of thirty-five hours' flying time. I had my student's license and no slip of paper was ever more cherished; for it meant that I could continue to fly, both under instruction and by myself. The unhappy part of the picture was that my serious flying was still dependent upon my weekly salary of four dollars.

I had no time for anything else but school, working six days a week, and spending my few dollars in what time was left at the airport. Finally I quit my job at Fred Gray's cabinet shop. I still needed money, however, and I sought my finances through a weekend job in a grocery. This way I could satisfy a growing urge for football by playing after school, and still earn the money I needed for my precious moments of flying.

Life in those times was wonderful. I just didn't have any problems. I got along fine in school, I was able to stay on top in any of the sports that attracted me. I didn't make any fortune at that grocery, but it was cash, and enough to cover my flying. Life was wonderful, and it was wonderfully simple.

Without warning, disaster struck. I discovered girls. To me this was a unique situation. The other fellows were dating. They talked about girls, but these were strange creatures whom I saw in town, or spoke to, or mostly ignored. Of course, I had my two older sisters at home. But they weren't *girls*. They were my sisters!

The awakening to this strange and wonderful female creature proved calamitous to my carefully nurtured finances and little spare time. Between the needs of the young ladies who suddenly appeared on the Johnson horizon, I was kept flat broke.

My social life was suddenly active; indeed, it flourished

in grand fashion. This turn of events brought about a woeful neglect of my flying. The desire for both was nearly overwhelming, and I was facing what was to me an epochal decision. I wanted desperately to continue my flying, and I wanted with equal intensity to revel in my amazing new social life, in which one Barbara Morgan played no small role.

The wings and propeller lost. It grieves me to admit that the gentle sex was triumphant.

Fortunately for what I considered a precarious peace of mind, I was befriended by Dr. Clarence Breedlove, the dean of Cameron Junior College, which I attended at eighteen. Unexpectedly, he summoned me one day to his office. He went right to the point. "Bob, would you like to take this CPT course; you know, the Civilian Pilot Training program?"

Would I! It was an amazing life; suddenly the girls were shoved into the background. "Sure!" I answered eagerly. "How do I go about it, and what will it cost?"

The reply dashed freezing water on the prospects of serious flying. Dr. Breedlove revealed that the CPT course would cost me at least fifty to fifty-five dollars.

"I don't have that kind of money, Doctor," I explained. Then, hardly able to believe my own words—for I was quite attached to my very valuable transportation, a twenty-five-dollar, 1929 Model A Ford—I added, "But, I'll do anything to fly. I'll sell my Model A if necessary, and I'm sure I can get the rest by taking on some extra job."

Doc smiled. "It won't be necessary to sell your car, Bob," he offered. "I know you have done some flying already. I'll make you a personal loan of the money; pay me back whenever you can."

That loan completed the cycle. The skirts had enjoyed

their flourish of triumph. Now nothing was going to keep me out of the air.

My return to flying didn't leave time for much else. I was taking an engineering course in college, which demanded concentration of effort and considerable studying at home. I played football. I had a new job in the evenings, one that surprised even me. At night I'd travel to Lawton to work in a Ladies' Ready to Wear store, where I helped to dress windows and held down the "executive position" of general cleanup man. When I finished this job, I went down to the Lawton Fire Department and donned the clothes of a fireman. This latter position, at least, enabled me to put in some extra studying when I wasn't out spraying water on burning buildings.

From these jobs I planned to gather the money with which to repay the loan from Dr. Breedlove. It was worth all the effort. I was back in the air, this time in earnest.

5

This was the way to fly! No scrounging for every dollar, no need to count every nickel before I could begin the long hike to the airport for the brief lesson. Besides, I was now a wheel, and the Model A made the trip to the airport infinitely more pleasurable than the long hike on short legs.

My new instructor was Duane Huscher, who introduced me to flying in a more leisurely style than I'd known in the Wiley Post. We flew a high-wing Taylorcraft sportplane, with dual wheel controls in side-by-side position. After some fine points of instruction, Duane turned me loose. At the close of the official thirty-five hours of the

Civilian Pilot Training program, I had logged a total of seventy-five hours as a pilot.

I flew every time I could find the opportunity. Some flights were only of fifteen- or twenty-minute duration, but my flying was spiced with wonderful intervals in which I went aloft alone for several hours of bliss in the blue. Switching from one type of plane to another was in itself valuable training, for I became adept at flying different control systems and meeting the demands of each individual ship. By my second year in college I was nearing the coveted century mark of the new pilot—one hundred hours' logged time.

In 1941 I reached my twenty-first birthday, and read with no small joy of the accelerating program of the Air Corps to train pilots. By now, of course, there had been an air war in Spain. Chinese pilots were battling against the superior training and equipment of the invading Japanese. And each air battle in the English skies, with fighters and bombers engaging in enormous running fights, had whetted my appetite and that of several of my friends for a future as fighter pilots.

I *knew* I could meet all the requirements of the Air Corps for their cadet program, and at Fort Sill I signed my enlistment papers. Soon after, I found myself at Post Field, where, in 1928, I had watched with wonder and in awe the three Army pursuits being wrung through their dazzling aerobatics.

There are various incidents in military life which remain with one forever, and the day of my physical examination as a potential cadet became one of them. With the mercury pushing past 100 degrees, it was a typical Oklahoma summer day—brutal and sweltering. Forty-six hopefuls, of which I was one, collected at the airfield to subject ourselves to the physiological inquisition of the Army medical staff.

In charge of our medical examination was a Captain Schmidtke, a flight surgeon of vast experience who exhibited a remarkable Dr. Jekyll and Mr. Hyde personality. He could, as I discovered, be a nice guy. And he could also erase a smile from his face in the fastest transformation of personality I'd ever seen. To say that I was wary of the good doctor is an understatement; as the day wore on I eyed him like a rabbit staring at a leering hound who had a snoutful of sharp teeth. My tenseness, well aggravated by the smothering heat, made me feel and look like a wet sponge, incessantly and vigorously squeezed from within. From head to toes I was soaking wet.

I learned during this illuminating introduction to the military that much of the heroic uniformed life consists of waiting. So—while the other volunteers opened their mouths and gurgled, bent over, stood straight, peered at strange symbols on eye charts, hopped idiotically from foot to foot, coughed, spat and urinated—I waited.

These were not yet the days when Uncle Sam was desperate for people in staggering numbers to drive his airplanes. To be accepted as a cadet you simply had to pass *all* of the existing and rigid requirements. In this respect the good Doctor Schmidtke was unshakable. A single slip, one mistake, was enough to bounce you out of the prospects' waiting line—as several hopefuls learned to their sorrow.

With several other enlistees I sat in the hallway, waiting in a pool of sweat to be called in for my own examination. Tense and overexcited, some of the boys worked off steam as best they could. One blond fellow, in an obvious state of mental distress, paced back and forth in the hall outside Schmidtke's office, whistling tunelessly, and switching to a dull, droning, horribly monotone hum. This unfortunate soul not only performed for an equally distressed and unappreciative audience, but he was hapless enough to contribute his dubious talents directly beneath a sign which, in large red letters, screamed: QUIET!

He was embarking on his sixth or seventh round trip of mournful noise along the hall when the door to Schmidtke's office opened, and the Figure of Doom stepped out. For several seconds he impaled the offending youngster with his frigid stare, and then lifted his eyes to the sign. To the boy, withering beneath the captain's remorseless gaze, the sign now seemed to be in bright neon lights.

"Young fellow," Schmidtke snapped, "pack your things at once. Then, go home. You're too nervous to be a pilot." With this devastating remark he slammed the door.

Strike One! Forty-six of us had signed up, and the rigorous requirements for cadet acceptance soon were sweeping our perspiring ranks like a sharpened scythe through yielding wheat. I just *had* to stop sweating like this!

The harder I tried, the more the perspiration seemed to ooze in a steady stream from my pores. My imagination went wild on me, and I conjured visions of a Johnson covered with a thick film of glassy water. The more this went on, the more fretful I became—several boys had actually been rejected because they were sweating as much, if not more, than I was.

"This perspiring," the Voice of Doom informed each of these very wet and uneasy people, "is a sign of excessive nervousness. You cannot be a pilot if you are so nervous. Sorry, we can't take you."

And there sat Johnson the Sponge.

When my name was called, I arose with misgivings and entered what had become, through fearful anticipation, the chamber of horror and rejection. Yet, the Figure of Doom smiled when I entered and said, not at all unkindly, "Be seated, son."

As I did so, I slid my hands along my thighs, drying off the palm and heel of each hand against my khakis. I congratulated myself on such shrewdness, yet . . . I could have sworn I saw Captain Schmidtke smile. If so, it was no more than a flicker.

The good doctor hadn't missed the motions. Several minutes later, without any warning, his hand flicked out like a snake and grasped my wrist. He turned my palm up and I winced—for there it was, more perspiration than I had so "shrewdly" wiped away. Wonder of wonders, Schmidtke smiled; in fact, he even grinned at me!

He turned away to note something on my papers, and to my immense relief he never said a word, but chuckled to himself. I knew that I had passed the hurdle that I feared most.

Schmidtke introduced me to a few tricks I hadn't expected. I sat in a wide chair and, surprised, settled back to make myself comfortable. Schmidtke's hand banged against the chair and it began to spin. Around and around went the chair, faster and faster, around and around went Johnson, and soon I was afraid that the room would begin spinning even faster than I was going.

Schmidtke's outthrust foot slammed the chair to a jarring halt. Before I knew what was happening the captain shoved his face up against mine and was peering intently into my eyes. He grunted something unintelligible, and scribbled some more gibberish on the Johnson medical paper. The gibberish, however, seemed to be in my favor.

Before Schmidtke was through with me, I had taken balance tests, special vision tests, examinations for depth perception, *ad nauseam*. I was physically and psychologically prodded, poked, inspected and judged. I felt like a trained white rat running through a maze filled with hidden trapdoors, any one of which would stamp me REJECTED and bounce me out of the camp.

When the captain was through, the survivors of his incisive medical and psychological examination were ordered to report immediately to the hospital at Fort Sill to receive eye-dilation fluid for still more of Schmidtke's tests. As we left the hospital, I was startled to note that—of the forty-six boys who had reported to Post Field that morning—only nine were left. Thirty-seven out of forty-six rejected the first day!

The next morning three more luckless lads were rejected, so that in the end only six of us survived the medical examinations. Of this number I received special attention. Captain Schmidtke told me to have my tonsils removed (why, I do not know, but that's what I was ordered to do), and to wait at home for notification by mail of the call to active duty.

I waited. And I continued to wait, impatient and fretful, as one by one the other five boys received with cries of delight their letters from the Army to report for flight training. Each day I stared with hungry eyes at the mailbox, and finally reached the point where I could sniff out the mailman a half mile down the block. I waited, and the summer of 1941 disappeared into history. Every time I read of the air war raging over England, of the Spitfires and Hurricanes and Messerschmitts, I became sicker.

Then everyone was gone, and only Johnson waited at home, something like the hapless groom left at the postal altar. By now I was convinced that the war would be over and done with while I stayed at home, passing time at college and meeting the mailman with ever-beseeching gaze, hoping for the letter that failed to arrive.

I was learning fast. I decided that if the Army wouldn't come to me, then I'd go to the Army. I drove to Oklahoma City and checked in with the cadet board.

A frozen-faced and noncommittal sergeant listened to my tale of lament. After much noise and prodding on my part he looked through my file. "Oh, yeah," he yawned, "there's a piece of paper missing from here."

I didn't know whether to hit him or simply to resign myself to fate. The sergeant decided the matter for me. He looked up and grunted, not too unlike an orangutan, "Here, Johnson, get a copy of this certificate and bring it back to me."

I suppose that if I hadn't gone to Oklahoma City, I'd have sat out the entire war in Lawton. Two days after my enlightening conversation with the sergeant, on Armistice Day of 1941, I reported back to Oklahoma City. About one hundred and fifty cadets, boys from all over the southwest, were with me. We stood at attention, each of us grateful and solemn, and repeated word for word the oath that swore us to the Army. The next morning I plunged full into my new life; we left by train for Kelly Field at San Antonio, Texas.

It did not take long for me to appreciate just how different a cadet's life would be. We were the first preflight class ever to take training at Kelly Field, and this fortunate event placed us in spanking-new barracks which sat on a hill at the airfield—surrounded by a sea of thick, oozing mud.

And there to welcome our Class 42F were several of the boys with whom I had taken my physical back at Post Field. I also saw some of the fellows with whom I had played football at Cameron Junior College. The sight of familiar faces was cheering, and I prepared to greet the friends with whom I'd grown up.

It was a disastrous error. I had yet to learn that they were no longer the same human beings I had once known. In the time that had passed since our last meeting, they had undergone a strange metamorphosis. Their bodies had been straightened, their heads squared, and whatever diabolical characteristics had lain submerged in their minds had been brought to the surface to be whetted like a sharp knife.

This was my introduction to the creature commonly known as the second lieutenant, and with less flattery as the shavetail.

A withering blast which sounded remarkably like a raucous foghorn smote my ears. As the wind whistled past I recognized the unfamiliar words: "YOU, MISTER! HIT A BRACE, MISTER!"

I was bewildered. I glanced around in a sudden daze, and immediately another sonic barrage flailed me: "WHADDYA LOOKING AROUND FOR, MISTER? YOU WANNA BUY THE PLACE? EYES STRAIGHT AHEAD, MISTER!"

Was this possible? these were my *friends!* "CLOSE YOUR MOUTH, MISTER! YOU'RE NOT CATCHING FLIES TODAY!"

I stared straight ahead. A sea of faces, clean-shaven, all menacing, danced in front of me. I wasn't sure of things. . . . Didn't we once go to school together, play football?

"LOOK AT THIS THING! IS THIS A PHYSICAL SPECIMEN?"

"IT'S A MYSTERY. I THINK IT'S HUMAN."

"WHAT'S ITS NAME? UMM, JOHNSON. IS THAT A NAME? WHO TOLD YOU TO TURN AROUND, MISTER?"

Silence, then. For all of four seconds. Another voice, loud, raucous, mad with power:

"GRAB SUITCASES! REACH!"

"CHIN DOWN! CHEST OUT! SUCK IN THOSE GUTS!"

"WHERE'D YOU GET THAT POT, MISTER? YOU STEAL IT? SUCK IN THAT GUT!"

So, I stood there. It must have been a remarkable sight. My chin was jammed into my chest, and I swore it threatened my ribs. My neck felt like a layer of coiled springs, and you couldn't prove by me that my stomach wasn't pressing hard against my backbone. In this stance of impossible rigidity, affectionately known as a brace, I stood rooted to the muddy ground and subjected myself to the gentle torture of the Exalted Ones.

"WHAT'S YOUR NAME, MISTER? C'MON, SPEAK UP!"

What was the matter with this guy? I'd known him for ten years; he knew my name.

"YOU DEAF? WHATTSA MATTER, DIDN'T YOU LEARN HOW TO TALK? MAYBE YOU DON'T KNOW YOUR NAME! YOU *DO* HAVE A NAME, DON'T YOU? *SPEAK UP!*"

I started to speak. "Joh——"

"YOU HIT A BIG ONE, MISTER! SHADDUP! GRAB SUITCASES. GET SOME WRINKLES IN THAT CHIN! *TURN PURPLE!*"

What a way to start off on a new life. At least I couldn't say that anyone *ignored* me, not with my own private squad of imps sporting sharp horns, barbed tails and brand-new shining gold bars. I could have sworn that I'd known these guys . . .

We stumbled into our barracks with our gear. Fate was kind to us. With the other still-dazed cadets, I sank down to relax.

It was wonderful! We actually had ten entire seconds all to ourselves before lightning crackled and thunder boomed, announcing the arrival of the Welcome Wagon squad.

"TENHUT! YOU, MISTERS! HIT A BRACE, MISTERS!"

We leaped to our feet, and snapped to attention, each man at the foot of his bunk. Next to me, inflexible as a beam of steel, frozen solid, stood a Polish boy with the name of Gracyalyn. I don't know what his name sounded like in his native tongue, but in English it was, exactly, Gracie Allen.

A lieutenant stomped his way down the barracks, crashing to a halt before each cadet, who stood unmoving before his bunk. Each time the Exalted One stopped, he shoved his face nose to nose with the cadet, and bellowed, "WHAT'S YOUR NAME, MISTER?" As each cadet shot out his name, the lieutenant spun away and trod heavily toward the next offender.

Everything went smoothly until the Exalted One rocked to a stop before Gracyalyn, and barked, "WHAT'S YOUR NAME, MISTER?"

The reply was crystal clear: "GRACIE ALLEN, SIR!"

The lieutenant's eyes bugged out at such incredible insubordination. Joking with an officer, was he? "YOU HIT A BIG ONE, MISTER!" came the roar, and the shavetail clumped away.

He went down the line and then, with a look of sheer savagery on his face, returned ominously to Gracyalyn. Again the Face lunged forward in its nose-to-nose position, and the thunderclap burst forth: "OKAY, MISTER! ATTENTION!"

Gracyalyn was already as rigid as a steel beam, but we learned quickly enough never to confuse the minds of the shavetails with either facts or logic.

"Now, MISTER, WHAT'S YOUR NAME?"

"Gracie Allen, sir!" came blurting out.

I thought I'd split my sides, but I was afraid even to twitch an eyelash. I was able to see the fine shade of crimson starting up along the neck of the Exalted One.

At the end of the sixth bellowed "ALLRIGHTMISTERI'VEHAD ENOUGHOFYOURNONSENSE—WHAT'S YOUR NAME?" and the sixth "Gracie Allen, sir!" the shavetail was a brilliant mixture of red and purple.

By some incredible stroke of genius, the Exalted One finally hit upon the thought that perhaps he might find it wise to look at the offending cadet's dog tags. He jerked them up before his eyes and stared—and stared—and stared. . . .

In a weaker and even somewhat tremulous cry he shouted, "AT EASE, MISTER!" and the grateful Gracyalyn— alias Gracie Allen—softened a bit in posture. The lieutenant made no further comment, but walked, a bit less heavily, out of the barracks. It was a fabulous moral victory, and earned Gracyalyn the eternal gratitude of all.

To be a cadet in the Air Corps was not merely to learn to fly, I soon discovered. There were the drudgeries of introduction to military life, which I experienced in 1941, and which were to be shared in the following years, in one form or another, by millions of other men who discovered these strange new facets of life. Perhaps, as a cadet whose goal was flying skill and proficiency, I found little reason to be overjoyed with close-order drill, the niceties of handling rifles in a particular military fashion, including the manual of arms, and so on. There were other things to learn: the boring yet ominous Articles of War, and the mysterious and profound implications of that Great Game Played by Everyone—Military Courtesy.

I was already familiar with rifles. I was skilled in the use of everything from a .22 on up to a gun that could stop a grizzly in its tracks. This experience and skill, I was to discover, mattered little in the life of the air cadet and his rifle. Our shavetails honored us by demonstrating, in the briefest of lessons, the manual of arms. This allegedly prepared us for full and masterful use of the rifle, not only in respect to drilling but also in relation to the hazy requirements of military courtesy.

It was a cold November day when I came to appreciate the expediency of demonstrating with my rifle the proper courtesy to a lieutenant. Johnny Eaves, a classmate, and I were outside our barracks, leaning back against the building, with our elbows resting on the rifle muzzles, stock against the ground. We had always relaxed this way back in Oklahoma, and I saw no reason to change now.

Out of the barracks loomed one of Satan's disciples, a brand-new one, not even a smudge on either brightly gleaming gold bar. The truth struck both Eaves and myself; we were supposed to salute. We realized that we enjoyed a slight intimacy with the Air Corps (three days' worth) and that saluting was required of us.

We saluted. The Exalted One fairly turned green. For, remaining in the same position, feet unmoving, we threw our rifles to the left hand, and saluted with the right to the forehead. I understood soon after that this was not accepted procedure.

Such display on our part, we were informed fulsomely, could be calculated to throw even the most stolid veteran into sorrow. You may imagine, then, what this did to a spanking new second lieutenant. In a marvelous and an unforgettable exhibition of apoplexy—during the next thirty minutes—the shavetail revealed a terrible affliction that caused him to shriek, bark, shout, screech, and make other unintelligible sounds.

That night, however, I reflected again that I could never complain about a disinterested attitude on the part of my officers or my instructors. . . .

The weeks passed in a morass of drilling, instruction, and

general whipping into the shape that the Air Corps deemed necessary to render us fit for more advanced training. One day early in December we tore through our schooling, athletics, close-order drill and other work and—miracle of miracles—were told we could relax for the next several hours.

We held a raffle. No one had much money, but we figured that if everybody threw a half dollar into a kitty, the winner of the raffle would have enough money to buy a radio—which would be used for the entire barracks, naturally.

Frank Funk of Indiana was the winner, and shortly after he went off waving aloft the ticket of triumph, he returned to the barracks with our only source of contact to the outside world. It was a rare moment for all. We were in shorts and T-shirts, lolling on our bunks and soaking up relaxation. Frank plugged in the radio, and the barracks shook happily to music. I think the music lasted perhaps five minutes.

It stopped. The cadets turned to see what had happened, and all conversation halted as the announcer shattered our private worlds with the news that, on this morning, Japanese planes had bombed Pearl Harbor in the Hawaiian Islands.

All sound died, except the deep voice of that unidentified announcer who related the meager details of the attack against Hawaii. We heard phrases, I suppose: ". . . heavy casualties . . . the nation is at war . . ."

Not a man in that barracks spoke. We listened, each with his own thoughts, each struck in a different way, but struck deeply by the realization of what was happening.

War . . . we were at war. People in the United States; we were at war. I thought of what I had read of those savage melees so high over England, of the strangeness and alien substance of that conflict thousands of miles away.

But now . . . it was to be our fight. I realized these things; I *felt* the sudden change, I imagine, rather than being able to rationalize or to consider specifics. Everything was different. It was a feeling, a sensing, that came to all of us together, yet to every man alone.

War!

6

The first sound to be heard against the continuing news of the disaster was the incredulous voice of a cadet who cried, "Why, the bastards! The dirty, stinking bastards . . ."

We cadets were young men with limited practical experience in the world. Residence and schooling in a town like Lawton, Oklahoma, with a life filled with study, sports, flying, social and family activities, were perhaps not the best crucibles for forging a sensitive appreciation of wars that were being fought many thousands of miles away. No newspaper ever truly conveyed the screams of wounded and dying, and black and white newsprint is wholly inadequate for portraying the bright splash of spilled blood.

We lacked—by the very isolation of geography, by the in-
adequacy of newspaper and radio commentary and descriptions, and by our limited experience—an intrinsic grasp
of the roles we were destined to play in this new war. We
could and did realize, of course, that our position as flight
cadets would lead us inexorably into that vast arena of conflict. We knew that among our number there were boys who
would be killed in this fight. We *knew,* but it was impossible
to understand the full implications of what we knew. Not
then, not in those moments fresh with the news of a war
that was still thousands of miles distant.

By the close of the following week we had all been selected for our primary flight-training schools. With Gracyalyn, Eaves, Funk and several others, I shipped out to the
obscure town of Sikeston, Missouri. Here we would report
to a civilian contractor flying school to take our primary
flight instruction.

We cadets journeyed to Sikeston under our own steam, a
scattering of small groups who traveled by train, automobile
and bus. Three joined me in my car, and we formed a
ragged sort of convoy with three other cars, bumping our
way across the countryside.

The drive to Sikeston from San Antonio required three
days. At that time every radio station kept up a running
commentary on the latest developments in the Pacific, of
air battles and ships battered. Looking back now, I am
surprised to realize that we didn't stay glued to the car
radio. We'd received our shock and recognized that we
were at war. It was equally obvious to us all that no matter
what personal urgency impelled us to reach a combat area
at the earliest possible time, we were far removed from any
fighting, and that the state of affairs would prevail for many

months to come. Accepting this situation, the actual events of the combat raging those thousands of miles away were pushed to a secondary place in our thoughts, and our talk was almost entirely of flight maneuvers, of what we could expect at school—in short, strictly of flying.

The change in status imparted by our cadet uniforms was revealed in a small yet meaningful manner. We stopped in a little cow town in Oklahoma, a dusty place lost in loneliness on the vast plains. In a diner, our anonymity fled when the townspeople of the forsaken hamlet took full notice of our cadet uniforms. They had little to offer other than hospitality, but their warmth was an aura evident in their speech and attitude. As a parting gift we received what was perhaps the best they had to give at the moment, a sixteen-pound bag of pecans.

Our first impression of our future home and flight center at Sikeston, Missouri, was impressive. Before us lay beautiful fields, well tended and cropped. It appeared to be perfect for flying, until one of the cadets noticed a sign that identified the beautiful fields as a bull farm. It turned out the bulls were far more important to Sikeston than our flying, for the Army contract school squatted in mild squalor on a grassy field, resplendent in its single and somewhat aged tin hangar. Fortunately for us, our enthusiasm for flying still flamed brightly. In a little town stuck by itself in the middle of nowhere, with the ground frozen solid beneath our feet, the wind whistling and the thermometer at barely ten degrees above zero—we needed *something* to keep us warm!

With our supplies loading us down, we were assigned to our barracks at the field. The Air Corps at times could be downright efficient, and the cadets were broken into three

groups, identified as A, B and C Barracks. The latter was
for the "little fellers," known to one and all as the "sandblowers." This included, naturally, yours truly, Robert S.
Johnson.

Our new home was—well, let's just call it different. We
moved into single-story temporary wooden barracks, and
every man who once wore the uniform knows as well as I
that the "temporary" barracks of the Army are likely to be
kept in use for the lifetime of the Washington Monument.
Standing in perfect position to block all traffic in the barracks aisle were two potbellied stoves, which reminded me
not so much of a source of heat as of a setting for one of
Jack London's tales of the far frozen north. Once we were assigned to our bunks—the regular Army steel cot—our
"Brother" introduced himself. Each upper classman accepted as his charges several cadets, and it was his responsibility to provide leadership, discipline and—oh wonder!—protection from the *other* upper classmen!

Before the first day had passed we came to realize that
the days of close-order drill and the manual of arms belonged to yesteryear. Big Brother gathered his flock about
him and in no uncertain terms gave us "The Word."

"We're here to separate the men from the boys," was his
cheering salutation. "The purpose of this school is to complete your primary flight training as pilots. We have no use
for eight-balls. Those of you who are anything but letter-
perfect are going to be bounced out of here, and damned
quickly.

"You'll get along if you listen carefully to what you're
told, obey orders, and fly the way we expect you to fly.
The best advice I can give you if you want to complete
this course and go on to basic flight training is simply to
stay on the straight and narrow."

Merry Christmas, everybody!

Demerits were the price of disregarding this fraternal advice. Big Brother meant what he said about staying on the straight and narrow. To save the expense of haircuts, Gracyalyn and I each clipped the other's hair. The cut I received was more barbaric than a barber's clipping, and at inspection my shorn skull drew an incredulous stare. It took me four hours of marching at attention to "walk off" the demerits. This was the unique way we kept down the snow which fell frequently. I never appreciated the fact before that the tramping of cadet feet could beat even a blizzard into the ground.

The Air Corps instructors emphasized strongly in their training schedule the value of athletics and calisthenics, and in this respect I experienced no trouble at all. I was in excellent physical shape, and the routines regarded by the upper classmen as "rugged" were a cakewalk for me.

This fact one day plunged Cadet Johnson into hot water. Every so often upper classmen would instruct a cadet to give the orders for calisthenics training, and, when the finger pointed my way, I seized quickly upon the golden opportunity.

"AWRIGHT!" I shouted. "Assume positions for duckwalk!" This is a minor sort of torture which after a few minutes leaves the average person tied up in a combination of breathlessness, knotted muscles and an aching back. I dropped to a full knee-bend position, and ordered the group to place their hands on their hips, trunk straight, head held high and at attention. When propelled forward in this fashion, the human figure comes close to resembling our web-footed friends in motion. It is a sort of waddle which, if the individual is not in excellent physical shape, can become excruciating after a while. And for fifteen minutes I led the cadets—and the upper classmen—about the field in a rather hilarious, mass duckwalk.

That night another finger pointed at me. Unhappily this was one of retribution. Barely was the day over when two upper classmen stalked into the sandblowers' barracks, and stopped at my bunk.

"You hit a big one, Mister!" they shouted in chorus. I was informed fulsomely that they had come to appreciate my talents at duckwalking. "Cadet Johnson," one of the upper classmen purred, "we would deem it a disgrace not to enjoy the benefits of your obvious superiority in this particular endeavor. You are, sir, in popular demand with the upper classmen. You will follow me."

Led unerringly to the upper-classmen's barracks, I was greeted by the Exalted Ones, assembled in a group to partake in a feast of well-done Johnson Dinner. With the friendly smiles of a ring of crocodiles, they piled heavy textbooks beneath each of my arms, and bade me assume the duckwalking position.

For the next thirty-five minutes I marched in this fashion up and down the barracks, wending my way around the potbellied stoves, while the upper classmen indicated their pleasure at my talent with shouts of "Quack, quack!"

I still say it was worth it. To this day, despite those moments in the past when my ears sang with the stinging remarks of the upper classmen, when my back ached from those braces, and my feet despaired of the long marches to walk off demerits, I believe the hazing was worth all the troubles of endurance. Truly it did separate the men from the boys. One day we would be committed to battle, not as lone wolves, but each man as a part of a team, upon whose conduct the lives of many others would rest. Before a man could be entrusted with so great a responsibility, he had to prove, in the company of the same men with whom he might one day fight, that he could "take it." I never once forgot that the very men who bellowed heartily into my weary ears, who gleefully baited me, and enjoyed their lofty positions of superiority, had once endured the very same routine. Before a man could ever give orders or enforce discipline, he had to prove his ability to take orders and to be disciplined.

Before our first week at Sikeston had passed, we started on our flight lessons. H. E. Fulk, mild-mannered and a fabulous flier, was my first instructor. Two days before Christmas of 1941, I went aloft for my first flight as an Air Corps cadet, the details of which remain with me to this day.

The Fairchild PT-19A was a big airplane compared to what I had flown. A sleek, low-wing trainer—Army Number 26—it had 175 horsepower, several times that of the Taylorcraft I'd flown in the Civilian Pilot Training program. Fulk introduced me to the ship through a careful line inspection. Just before we climbed into it, he said, "Johnson, I know you've done some flying. But the Air Corps has a specific pattern of instruction, and with good reasons. Make it easier on yourself. Forget everything you learned in the past, and start out from scratch. Things will be a lot easier for you this way."

Fulk gave me my first chandelle, as well as other maneuvers still new to me. After several familiarization flights, he told me to follow him through lightly on the controls. First the right rudder bar went down a bit, and then I felt the stick coming back and easing over to the right. The PT-19A lifted up and around from cruising flight into a maximum, near-stall climbing turn. At the top, heading in the opposite direction, Fulk eased the laboring trainer gently out of the turn and climb and—presto!—we again slipped effortlessly through the air.

The five hours spent in the PT-19A were a dream. The lazy eight maneuvers were graceful swoops through the air. I'd simply apply slight left rudder and stick, and pull the trainer up into a climbing left turn, just as in the chandelle. The ship soared up and around and, just as she hung near a stall, I'd start a long, gentle swoop to the right.

And that was it, the gentle and lazy swoops and turns through the air, rising and falling like a leaf borne by the wind, following a great lazy figure eight. Perhaps the Air Corps considered this as training and as work, but to me it was wonder and freedom and joy, advancement in skill, a fulfillment of that wondrous moment of my first solo seven years before when I was fourteen years old.

No training schedule or ordered maneuvers could dampen my enthusiasm. What difference whether the gentle swoops or the violently rotating horizon and sky as the Fairchild whirled for the earth in a spin—this was flying! A difference was to be found only in that these flights were made not for pleasure alone. Each had to follow a specific schedule, each maneuver had to meet exacting requirements. The spins were not merely a free whirling plunge toward the snow-covered ground. Each was made as required. Spins to the left, to the right. Each recovery maneuver exactly so. Stick forward, opposite rudder, straighten out the airplane, bring her out exactly on point. Then stick back and level her out—or incur the wrath of the instructor.

After that the period with the Fairchild, new and yet immediately an old intimacy, was done. Fulk introduced me to the next step, a more powerful and sturdy machine, double-winged, solid, fairly itching to be taken aloft and wrung through the best that her pilot could do. She was a Stearman, a PT-18 with Number 39 painted on her fabric. Looming before her open cockpits was a 225 horsepower engine, a snarling promise of new freedom, a willingness to cut free and to fly.

My first flight in the Stearman revealed at once the beautiful agility of the rugged biplane. The primary trainer was sensitive and alive, responding instantly to even the barest touch of the controls.

Fulk separated each flying day into periods of dual instruction, and solo flights. Takeoffs and landings taught me the little tricks of the biplane in critical speed ranges. Fulk followed through with much of the same training routine I had known before. Yet each flight was different, each maneuver more demanding—225 horsepower was a far cry from the thirty-five horses of the little Taylorcraft.

One beautiful morning I found myself in the pilot's heaven I had come to know so well. Below us clouds drifted over the frozen Missouri countryside. This was a dual flight, and I had just completed a chandelle with the Stearman when Fulk came on the speaking tube: "Cadet Johnson, I've got it." I released the controls and looked forward in the small mirror. For a moment I could have sworn the quiet, soft-spoken instructor had a gleam in his eye; knowing Fulk, however, I dismissed the thou——

WHAM! Earth horizon and sky and clouds and Stearman engine whipped crazily around in a whirling streak. The trainer's nose snapped up and around, a stomach-wrenching whip combined with a rapid rolling motion.

"What was *that?*" I shouted.

Fulk laughed. "A snap roll, Johnson. How did you like it?"

"I don't know what to . . . I loved it, sir! But if I still had those tonsils the Air Corps had me take out, they'd be somewhere up here on the edge of my tongue by now!"

He chuckled. "Hang on," he called. "Here we go again. A bit more gentle this time; I'll slow roll her through."

The wings tilted to the left as Fulk swung the Stearman into a turn. But . . . as we reached a bank of forty-five degrees from the horizontal I felt Fulk's foot holding opposite rudder. Instead of turning, the Stearman continued to roll; the wings kept swinging around until, for a split second, they stood vertically along the horizon. Then we were going over, rolling smoothly into inverted flight.

I didn't know what to expect, but I followed Fulk through on the controls to feel the reactions of the ship in the slow roll. Then we were inverted—and I never expected the stream of dirt, nuts, paper and other debris that dropped from the cockpit floor and fell past my face. For a moment my sight was obscured by this flow of debris that swirled about my face before the propeller blast whipped it away.

Before I had time even to think about the dirt flying past, I dropped suddenly. The belt tugged against my stomach as I hung suspended. Unhappily I realized one disadvantage of being a sandblower—my feet fell away from the controls. There I was, hanging upside down, my feet unable to reach the controls. A fine picture of a pilot I was *then!*

I waved my left hand about frantically, trying to grab something to give me support. Still inverted, I found a metal tube along the side of the seat and hung on tightly.

I had sense enough to look about. My first sight of a world flung upside down was fabulous. Looking straight "up" I saw trees black against the snow, and "below" me stretched the deep blue sky. The wind streamed past my helmet and goggles, and strangely, the roar of the engine had become a muted and pleasant sound. And then we were coming out, rolling around again until the earth rested below and the sky stretched away above me.

The first thing I did was to reach down and tighten my safety belt as far as it would go.

"Johnson, do you want to do one?"

Did I! "Yes, sir!" I fairly shouted. So I tried my first slow roll. The trick, I knew, was to roll the airplane along its axis of flight, maintaining a heading by keeping a point on the horizon always in the same place over the nose.

I eased the stick to the left in a smooth but rapid movement, and simultaneously applied pressure on the left rudder pedal. The horizon tilted over and, as I approached a bank of forty-five degrees, I began applying pressure to the right rudder, making a gentle but definite transition.

The control movements seemed to me to be in slow motion, but actually the Stearman was rolling over into inverted flight in a steady and paced maneuver. At the forty-five-degree bank the change in rudder had resulted in a neutral control position, but only momentarily, as I continued to apply right rudder. Now I eased forward on the stick, still holding it far over to the left.

At the full ninety-degree bank, I had full right rudder and full left and forward stick. As the wings continued rolling into inverted flight I again worked the rudders to keep the nose of the ship rotating along its axis of flight. By the time I was fully inverted, the rudder was neutral again, the stick still to the left, but all the way forward to hold the nose up so that my elevator control was exactly the reverse of normal flight.

The Stearman rolled through beautifully, but *I* didn't. My control movements to this point had been smooth and continuous, exactly as the book said. But in the thrill and excitement of the moment—maybe I can blame it on my short arms and the fact that I was still hanging dearly to that pipe on the floor boards—I fouled up.

As I rolled into the inverted position, I should have kept the stick full forward. Instead, busily enjoying myself and clutching that pipe, I relaxed and allowed the stick to come back toward me.

Immediately the Stearman dropped her nose and ran for the earth, picking up speed quickly. And Cadet Johnson ended up in what is quaintly known as the "Hairy Maneuver"—falling out of the slow roll. As I moved the controls in corrective action the Stearman swooped up and around in a gigantic roll, exactly as though it were sliding along and around the inside of some enormous barrel in the sky. I didn't know it at the moment, but I had managed to blunder my way through something of a combination slow roll and a barrel roll, a maneuver packed with varying pleasant sensations, but hardly calculated to impress my instructor with my skill.

However, it was the first time, and Fulk only grinned. That afternoon we had a picnic in the sky. Fulk was feeling his oats, and he slow rolled, barrel rolled, and snap rolled, easing the Stearman through her maneuvers as if he were part of the biplane's nervous system.

Fulk kept me at it, too, rolling the ship around and around until I reached the point where I could go through the maneuver in fair condition. Again and again we went at it, each time with my eyes glued to a horizon reference point, and the engine, snow and trees, sky, the horizon, and the cockpit rim moving in a blurred circular streak before my eyes. By the time we were through, I was able to slow roll the Stearman to the full satisfaction of the instructor.

I never did like the slow roll. It looks pretty to the pilot of another airplane, and it is an impressive maneuver to the person on ground. But it's uncomfortable to the guy in the cockpit, and as far as I'm concerned, it's an unnatural way to fly.

I much prefer the barrel roll. In this case the airplane slides around the inside of the giant barrel in space, describing a wide circle around its axis of flight. It's a maneuver beautiful both to watch and to experience. As I swing through the roll, centrifugal force keeps me pinned to the seat. I don't hang down, suspended by my seat belt. I never did a slow roll in that Stearman without hanging on for dear life to that tubing at the bottom of the cockpit.

One morning, like so many others, I took off still half asleep for an early morning solo aerobatic mission. I was supposed to do a series of maneuvers, including slow rolls and the split-S. Somehow I didn't feel like running through the entire routine, and confined my aerobatics to barrel rolls and to spins. At the end of my flight time I landed at the field, and reached down to release my seat belt.

The belt had never been fastened. I had been doing my spins and barrel rolls without the fastened belt! The thought of myself dropping out of that airplane suddenly, caught without warning and dumped into space, if I *had* flown either a slow roll or a split-S . . . *whew!* I never made that mistake again.

Everything in a training program can't be good news. We had lost several cadets in accidents, notably a case in which a hapless student spun wildly out of a snowstorm to crash into the ground. But now we were losing them in a different way: the men were being separated from the boys, and more and more of the cadets were being washed out.

Some of the boys who got sick, or froze at the controls,

or who were unbalanced by the sensations of height, managed to fight their way through what can only be described as monumental emotional obstacles. Others just couldn't make it. It had nothing to do with a desire to fly, or with a lack of courage. The same man who washed out of flying because of a severe physical and emotional reaction could be a roaring terror in combat on the ground.

It pained us to realize that one of our very best friends at Sikeston had to be scrubbed from flight training—Gracyalyn. He had been so tense at the controls that his airplane was banged about with forced, jerky movements. One morning Gracyalyn's instructor took him up for spins, and that did it. That night in the barracks Gracyalyn told us his tale of woe.

"I do everything the way he tells me to," Gracyalyn explained, "and for a while it all goes fine. I haul back on the stick and she goes up steeply. Just when she hangs on a stall, I kick the right rudder.

"Everything works the way the book says. I hold the stick in my stomach and she hauls around, rolling into the spin to the right. Down we go, around and around, everything like clockwork. Then the instructor tells me to pull out.

"This is easier said than done." Gracyalyn shrugged. "What can I do? I want to pull out, but my right leg has other ideas. I shove the stick forward and I try to kick opposite rudder. But my right leg freezes! I grit my teeth, trying to get my right leg off the rudder. It won't move, and by now we're out of the spin, all right, going down in a wicked tight spiral.

"I don't know what to do. I kick hell out of my right foot with my left foot, but all I get for that is a couple of bruises. Finally I let go of the stick, reach down with both hands, and I lift that damn foot off the rudder. By now all

I want to do is to get out! I grab that stick with both hands and haul back—and out we come."

And how they came out of that spiral! Gracyalyn finished his story there, but it seems that he hauled the stick back suddenly, literally jerking it back into the pit of his stomach. And that Stearman was made to respond! The biplane whipped out of the spiral and shot from a near-vertical dive into a brutal pullout. Instructor and student sagged down into their seats from the g-forces and when they could look up again the Stearman was clawing her way back upstairs in a near-vertical climb.

In this case it was obviously the instructor and not the student who had received a "thrill." Gracyalyn was told to keep his hands in his lap, and the instructor brought the Stearman home to roost. The next morning Gracyalyn was given a thorough checkride—and at the end of that flight he was washed out as a cadet. Soon after, the unhappy cadet shipped out from Sikeston. Not until many years later, after the war, did I hear from him again.

We sandblowers from Barracks C sometimes had a knack for—well, let's say we didn't always do things exactly as the book stated they should be done. One of my fellow sandblowers was another little guy, named Frank K. Everest— for some strange reason called "Pete" by the rest of us. Perhaps the reader will recognize the name; Pete Everest became an outstanding fighter pilot in World War II, fought in Europe and then in Burma and China. Several months before the war ended a barrage of Japanese slugs caught his low-flying Mustang, and Pete went down. He finished out the last few months of the war as a Japanese prisoner.

Pete Everest later became one of the greatest test pilots in aviation history. As the top man in the Air Force Flight

Test Center for test flying, Pete became recognized as one of the world's outstanding authorities in this dangerous and precision work. He's been in airplanes that have exploded, burned, torn apart and crashed. He once held the world's speed record in the X-2 at 1,900 miles per hour. Who would ever have thought back in 1941, at that little grass field in Sikeston, that Sandblower Everest would become Colonel Everest, one of the fastest pilots in the world, and slated to become one of our first spacemen!

There had been a few moments at Sikeston, however, when Pete thought that he'd never even last out primary training. He was on a solo flight and behaving himself when he sighted another trainer. This was too good to miss . . .

Pete rolled over and came charging down at the other plane, sliding in to a tail firing position. The other ship jockeyed frantically all over the sky while Pete hung grimly to his tail, and managed to do a pretty fair job of staying there. Then he eased off the tail slot, and pulled alongside the other trainer to wave at the pilot.

Poor Pete. His grin faded to a horror-stricken expression as he noticed that the other flier was not a student—but a check-pilot lieutenant, a *fighter* pilot, mind you! Immediately Pete banged the stick over and kicked rudder to get out of there, but the lieutenant was right on his tail. Perhaps this was a measure of Pete's skill in the air—the lieutenant couldn't stay with his wild evasive action. He shook the lieutenant and lit out for home at full throttle.

He fairly crawled out of the airplane, and drooped his way into the barracks, scared stiff. He told us what had happened, and that the lieutenant would sure be after his hide. Pete was convinced that his flying days as a cadet were over.

At the messhall that night, Pete sat picking at his food,

a picture of dejection. His face drooped some more when he saw the lieutenant making a beeline for our table.

"What happened to you out there today?" he asked quietly. Pete mumbled something, fearing the words of disaster that he expected. The lieutenant grinned. "I'm sorry you got away like that," he said. "We could have had a ball. I haven't mixed it up in a free-for-all in a long time."

Pete stared at him, eyes bugging. He wasn't sore. . . . As the lieutenant walked away, Pete could scarcely believe his ears. ". . . maybe we'll get the opportunity again to give it a whirl. Only stick around for a while and give me a chance!"

On January 28, 1942, I received a new instructor. This wasn't to my liking, since I'd accumulated thirty-two hours under Fulk's wing and had become fond of him both as an instructor and as a friend. One of the cadet officers, however, had become afraid of his own instructor, and his flying and peace of mind suffered accordingly. He requested a change. The C.O. in turn "requested" that I exchange instructors with the other student pilot. I didn't like it one bit; not only because Fulk had been wonderful but also because I hated to be placed under a man who, obviously, was having difficulty with at least one, and possibly more, students. Oh, well! He was an instructor, a competent flier, and he could teach me to fly. After all, that's what I was here for.

My first flight with Phil Zampini was not exactly a joyride. Every time I looked into the rear-view mirror, I noticed his eyes glued on me. I was well in focus; Zampini was not the sort who relaxed in the cockpit. The sight left something to be desired; he was anything but a gentle-looking man.

After several flights together, we landed at south field

and were relaxing with some coffee, waiting for a plane to be readied for another flight. I discovered during these few off-guard moments that every flight school had a specific quota of pilots to graduate, and a specific number to eliminate from the training program. Unfortunately for Zampini, they had fingered him as the man to eliminate a certain number of pilots. He was finding it rough living with this problem, for he did not dare to make a friend— and then bounce the man.

The heart of the problem was that, though all of his students might fly well, he had to find a reason for washing some of them out. In the class before mine he had eliminated five pilots . . . *all* of *his* students. In my own class he'd already washed out three out of five students. I didn't envy his position.

Phil Zampini was one of the finest precision pilots with whom I've ever flown, and an instructor second to none. We hit it off together and in the short period during which he was my instructor we became good friends.

On our last flight—after some thirty hours with Zampini —he pulled out all the stops. This was just before graduation, and Zampini was out to teach me a few extra tricks that weren't in the curriculum.

On a beautiful, cloudless day, we went up in a closed cockpit Fairchild trainer and rewrote the book on aerobatics. It was one of those priceless times in the sky when a student is swept up with the desire of an outstanding flier to impart his knowledge and skill to his ward, and Zampini gave me everything he had to give.

I couldn't help thinking of those three little pursuits I'd seen when I was eight years old. Zampini did everything they had done. We dove and climbed, we soared, looped, skidded, slipped. He hung on our prop and staggered off right and left. Falling leafs, Immelmanns, loops, snap rolls, great barrel rolls, hammerhead stalls, vertical reverses— *everything*. It was one of the finest hours in my life.

On February tenth, nearly three weeks before I met Zampini for the first time, one of the boys brought an Army-Navy Journal into the barracks—with a news item outlined in red. He showed us a new regulation which authorized the acceptance of married personnel as flight cadets.

During my college days I had started going around with Barbara Morgan, and since I had always believed that a man's personal life was pretty much his own business, few people knew that Barbara and I had decided on marriage. The time was something we couldn't decide by ourselves, since one of the requirements for flight-cadet training had been single status.

But now . . . I knew that the base commander, Major Rockwood, was very fond of a girl living in a nearby town, and I thought he might be disposed toward permitting one of his cadets to get married. With my mind made up—why waste time?

I knocked on his office door, and walked in. I never held a better brace in my life, and snapped up a salute. "Sir! Cadet Johnson, R. S. Major, I would like your permission to get married."

He stared at me. Without giving him a chance even to open his mouth, I went right on talking. I put him on the spot by referring to his own girl; at least he couldn't immediately yell "No!" and throw me out of his office. When I finished, he told me he would see the Cadet Board and that the Board would see me that evening.

As far as I was concerned, however, I'd abided by the rules and regulations. I had requested permission from my commanding officer and, frankly, I didn't care a hoot what his decision would be. That afternoon I wired Barbara in Lawton to come to Sikeston just as soon as she could so that we could be married immediately.

That evening the cadet review board decided—naturally —that I should not get married. They refused permission on the basis that as a cadet I had signed away everything, life, liberty, happiness. It was a great little speech they made, but I don't believe I listened closely. Who cared? Even then Barbara was on her way to Sikeston!

By now all the cadets knew about the oncoming wedding. How the officers were kept in the dark is still a mystery to me, but they never even got wind of the mass conspiracy being practiced at the field. Comstock, Pete Everest, Stinky Miller, Eaves, the whole gang pitched in nickels, dimes and quarters to buy us a wedding present.

Late on the evening of February twenty-first (my birthday) Barbara arrived in Sikeston. Another cadet and his fiancée piled into the car with us to be our witnesses, and we drove to the parsonage of the Methodist Minister, Reverend Bess, in the little nearby town of Benton. It certainly wasn't the biggest wedding ever, and the crowd was kept small (the four of us!), but no two people were happier than Barbara and myself.

The following day we were to leave for Randolph Field in Texas to report for basic flight training. Barbara and I stayed in a small hotel in Sikeston that night. We were rich! The cadets had chipped in a total of sixty-three dollars as a wedding present.

The next morning Barbara and I climbed into our car, a disreputable 1936 Chevrolet, with two cadets in the rear for company, and three other cars filled with cadets as a convoy. We were off on our honeymoon!

7

On the morning of February 26, 1942, Barbara left San Antonio for the long bus trip back to Lawton, Oklahoma. We had been married only a few days. Our "honeymoon" —forced by circumstance to be crowded into that brief interval between departing from Sikeston and reporting to Randolph Field in Texas—left something to be desired.

Brief though it was, and attended by our flock of laughing and boisterous cadets, the several days on the road were as wonderful and as happy as the traditional trip to Niagara Falls. Of course, our honeymoon was somewhat different than the kind a couple normally anticipates. I'll venture few people have ever spent their first several days of wedded life in a car convoy of exuberant air cadets. But no bride ever received more doting attention than did the new Mrs. Johnson during those hectic days.

The moment Barbara's bus disappeared from sight, I reported for duty at Cadet Headquarters on Randolph Field. The feelings of uninhibited enthusiasm which had so deeply infected all of us during our first days as cadets had vanished. The air was charged, it seemed, with a grim sense of urgency. People at Randolph were possessed with a determination to keep the training program rolling in high gear.

On the morning of the twenty-seventh, barely twenty-four hours after I reported to Randolph, I was back in the air as a student pilot.

No cocky primary trainer any more for Johnson. The wonderful days at Sikeston, with the sensitive dervish we knew as the PT-18, were replaced with a grinding and relentless instruction in the North American BT-9 Yale, big and husky in comparison to the agile primary trainers. The snarl from the slamming cylinders up front came from 450 horsepower, more than twice as many as had ever roared under my throttle.

Lieutenant M. R. Burgess made the introduction to the Yale, and I was taught the eccentricities and the characteristics of the new ship. Even here I felt the change from the past. Burgess and the other instructors were not in the air to accommodate slipshod piloting or to wipe the wet nose of an unqualified cadet. Such ministrations were the sole domain of primary school, where personalities could be considered and difficulties ironed out. Now, as primary-flight-school graduates, the Air Force expected us to be able to fly.

The first hours spent aloft with the Yale were a challenge to learn her tricks, and to recognize her faults and dangers. I repeated the same maneuvers I had learned so well at Sikeston, whetting my ability with the task of guiding the greater weight and power of the BT-9 to respond smoothly and effortlessly in the sky.

This was the time allowed the new basic student to play tag with clouds, to swing up and around in chandelles and loops, to stand on a wing, to arc gracefully through the sky, soaring, gliding, flying as a man was meant to fly. Once I learned her tricks, the BT-9 and I settled down to serious business. No more swirling maneuvers. No more wonderful sound of the engine straining to pull the ship up and over the top of an enormous soaring loop, then singing of power as the earth rushed upward at the suddenly descending metal creature.

I moved into instrument training, a period of flight far removed from the early days of cold air and the shrill cry of wind past my open cockpit. Instrument flying is a precision business, demanding patience and an unflagging attention to the dials and needles which must, under certain conditions, replace entirely the natural instincts and feelings of the pilot. It is the only means of survival for the man lost at night, trapped in or over thick and opaque clouds, or battered by storm. It is indispensable to teamwork in the air.

My first "flight" on instruments was made in the weird contraption known as the Link trainer, an electronic, boxlike nightmare into which a pilot is clamped and sent out on "instrument flights." Cut off from the outside world except for radio and electronic devices which reproduce on instruments the motions and attitudes of an airplane in flight, the fledgling is dispatched on dangerous forays in the sky without ever leaving the ground. The faithful reproduction of aircraft controls, dials and instruments at times has proven overwhelming to students, with several riotous occasions when the fledgling in his electronic coffin has succumbed to the sensation that he was, literally, in the air, and, caught in a "violent power spin," has hurled back the cockpit hatch to dive in a crumpled heap on the floor as he "bailed out."

Much of my flying had been done by "feeling" the airplane's motions. The Link taught me—in absolute safety— that under certain blind flying conditions a stubborn reliance on my "senses" could kill me, and quickly. In flight under clear visual conditions no pilot worth his salt requires instruments except for navigation, but when the clouds boil and mix and close in, the man who cannot fly by his instruments is not long for this world. Under turbulent conditions and total lack of visibility, a pilot in a steep diving spiral may be absolutely convinced that he is flying straight and level, and disbelief of what his instruments tell him can prove lethal. Yet, I've also discovered that experience in aerobatics is an invaluable teacher in the matter of recognizing the attitude of an aircraft under a variety of flight conditions.

My old friend Burgess started my instrument training under the tried-and-true program of proving to the student that he's not really so hot. It's an old formula which works —most of the time. It didn't work with me, to my joy and the unhappy consternation of the lieutenant.

In the rear cockpit, I was "sealed in" beneath a canvas covering which blinded me to the outside world. I could fly only by instruments and by my own senses. Once in the air, Burgess climbed to a safe altitude and then ran wild with the BT-9. Knowing that under the hood I could see nothing of the horizon, he rolled, looped, chandelled, stalled, spun, spiralled, dove—did everything he could do to disorient me.

At the worst possible moment of flight, with the ship on the verge of snapping out of control, he'd yell, "Okay, Johnson, you've got it—bring her out!"

It was a shock, every time, to my instructor when I did exactly that. Several times I found myself hanging by my belt as Burgess kept the Yale in inverted flight. Normally I kept my hands in my lap while Burgess went through the aerobatic book. One of his favorite tricks was to pass the controls to me when the airplane was inverted and in some crazy attitude. Each time I'd hold my right hand poised to grasp the stick, and the moment he'd yell, I'd bang the stick over and kick rudder to roll her into level flight.

With each passing moment my instructor became more and more unhappy with his cadet. All the established rules of cowing the student pilot by demonstrating his inability to cope with the airplane under blind flying conditions were being thrown out the window.

"Johnson! Goddammit, stay off those controls until I give you the order to take over!" he roared. Slowly his voice kept rising in pitch as he became angrier. "You keep your hands in your lap, Cadet Johnson, until you're told to take over. Now stop jumping the gun on me!"

He couldn't understand that I was that quick on the controls. Every time I sat back while Burgess dished it out, I did exactly what he told me, hands in my lap, feet off the rudder. But at just that second when he yelled, my hand went out like a cat and grabbed the stick.

I could almost hear him muttering to himself in the cockpit. I knew that his patience was disappearing like steam in the wind. He mumbled something to me and then the BT-9 went wild. The first time he started to show that smart-aleck Cadet Johnson a trick or two, he called out just as the trainer soared upward in a climb, inverted, and ready at the slightest misuse of controls to whip out and tumble earth-ward.

I had my eyes glued to the gauges, and my hand poised. Burgess called for me to take over and just as pretty as you please, I rolled her over and slid out into level flight. He got trickier the longer we were aloft. His next stunt was to pull the trainer up on her nose, kick her around in a hammerhead stall, and throw the plane into a steep diving spiral—a death maneuver for the pilot caught without instruments in bad weather or at night. Quickly I leveled the wings, chopped power, and hauled her out.

Finally Burgess completely lost his temper. He whirled the trainer about in gyrating maneuvers. I had my feet rest-ing on the heels, ready to hit the rudder pedals. Then Bur-gess banged the stick rapidly from side to side. The metal tube smacked painfully against my knees with each full movement, and he kept it up. I had to lift my legs high off the floor boards and move them off to the sides.

"Now, Johnson, now!" he shouted. "Bring her out!" Down stamped my feet, and I swung the trainer hard out of her tumble through the air into straight and level flight.

Burgess was fairly foaming by now. "What in hell's the matter with you, Johnson?" he screamed. "You're trying to kill me! For God's sake, man, I've got a wife and three kids at home. I want to get back to land!" He ranted and raved for a while, then whipped the trainer up and over in an im-possible corkscrewing climb. He chanted his complaints of life and limb and then abruptly went quiet.

I must have been quite a sight in that enclosed cockpit, left hand poised over the throttle, my right hand fairly coiled to spring at the stick, and my feet ready to hit the rudder as Burgess hurled the BT-9 through her gyrations, straining my body against the seat belt.

When Burgess went quiet, I anticipated another knee battering. I kept my eye glued to the stick, and the moment it started to swing hard over to the side I grabbed it with my right hand. The struggle had taken a new turn—a test of strength! I could feel my instructor straining to move the stick, but I clenched the offending object as hard as I could and just hung on. After several minutes of Burgess hauling at the stick with both hands, and me clinging grimly to the control, the fight ended. It was a quiet showdown, with not a word spoken between us. Burgess told me to peel back the hood, and we went home.

I discovered later that this victory might well cost me dearly, much more than I ever wanted to pay. One afternoon, standing by the trainer after a flight, I asked Burgess if he would sign my logbook at the completion of my training at Randolph.

The lieutenant stared at me coldly. "What makes you think you're going to graduate from here, Johnson?" he grated. "How do you know you're not going to wash out?"

I stared at him. The man was crazy! Why, the possibility of washing out of flight school had never even entered my mind! I grinned at him. "Lieutenant, I've waited all my life to get into the Air Force, and I have no intention of ever washing out. That's why . . ."

Burgess didn't say a word, but from that point on he did everything possible when we flew together to "knock the cockiness out of you, Johnson." I didn't understand his attitude. To me a fighter pilot *had* to be aggressive and self-confident. Everything I had ever learned about air fighting taught me that the man who is aggressive, who pushes a fight, is the pilot who is successful in combat and who has the best opportunity for surviving battle and coming home. If Burgess meant to haze me, that was one thing—but the man appeared to be serious.

When we prepared for flight training, he ordered me to stand by the wing of the airplane, heavy flying clothes and my parachute buckled on tightly. And here he would keep me in a wicked, stiff brace, while he leaned against the wing with another cadet and had a chummy talk.

Our flights became even rougher than during the little showdown we had had by ourselves in the sky. Burgess made my flying hard work, and never missed an opportunity to push me as hard as he could. It kept growing worse. For the very first time since I'd taken my oath, I had doubts about my final outcome in the Air Force. The more I thought about the problem, the more I entertained thoughts of requesting a transfer to another instructor before Burgess could manage to have me booted out of flight training.

My greatest fear was that one day he'd push me past my limit, and that I'd cut my own throat by losing my temper. If that happened, I knew that I'd be all over Burgess. And that would mean the end of Cadet Johnson, R.S.! But the more I thought about the private war between Burgess and myself, the more repugnant became the idea of quitting. Requesting a transfer meant to me that I couldn't take what Burgess had to dish out. I swore that I'd show that old so-and-so by taking everything he had to give, and that I'd beat him at his own game.

Five hours of instruction time later I couldn't have been happier with this choice. Burgess received orders transferring him to another command, and he was whisked out of my student life, along with his self-made problems.

Burgess was a big man. His replacement was even bigger Lieutenant T. M. Maloney was a rough, gruff Irishman, bulging with muscle, who towered over me. But how that man could fly! It was almost like having Zampini with me in the air again, for here was another of those rare instructors, gifted with brilliant piloting skill, who bent every effort to impart his skill and knowledge to his students. Maloney and I flew together for twenty hours, and the time spent with this man was invaluable to me. What Maloney passed on to his cadet student wasn't to be found in any book.

It was this personal touch, the willingness to turn the fledgling into an eagle, for which I shall always be indebted to men like Zampini and Maloney. They are the difference between learning to fly by the book, and learning to fly as a part of the airplane's very steel sinew. The small tricks I learned from them, the little touches of experience, were the things which later proved so invaluable in the air war over Germany.

A new name appeared in my logbook, that of Lieutenant L. B. Farnell, Jr., who was to teach me to fly in formation, to guide my airplane with patience and skill in the closest possible proximity to other machines in the sky. My first sight of Farnell was a shot in the arm to my morale. After the bearlike size and the bulldog countenances of Burgess and Maloney, little Farnell in comparison seemed like a Pekingese! I swear I suddenly seemed to expand in size; I felt bigger and more on even terms with an instructor than ever before.

For our first flight the diminutive Farnell strode briskly to the airplane, a big grin plastered across his face. He looked like a man who could fly well and who, on this partic-

ular morning, was going upstairs to enjoy himself. Except—
well, for a while I didn't know whether Farnell had dismissed
his senses, or simply was determined to scare his students
half to death.

He revved up the BT-9 and with judicious use of the
brakes, rudder and throttle, squeezed his way directly behind another trainer—which seemed also to be occupied by
an instructor similarly afflicted with madness. When our
plane stopped, the wingtips of both trainers were barely
twelve inches apart. And here they stayed as both planes
started their roll down the grass. Only experience with instructors prevented me from asking Farnell if he knew what
the devil he was doing. Neither plane moved an inch apart
as they roared in tight formation down the field. I stared at
the two wingtips, expecting anything to happen. . . .

Did I say *tight* formation? Our wheels were barely off the
ground when Farnell nursed the throttle and inched the BT-9
forward. I was fascinated by the sight of our wing moving
closer and closer to the other airplane, whose pilot seemed
utterly indifferent to the formation. No sooner had Farnell
placed several feet of our airplane's wing in such position
that it hovered barely inches above the wing of the other
BT-9 when the trainer banked steeply and rolled into a
turn. I blinked. When I opened my eyes Farnell had our
ship in exactly the same turn . . . both wings were exactly
in the same position!

And away we went, two ships seemingly bolted together
as one plane, turning and banking, gliding, climbing, in an
astonishing firsthand demonstration of a piloting skill of
which I was virtually ignorant. This was the beginning of
my training in patience and air discipline. The lessons in
formation flying taught me air teamwork and a degree of
co-ordination in flying with other airplanes which seemed

all the more remarkable when I realized that I, too, could fly these tight dual maneuvers.

Hour after hour piled up in my logbook. Formation take-offs, made with sensitive and constant minor adjustments of throttle and rudder and stick in order to remain exactly in position. Formation landings, each ship sliding down from space on its own invisible guiding wire, each hand in each cockpit invisibly alike, curling around the throttle knob. Where once I considered a good crosswind landing a noteworthy accomplishment, I gained skill in the infinitely more difficult procedure of landing in formation in a cross-wind, constantly adjusting for wind shifts and gusts and the minor eccentricities of flight of an airplane descending at minimum speed and power.

Then into gentle turns in formation, our instructors work-ing with us every inch of the way, teaching us the little tricks of lifting up and over, of holding position in the two and three slot with skill sufficient to allow the lead pilot to ignore completely the two flashing, deadly propellers so close to his own naked airplane.

We learned how to drop into and to leave echelon forma-tion smoothly and quickly, each plane moving with the re-hearsed precision of a ballet dancer. We learned the value of using the rudder for skidding in and out of formation.

As the weeks passed we were able virtually to slide the BT-9 on invisible rails into and away from the vee and ech-elon flights. These were the early moments of not merely learning, but accepting on the basis of our very own life and skill, the airmanship and competency of the men with whom we flew formation. For when, as a pilot, you fly this closely in the air at 150 miles per hour, and maneuver in steep turns and banks, in glides and in climbs, you can no longer look constantly at your teammate and protect yourself from his possibly inadvertent moves. You come to rest your life on *his* skill, as he does on yours, or you simply get out, and stay out, of the air.

From the beginning Farnell taught me not to be wing-shy. At first sight two wings so close together appear start-ling and dangerous. Yet it is within this very proximity that safety rests, for even should two wings bump (as they did on several occasions) their movement is so slight that not enough force is exerted to cause much damage, if any.

To the pilot flying by himself in the vast sky arena, the blast of air following behind his own airplane is nonexistent. It can be encountered only when the pilot practices turns of 360 degrees and 720 degrees, and only if he maintains his altitude with sufficient precision to suddenly encounter a definite and even a sharp bump in the air—the stream of tur-bulent air caused by the passage of his own airplane. But in formation flying, propwash, as well as the wash of air from other wings, is an invisible enemy, always waiting to jostle an airplane about severely, to shake it up, to send a wingtip skidding with dangerous force into the fuselage or tail as-sembly of another airplane.

In my student flying with Farnell I suffered no dangerous incidents. But how I came to respect this streaming and turbulent air! Again and again both Farnell and continued experience hammered home the lesson of the pilot maintain-ing use of his controls with extreme sensitivity, always stay-ing on the throttle, always ready to move the rudder pedals with his feet, to use the stick, all separate motions to be in-tegrated into agile response from the airplane.

I had sense enough to realize the necessity of such flying. No pilot ever flies alone. The days of the daredevil aces of World War I that I had read about so avidly were moments of history long past. The tactics of Lufbery, of Fonck, of

Boelcke, and the greats of that historic melee in the air were not for today's air battles where teamwork and precision were the key ingredients to success, and continued life. This Farnell and my own experience taught me, but not for a moment could I have anticipated the near future when I would fly as a member of the most devastating air killer team in Europe—Zemke's Wolfpack.

The days passed in an increasing blur of studying, flying, training, and more studying. From early morning until well into the evening our instructors hammered flying, flying, flying into our minds and bodies. Then our flying beneath the sun was completed, and we prepared for night training.

My first flight under the stars was a journey back in time, when I had scampered so eagerly into the cabin of that ancient Ford Tri-Motor in Lawton. The passage of years had brought with them piloting ability, and even foreknowledge of what to expect in the sky stripped of light; yet, not even the intervening years could diminish the sense of beauty, or the impression of the infinite depth of world and space that I had found on my first flight.

I have rarely known skies so utterly black as those I encountered high over the San Antonio area. Usually even the absence of a moon in a clear and star-filled sky cannot prevent a soft and diffused glow from filling the night heavens. Starlight and the very glow of the upper air are usually sufficient to permit the pilot to distinguish where the inky silhouettes of mountains cleave the night air.

But not during those moonless night hours of training when I flew from Randolph Field. Once the trainer had gripped the cool air with her wings and soared away from earth, not even the vast display of celestial light, the infinite range of stars, blue and white, sparkling and gleaming, could pierce the gloom. On these occasions the stars were to be marvelled at, a miracle of a strange and sparkling canopy of light that seemed to reach only the eye of the viewer and nowhere else.

Far below, oases of shimmering colors, of diffused red and blue and yellow and green, pinpoints of pink, sudden flares of harsh hues, sliced through the night. Small farmhouses, common and unworthy of attention by day, became important and eye-catching by the sole virtue of a needle-pointed gleam against a bottomless backdrop of velvet. Distant towns announced their presence on the vast ocean of sand by dim tendrils of softly glowing highway lights, leading to a stationary, self-illuminated pinwheel.

Sometimes the lights below became alive: the caterpillar glow of a passenger train gliding across the black, preceded by a tiny shower of sparks and tinted orange flame from the locomotive; or the firefly gleam of a lonely automobile in the midst of darkened earth slowly piercing the silver gloom.

There were sometimes lights in the sky as well: the hard glint of moonlight running as flashing quicksilver along the trainer's wings, the reflection of moonbeams in the glass canopy, dancing streamers of cold fire flitting through the propeller. Sometimes there was company in the air, the harsh sheen of blue exhausts of other trainers, ghosts in the air, captured by a reflected flash of moonlight and the red and green marker lights outboard on the wings and at the tail.

These were strange and mystical hours of flight, for if I allowed my imagination free rein, especially when I flew beneath a canopy of high clouds, the world became like a deep and dark ocean, the lights of the other planes becoming the iridescence of deep-sea creatures able to glow of themselves. These were moments of beauty, utterly different and yet in every sense as enchanting and alive as those spent soaring through sun-drenched clouds. They were moments for pilots only, unknown and a thousand worlds away from the people over whom we flew, captured and wingless, lost in the velvety black of the darkened earth.

Suddenly it was over. I had lost track of days fleeing from the calendar. The weeks had passed in a flow of hours of flight and of study and there before me stretched the completion of basic training. Now, another step in the long ascent of skill and proficiency had been made, and I was that much closer to the final goal where I would streak into the blue on fighter wings.

I was advised to do otherwise. Our instructors conferred with us and discussed our future as pilots. When we waxed enthusiastic about fighters, they did their best to dissuade us. I was as imbued as any with the dream of fighters, yet I had come to respect highly the opinion and the experience of those same men who were imparting to me their own talents born of many years in the air.

"Look, Johnson," they explained, "there's no future in fighters. Sure, it's a big deal now because we need a lot of people to jockey these things around the sky. But what comes after? You want to keep on flying?"

What else? I nodded assent.

"Then fighters aren't the answer. If you want to keep those wings you're working for active after this war, then you'd better get into multi-engine. The big stuff. When this fracas is over they're going to need airline pilots. Think of the future, Johnson; a couple of years pushing around bombers or transports means clinching an airline seat later. Fighters won't get you anywhere."

And so the arguments went. I'd always wanted fighters so bad I could almost taste the sound and feeling of the powerhouse killers. Why I gave in to these arguments I'll never know. But the pressure was on; many of the cadets with whom I flew had signed for multi-engine work, to fly bombers and transports. My heart wasn't in the decision, but somehow I muttered, "Okay, okay, I'll take multi-engine school." And I signed for bombers.

I'd always wanted to fly at Kelly Field in Texas, and my decision for bomber training at least meant realizing this wish. With most of my cadet class I moved to Kelly, swept along with the increasing clamor for more and more pilots. If there had been a sense of need before, the feeling that pervaded Kelly Field was now one of extreme urgency.

On May 2, 1942, I made my first flight at Kelly Field as a bomber student pilot. I had accomplished another move toward wearing those coveted silver wings, for now I broke away from earth in a North American BC-1, a rugged and sleek trainer pulled through the sky by a snarling engine of 650 horsepower. The BC-1 was a demanding airplane, beautifully designed, clean with retracting gear—and unforgiving of an erring pilot. You knew you had the stuff when you put this ship through her paces, and between May second and June twenty-eighth, I spent 93 hours and 30 minutes in the BC-1 basic combat and AT-6 advanced trainers, bringing my total air time to 300 hours.

Again our flying was kept on a strict training basis. We were being taught to fly as bomber pilots, and since bombers aren't made for the wild aerobatics or free-soaring maneuvers I had learned to love so well, the two months at Kelly Field became a period of grinding perfection and versatility into our flying.

We flew by day and by night. Straight and level flight, in clear weather and in storms. Navigation under the hood, formations at night. Radio beams for long cross-country flights, hours on instruments, learning how to reach distant targets, taking evasive action. Days and nights of practice until even the most complicated instrument flight, which once had seemed overwhelming, became habit, a means of flight accepted and perfected. Only one flaw marred our training. Without twin-engined trainers, none of which were available, we were kept in the BC-1 and AT-6 trainers, single-engined machines which could never teach proficiency in the multitude of responsibilities which larger and multi-engined aircraft demanded.

I was assigned as first pilot off the ground for the long night missions, a role which endeared me to the other cadets. I was the first to fly into storms and turbulence, and the crowd on the ground chortled as I sometimes made my radio reports while the trainer was being whipped and buffeted by angry, towering thunderstorms. Then, rain drummed in impenetrable sheets of water against the canopy and the wings. Shattering bolts of lightning leaped from cloud to cloud in writhing energy, or disappeared through an abyss to hurl themselves into the earth far below my wings. Hail battered at the metal of the airplane in a machine-gun staccato, hurled by the wind and my own velocity to impact speeds as high as two hundred miles per hour, each hailstone a ragged ice bullet, exploding with cracking reports against the trainer.

Wings askew, nose whirling from a steep climb to a wild and plunging spiral, buffeted, hammered and flung about, the trainer brought me through the heart of the elements, each moment in this furious space at once a challenge and a victory.

Where was the time going? We had no time in which to read newspapers, or to listen to radio news broadcasts, or even to discuss with one another what was happening in a world writhing in blood and in mounting battle. Up at daybreak, often in the air by six A.M., flying through a sky painted with dawn, a broadening streak wiping away the smudge of darkness clinging grimly around the western rim of the visible world. Fly, fly, fly! Land for food, for critiques, for more and more instruction, and then again into the air. Land and refuel, receive new problems, hurry, hurry, time to take off!

And then that final *big* flight, the runways at Kelly Field reverberating more to the pounding of hearts near a goal than to the thunder of more than fifty trainers, each piloted by a cadet about to reach that final moment of graduation. Fifty and more silver-winged trainers, held straight and true in mass formation on course, winging from Kelly Field to Douglas, Arizona. A test, a final test, and a pageant for those on the ground as the final proof of our training, the return in the form of pilot skill for the investment of time, energy, money, airplanes, ground facilities, and the pouring out of a true instructor's heart to his fledgling.

The moment came. Standing rigidly at attention, a brace self-imposed and straighter than ordered by any shavetail with a penchant for hazing. A long line of cadets, proud, erect, not feeling the sun broiling the airfield concrete about us, a moment of wonder and realization as the small group of officers approached. The words said over and over to thousands of cadets, but new, sparkling, rich with meaning and a promise of tomorrow and the days after that.

The tugging of the uniform. Words of congratulations, a handshake.

And those silver wings! *Your* wings, Johnson, *your* wings! Silver, gleaming in the sun. The day finally come, the Moment, when your hand was gripped firmly and . . . Johnson, you did it—you're a pilot! Wings earned, forever yours, membership in that great fraternity in a world without end.

A moment never to be forgotten . . . cheering of men

around you, their dreams come true also. But a muted sound, for your eyes are on Barbara's small figure running across the broad concrete, fully as proud and happy as yourself.

When I think back today to those times, back to July 3, 1942, I can see those moments now, just as they appeared then. When I do, I can realize the passage of time, the stretching away of sixteen years. Nearly two full decades! After the passage of all these years, it is like looking back and seeing with pride a strange young man. It is then that I seem to be almost two people. Myself, today, and that pilot who just then earned those silver wings.

Barbara and I had unnumbered things to talk about. She was proud of all that had been done, proud of the gold bars that denoted my change in status from cadet to lieutenant. But to me . . . well, I'd have worn those wings as proudly on a pair of pajamas!

We discussed my future as a pilot, and I explained that I had made as my first choice training in A-20 attack bombers at Oklahoma City. Second in choice was the A-20 school at Seattle, Washington, and third, the A-20 school in Florida. The sleek, twin-engined ship was the closest thing to a fighter. Fast, deadly, charged with power, agile, bristling with armament.

I still thought wistfully of fighters, but—well, I'd made my choice. I would fly bombers.

My orders came through. Second Lieutenant Johnson, R.S., would report by 19 July 1942 at Stratford, Connecticut, to . . .

. . . to fly *fighters!*

8

The big aircraft hangar at Bridgeport's Municipal Airport resounded with mechanical, hammering sounds that came from an assortment of airplanes spread out in various states of disassembly. I walked around the naked engines and ducked beneath the wings of the aerodynamic labyrinth to reach a small office tucked away in a corner of the hangar.

My orders read for me to report on July nineteenth to the 61st Squadron of the 56th Fighter Group, and all through the seventeen days of furlough after leaving Kelly Field I fairly itched for this moment to arrive. I didn't know what the

56th flew, and I didn't care. The word *fighter* set my imagination afire, and I marvelled at the miraculous twist of fate that had assigned me to what I'd always wanted.

I was the perfect picture of the new second lieutenant, uniform so neatly pressed it looked as if I'd starched every crease into place. Those wings felt bright and silvery on my chest, and to the brim of my cap I was still filled with the military discipline and decorum pounded into me as a cadet. At least, I thought, the 61st was in the middle of things— you could hardly find the squadron officer for all the airplanes surrounding the place!

I knocked at a door marked with a wooden sign, entered, and snapped to attention. In the finest cadet form my hand arced up into a salute as I started to rattle off my name, rank and the proper words of reporting procedure. I never had the chance to finish. The captain seated behind the desk in a worn flying jacket grinned and rose to his feet. Suddenly a powerful hand grasped mine and shook it briskly. "I'm McCollom," the captain said warmly. "We're glad to have you with us, Johnson. Now, sit down and relax."

I never expected this; I suppose I was still groggy from the cadet routine of spit and polish. "The 61st is a fine outfit, Johnson," McCollom said. "We've got top pilots and ground crews in the squadron. Right now we're just boning up on fighters in general, sort of feeling ourselves out. The 63rd Squadron is with us on this field, and the 62nd, which completes the Group, is stationed at Bradley Field. That's at Windsor Locks; you'll get to see the place in several days when we all assemble there." He filled me in on details of the squadron, and then gave me the news I'd waited eagerly to hear. The 56th Group, he said, would be the first Army Air Forces fighter outfit to be equipped with the new P-47 fighter.

"You ever see a Thunderbolt, Johnson?" he asked. I hadn't, and a delighted grin spread across McCollom's face. "Well, just hold your breath until you catch sight of one. You've never seen a fighter quite like it. Two thousand horses, faster than hell, and eight big fifties in the wings. There's a lot more to say about this airplane, but first we'd better see to getting you a place to stay."

Barbara and I had driven in our 1936 Chevrolet from Kelly Field to Lawton for a ten-day vacation at home with our families. And then, with every possession we had to our name piled into the back seat and trunk of the venerable machine, we had travelled across the rest of the country to Bridgeport, which for the next six months became our home. We actually felt as if we were married, for the ten days in Lawton became a belated honeymoon, and we were able to set up housekeeping in Bridgeport. The breaks all came to us, as we found an apartment in the home of Mr. and Mrs. Victor Malmberg, a couple who bent every effort to make our stay comfortable and pleasant.

The first project on our personal agenda was to sell the car, which we no longer needed in Bridgeport. Months were to pass before I would recall the Air Force pilot to whom I sold the Chevrolet—Neel Kearby. Later, when I was flying combat in Europe, Neel took the first Thunderbolts to the Pacific. He was a brilliant pilot and a courageous leader willing to accept any combat odds. He ran his confirmed score of air kills to twenty-two Japanese planes shot down. One afternoon, he led three other Thunderbolts in a howling dive to plunge into the midst of forty-eight enemy planes. In the savage twelve-to-one melee that raged, Neel Kearby shot down six planes, while his pilots bagged another six. They escaped unscathed.

For this feat Neel received the Congressional Medal of

Honor. Unhappily, his luck failed to last. No Japanese pilot ever kept Kearby's Thunderbolt in his sights long enough to shoot him down, but as he raced low over a Japanese airfield in a strafing attack, enemy shells smashed into the Thunderbolt and sent it hurtling out of control into the ground.

Shortly after I reported to Captain McCollom, the 61st Squadron moved temporarily to Bradley Field at Windsor Locks, to check out in our new fighters. The Bradley Field runways were almost twice as long as those at Bridgeport, a vital safety factor in view of the Thunderbolt's extremely high performance. And it was here that I was introduced to the ship in which I would be subjected to the acid test of combat.

In every respect the Thunderbolt was an airplane that lived up to her name. After the BC-1 and the AT-6 trainers at Kelly Field, the Thunderbolt was a giant. I had been accustomed to 600 horsepower; beneath the P-47B's massive cowling was a great engine capable of 2,000 horsepower! She was big and on the ground she wasn't very pretty. But every inch of her structure was power, a rugged and sturdy machine with all the mass of a tank. Being left alone with the Thunderbolt meant a time of study, a careful scrutiny of the tremendous four-bladed propeller, the wide and straddling landing gear. In each wing rested four heavy .50-caliber guns, giving the Thunderbolt a fantastic punch, the ability to throw heavy lead at the rate of 7,200 rounds per minute!

It was love at first sight. Somehow I just knew that this machine and I were meant for each other. I itched to take her up, to run loose in the sky with 2,000 horses up front eager to howl freely. It galled me, but the truth was that with all my hours and all my experience, Second Lieutenant Johnson, R.S., was still a raw novice as a fighter jockey. And that meant studying.

I staggered under the weight of the thick manuals, handbooks and technical orders all pertaining to the P-47B. Nose buried in the printed pages, I came to appreciate the complexity that constituted the Thunderbolt. In all my flying to date, a speed of 105 and 110 miles per hour had been respectable. The Thunderbolt *stalled* out at 105 miles per hour!

My study period called for a great deal more boning up on all the technical publications that described the Thunderbolt. I spent hours studying every detail of the airplane. I talked to the mechanics and to other pilots, and sat attentively through instruction courses. Hours passed as I sat in the cockpit, feeling the stick and rudder, working the throttle, flap levers, gear controls, gun switches. Time after time I reviewed and then ran through control procedures. I memorized every last detail of the airplane I would need to know to check out as a pilot, and finally I took and passed all the written tests. Always before, I had simply climbed into a new plane with an instructor and learned her tricks. But there wasn't any second seat in the Thunderbolt—the first time was *it*.

First Lieutenant Gerald W. Johnson—destined to become one of our greatest fighter pilots before he was shot down, to end the war in the German prison camp of Stalag Luft—checked me out in the Thunderbolt. We spent the final thirty minutes on the ground with me seated in the cockpit, while Jerry stood on the wing and leaned over my shoulder and gave me a final run-through.

"Okay, Bob," he called, "she's all yours." He slid off the wing and walked back from the ship. Everything now was business. I ran through the cockpit check. Seat belt tight;

shoulder straps tight. Seat adjusted, and me all rigged out in flying clothes, helmet, goggles, oxygen mask, parachute and other gear. With full precision, following the book, I went over the instruments, buttons, dials, switches—a seemingly endless array of controls and dials.

Time to move out. The Thunderbolt requires the closing of thirteen separate buttons and switches to be prepared for flight, and I counted them off mentally. Now the primer to feed juice to the engine. Stick back, brakes locked. As ready as she'll ever be.

I hit the starter switch. Deep inside her belly the Thunderbolt groaned, a straining rumble sounding for all the world like a giant dynamo coming alive. Ahead of me the four propeller blades turned slowly, then began to move faster as the Pratt & Whitney gained in power. The rumble increased in pitch, the blades became a blur. Every inch of her body and wings trembled. Suddenly the cranking and rumbling vanished, to be replaced by a tremendous, throaty roar, a bass of power such as I'd never heard. I cracked the throttle forward a fraction of an inch and the fighter sang of power, a symphony of thunder, alive and ready to howl at the slightest movement of my fingers.

For ten minutes I sat there in one spot, cautious, feeling her out easily. Scared—just as if I were getting in the ring to fight. I wanted to sense the ship, to recognize her sounds and vibrations and movements. I scanned the dials again, checked pressures and controls. I knew the Thunderbolt would be a sweetheart, but a fighter demanding skill and ability and knowledge. Anything else, any failure on the part of the pilot, might easily be answered by disaster. The Thunderbolt was a killer in the sky, with her power and speed and armament literally a juggernaut. She demanded the best.

Finally all the checks were completed. I sat in awe and
respect of the enormous machine into which I'd strapped
myself, and wondered if I could really handle the monster.
I suffered no lack of self-confidence in my flying, and I'd
always accepted any new plane before without a second
thought. But *this* . . . ! Everything I had ever flown was a
toy compared to the Thunderbolt.

I called the tower and requested permission to taxi out
and to take off. Just short of the runway I braked the fighter,
locked the brakes, and spent another ten minutes going
through the cockpit check. I studied everything, the dial
readings, pressure readings, position of switches, handles,
toggles, buttons. The first time was the acid test with
the Thunderbolt, and I wanted to be positive that I kept
my part of the bargain with the ship.

Rolling out onto the runway for takeoff position, I still
wasn't certain! This was a strange sensation for me, and
I thought of the warning that no matter what a man had
ever flown before, it was the Thunderbolt that separated
the men from the boys. I reached up and slightly behind me
and grasped the canopy bar, squeezed the trigger and pushed
the canopy forward. I looked up to check. Canopy all the
way forward, trigger closed, locked into position.

"Okay, Army 961," the tower called. "Roll when ready."
I acknowledged, took a deep breath, and tightened my
hand around the black throttle knob, eased it forward. The
sustained rumble ahead of me changed immediately in
pitch, growling its way upward to a deep-throated roar.
Now: foot brakes—off. My feet came off the brake pedals,
and I kept moving the throttle forward, constantly increasing power.

The knob went all the way forward, stopped against
the rest. Inside the cockpit I both felt and heard the tre-

mendous roar of the Pratt & Whitney as acceleration shoved me back in the seat. The Thunderbolt didn't merely roll down the runway, she hurled herself forward.

I eased forward on the stick. At once the nose lowered and the tailwheel lifted. Engine torque was terrific; the fighter kept trying to swing to the left as a result of the tremendous engine forces. As the fighter's speed increased, I kept increasing right rudder pressure to keep her headed down the center of the runway. The needle swung past 70, then 85, past 90 miles per hour. She was almost ready for flight, more sensitive on the controls. Her wings grabbed at air. There was a solid feeling of air loads. I checked the airspeed indicator, and began the back pressure on the stick to lift her off the ground. Without hesitation the nose be-gan——

CRACK! Something struck hard against my head. For an instant, I saw red, and heard what seemed to be a loud explosion. A blast of air stormed into the cockpit. Head still ringing, I moved instinctively; without thinking I chopped the throttle and slammed both feet to the brakes. The Thunderbolt ground to a stop, brakes squealing. I blinked my eyes a couple of times, and saw with relief that I was still on the runway, with plenty of room before me.

The canopy latch had slipped and, under the rush of air the canopy had snapped backward. Both the trigger and the canopy bar had slammed with terrific force against my head, causing the "explosion" I'd heard. I called the tower and taxied back to takeoff position, checked out the cockpit, and wound her up.

Again that terrific surge of power as the Thunderbolt tore down the concrete. And again, at 95 miles per hour, a smash against my head! This time I said to hell with it, and kept her rolling. I didn't even feel the pain of the canopy bar striking my head. The needle swept around past 100 miles per hour, and at an even 110 miles per hour I eased back on the stick.

Abruptly the rumble and vibration of the runway disappeared, leaving only the deep singing roar of the engine and the rush of wind past the open cockpit. Even before I realized the fact, I was at 500 feet, wheels still down and airspeed building up rapidly. With the gears up, canopy closed and the airplane clean, the P-47 raced freely. Cautiously, I pulled back further on the stick.

I couldn't help it, I grinned from the absolute joy of the moment. It was almost like giving a racehorse free rein. The Thunderbolt reared her nose. No sluggish response against gravity such as I'd always known in a sustained climb! The powerhouse up front thundered sweetly, undaunted by the sudden change in attitude, and she howled her way higher into the sky. Fighter pilots have an expression for a moment of such freedom as a fighter seems to leap away from the earth; they say the ship climbs like a homesick angel. The Thunderbolt was no angel, but how she could run into the blue!

Without effort we soared to 10,000 feet, where the ground turned into diminutive slopes of green and brown. Stretching to the horizon were the green Connecticut hills, far beyond the deep blue of the Atlantic, seared by the brilliant reflection of the sun. The Thunderbolt had many thousands of feet to climb before she would even falter in the thinner air above me, but this moment was not for full freedom, for uninhibited flight. I still had to know the Thunderbolt, I still had much to learn of her characteristics to recognize the moments when she would not forgive the unwary pilot. I had yet to learn to forget many of the restrictions I'd known before in the air. Every plane I'd ever flown could easily be hurt, could be battered by excessive speed or a sharp turn or a bruising maneuver. And so I was cautious, I approached the Thunderbolt slowly, I suppose, feeling her out carefully, learning her tricks and responses and habits. For thirty-five minutes I cruised easily in the sky, banking and turning, running through climbs and glides, eager to let her run wild, but sensible enough to hold down my feelings.

On takeoff the Thunderbolt had warned of possible trouble in the snapping free of the canopy trigger lock. On this flight, at least, I expected anything to happen. The P-47 was a new fighter, only now being proven, and the only word for the moment was caution. It was up to *us*, the second lieutenants, to make the ship operational. Finally I eased back on the throttle and dropped her nose. Seven tons of fighter slipped earthward, steady as a rock, turning gently for our home field.

The runway grew larger. Nose up slightly, gear down, the fighter eased toward the concrete ribbon at 120 miles per hour. So big and heavy a fighter stalls out at high speed. At 105 miles per hour, I knew, the thin wing would lose its grip on the air. The invisible flow past the wings would burble, lift would vanish, and gravity would pull the Thunderbolt out of the sky. I flew the dividing line carefully, maintaining a gliding approach at 120 miles per hour, prepared to set her down at 110, just above stalling speed, keeping control in my hands.

I swung into the final gliding turn, swinging out of base leg on my final approach. I pulled on the flap lever, ready to drop her nose slightly as the flaps slowed her steady descent. Trouble! The right flap dropped obediently, but the left stayed up. All hell broke loose as the unequal pressure flipped the fighter into a vertical bank to the left, a disastrous maneuver at so reduced a speed.

Hands and feet moving by sheer instinct, I slammed the stick to the right, tramped down on right rudder, and shoved the throttle all the way forward. The engine roared and as I shoved the stick forward to lower the nose the Thunderbolt accelerated rapidly. I pulled up the gear and eased her into a turning climb to swing around the field. This first flight in the P-47 wasn't proving any picnic!

The tower had watched the fighter snap over to the right and my climbout. "Army 961, what's your trouble?" I told them, and received new instructions. "Army 961. Suggest you cycle the hydraulic flap equalizer. You may not be getting equal pressure for each flap. Try it a couple of times and let us know what happens. Over."

I didn't have much success. Something was fouling up the hydraulic line. After working the hydraulic controls about a dozen times I managed to lower the flaps to the halfway position. I swung the Thunderbolt around again, dropped the gear, and slid down toward the runway. After giving me a hard time, the fighter greased herself down in a perfect three-point landing.

The 61st and 63rd Squadrons returned to Bridgeport, and spent the next several months in shaking out the still-new Thunderbolt fighters. Our planes and the new R-2800 engines were fresh off the production line, and there were still mechanical bugs to be ironed out, kinks in hydraulic lines and electrical systems to be eliminated. The extensive training flights we ran with the new P-47B proved instrumental in effecting major modifications of the airplane, changes which were incorporated into the fighter models to follow the P-47B with which we were equipped. Unhappily, the conditions under which we flew cost us heavily in pilots killed and in planes lost.

The curse of the problem was that an airfield better than Bridgeport would undoubtedly have saved lives. Our accident rate was exorbitant. We were forced to fly from an airfield wholly inadequate to meet the performance demands of so new and hot a fighter as the P-47B. The maximum runway length on the field was 3,000 feet, enough to make any veteran pilot shudder, especially when you saw in the immediate vicinity of the airport high poles, steel towers, houses and rising hills.

It was bad enough to fly a seven-ton fighter from a short field, but when the wind died to a gentle breeze and the afternoon temperature rose, takeoff and especially landing required caution. One of the 61st Squadron's pilots, Robill Roberts, came in low on such a day in P-47B No. 26. By the time he realized that he might not clear a house facing him at the end of Runway Three, it was too late.

Almost on the point of stalling as he tried to pick up the fighter's nose, the left wheel and gear strut of the Thunderbolt smashed into the house, and like a giant bludgeon sheared through wood, plaster and plumbing. A crash shook the area as the wheel tore through a thunderstruck woman's bathroom. The noise, if one could have heard it, must have been fabulous, a combination of the Thunderbolt's screaming roar, the ripping and tearing of wood, plaster and piping, and, if she still had her voice, the startled shrieks of the distressed but unharmed woman.

The Thunderbolt, if it faltered at all, paused only momentarily, then burst onward, leaving behind it a jumbled mass of debris that spewed forth in a torrent from the side of the house. Unaware that he had achieved something of a world's record in bathroom demolition, Roberts brought the fighter in for a perfect landing.

Eighteen pilots lost their lives in our operational flight training, but the number would have been several times higher had we flown an airplane less rugged than the Thunderbolt. Roberts's escapade, which by a miracle avoided personal disaster, was only a sample of the ability of this airplane to absorb tremendous punishment and enable its pilot to survive. One pilot failed to clear the surrounding terrain on takeoff, and at 105 miles per hour crashed directly into a hill. He smashed his propeller, literally ripped the engine from its mounts, and tore the whole underbelly of the fighter to shreds—to say nothing of ripping up the local real estate. He walked away with nothing more than a few bruises.

No pilot was more blessed with a combination of Thunderbolt durability and sheer good luck than Milton Anderson. Just as his fighter cleared the runway his engine lost power as several cylinders blew out. Immediately Anderson shoved forward on the stick to lower the fighter's nose, the only possible procedure to maintain enough flying speed to clear the rolling ground. In this he was successful—except that at nearly 150 miles per hour, gear still down, the Thunderbolt smashed into Long Island Sound. We watched in horror as a mountain of spray leaped upward and the sound of the crash reached us. At once the stricken fighter cartwheeled, hurtling wingtip over tail, literally wadding itself like crumpled paper. The Thunderbolt was still tumbling helplessly as we raced to the shore. By now the P-47 was a crumpled mass, and our concern was to find Anderson's body before it sank or drifted away with the current.

Anderson wasn't dead! Strapped tightly into his seat he had survived the tremendous buffeting of the crash, suffering only a bump on his head and shoulder bruises. The moment the wreckage came to a stop, he wriggled out of his straps and half waded and swam to shore. He was waiting patiently for us, and wanted to know what took us so long to get there!

We learned soon enough that unless we plunged nose first into the ground, we couldn't hurt the Thunderbolt. The ruggedness of the airplane was simply fantastic. For several months we took every opportunity to engage in wild dogfights with each other, whetting our own skill as well as learning to fly as a team. The best moments came when we discovered some unfortunate soul in another fighter in the air. When that happened—*Go!* Thunderbolts plunged from the sky in mock attack, sweeping down to bounce anything that came before our gunsights. Our favorite opponent was the Corsair, a gull-winged Navy fighter with the same engine that powered the Thunderbolt. Fast and maneuverable, the Corsairs proved excellent bait for our assaults, and many an hour was spent over Long Island Sound as we tore at one another in the high air.

As the hours accumulated, I learned, as did the other pilots, that we were free in this airplane to engage in any maneuver we pleased. This was no small advantage, for we came to trust to the fullest the capabilities of our weapon. We knew that the Thunderbolt would never fail us, that we could literally hurl the airplane in any attitude through the sky. Such trust was a wonderful thing to have; we knew we would never hesitate to subject our fighters to the worst rigors of aerial combat.

In yet another instance was the amazing structure of the Thunderbolt a means of survival. The first two fighters in the United States able to fly so fast as to run into a barrier of sound in the sky were the Thunderbolt and the Light-

ning, the latter a swift and large twin-engined fighter. On
the Pacific coast, where they were produced and flight-
tested, the Lightnings had revealed in alarming fashion,
through the death of several pilots, that a reef existed in the
air, a jagged wall that could tear an airplane to pieces.
We didn't know it at the time, of course, but this was compressibility. As our fighters gained speed in power dives, the
air piled up in steel-hard wedges around the airplane, creating tremendous forces and pressures which battered at the
wings and fuselage.

The first Thunderbolt pilots to hit compressibility and to
know about it—and live—were Lieutenants Harold E. Comstock and Roger B. Dyar. On November 13, 1942, they were
at 35,000 feet in speed-run tests, when they rolled the fighters over and dove for earth. In the high, thin air the Thunderbolt accelerated like a bullet shot out of a gun. Just below 30,000 feet both pilots tried to pull out. They couldn't.
The roaring planes were gripped in the steel wedges of
compressed air, controls absolutely immovable. Later, and
much closer to the earth, which seemed to leap upward at
them, the Thunderbolts began to ease out of their careening
dives and finally burst upward again.

Investigation revealed the problem for what it was, and
most of us in our flights encountered the wall in the sky.
My first meeting with compressibility was a frightening experience. I rolled the fighter on her back and dropped
the nose in a vertical plunge earthward. The engine howled
with power and the Thunderbolt ran wild. In seconds I was
in compressibility range—and absolutely helpless.

No man was strong enough to pull the fighter out of a
compressibility dive. I've gripped the control stick in both
hands, jammed my feet against the instrument panel for
leverage, and hauled back with all the strength I had. The

stick might have been imbedded in concrete for all the good the frantic pulling did me. All I could do was to hang on to that stick, straining with all my might, and wait until the fighter screamed her way into the denser air at lower altitudes. Between 12,000 and 8,000 feet the air was sufficiently dense to allow the controls to grab. Then came the brutal and crushing g-forces of the pullout, when my blood rushed downward and drained from my head, and the world turned grey and then black—and finally the blackout caused by a brain deprived of blood. I'd come to, groggy and shaken up, as the Thunderbolt hung on her propeller, rushing upward in a tremendous zoom climb.

The pilots who survived these early days of trouble and tests became the experienced veterans of the 56th Fighter Group. On September 16, 1942 we received a new Group Commander, Major Hubert A. Zemke, recently returned from a liaison mission to Russia and England where he'd gained invaluable experience in combat tactics. We were to know "Hub" Zemke well. His skilled leadership and genius for combat transformed the untried 56th Fighter Group into the famed "Zemke Wolfpack," the most devastating fighter group to storm into enemy skies over Europe.

On Thanksgiving Day, 1942, the 56th Fighter Group was alerted for overseas duty. The moment of trial under fire loomed closer.

9

On the heels of our alert notice came the order grounding
the 56th Fighter Group. No time was to be lost in preparing for overseas shipment, and toward this end the 56th
exercised high efficiency in taking itself apart at the seams.
It meant the end of our flying for several months. Yet the
necessity for our grounding order was cheering. We were
that much closer to the time when we would pit the Thunderbolt, and ourselves as well, against the best the enemy had
to offer—which enemy, we didn't know.

My education in the sometimes odd behavior of the military organization was resumed. Once our planes were gone,

we worked twelve and sixteen hours a day stripping the airport facilities and our own installations for shipment to the port of embarkation. It was hard work and, after the freedom of flying, incredibly dull. Only the fact that we were committed to a new assignment in a combat theater kept the griping to a low rumble. But then came that day when everything that could be pulled out of the ground had been sent on its way, and only the personnel of the 56th remained. The situation was unusual. Here was a fighter group, sans airplanes and operational equipment and, in the minds of the high brass, living an easy and slothful life. This could not be permitted; we had to keep in top physical condition. And so we treated the good citizens of Bridgeport to the astonishing sight of the 56th Fighter Group, bundled up in overcoats and boots, trudging on fifteen-mile hikes through the slush of the city's streets.

Two alerts to "ship out immediately" came and went. Finally definite word was received: we would leave Bridgeport on December twenty-eighth for transfer to our shipping depot. Early on the morning of the twenty-sixth, the day after our first Christmas together, I saw Barbara off for home. It wasn't a pleasant day, and it wasn't the best of moments. A cold and bitter wind sent snow flying through the railroad station, a dismal and bleak setting for our last moments.

We had been together for six months of our brief marriage. Barbara tried unsuccessfully to hold back her tears. It wasn't the realization that we would be separated for an indefinite time; Barbara was facing the possibility that I might never come home. How alone two people can be in such a moment! Alone, and yet the sharers of a personal grief of parting.

My feelings were a mixture of the sorrow of separation,

and the mounting excitement of the air combat that was to be. I had always wanted to fight in the air, to pit my skill and my strength against an opponent; for some reason, I enjoyed an absolute confidence that no matter what happened, I would return to Barbara. Time and again I had repeated these assurances to my wife. In these last moments together the conviction fled before the grim reality that in war people get hurt, and people are killed. There was nothing left to say, only seconds for a final embrace. Then the rumble of the train as it began to move from the station. I ran along the platform as far as I could, trying to smile, waving to Barbara. With tears streaming down her cheeks she did her best to smile back.

She became a diminutive figure as the train picked up speed. In the sudden blinking of my eyes, she was gone. Now more than ever the station was cold, a concrete bed of loneliness. I quickened my pace to reach the car waiting for me, and returned to the field.

We sweated out the next two days with growing impatience, waiting for the signal to move out. Our nights passed with the men huddled in bedrolls, sprawled out in the operations hut, hangars, or any available spot we could find. Few men slept well; the dank cold of a wooden or concrete floor penetrated effectively through the bedrolls. Then came the "word," and three days after Christmas the 56th boarded a troop train for transfer to Camp Kilmer in New Jersey—for more waiting.

For a week we shuffled miserably through the deep, sucking red clay of Kilmer, each foot sinking ankle-deep in the clutching mud. To the commander of such an installation, boredom is a disease to be rooted out at its inception. And so for a week we stumbled our way from room to room, from building to building, listening to a dull drone of speakers

who lectured us on everything from venereal disease to life-
boat drill. We stood inspection after inspection, packing,
unpacking and repacking our gear. Doctors who had nothing else to do poked, peered, pried and studied us from
head to toe, and then penetrated our skin with long, barbed
needles. It was a thoroughly effective demonstration that
the camp psychologists knew exactly what they were doing.
For at the end of that week, when we were notified to grab
our gear and prepare to board ship, even those who had
been most reluctant to move overseas received the shipping
news with delirious joy.

To the bitter end we lived our hours of frustration, dis-
comfort and waiting. Pier 90 in New York, where the giant
Queen Elizabeth awaited our arrival, lies only twenty-five
miles from Camp Kilmer, ordinarily a brief journey of perhaps forty-five minutes. It took the 56th Fighter Group no
less than five hours of halting, fitful movement by cold train
and freezing ferry to reach the great vessel.

No glorious or patriotic moments these. At three in the
morning of January 6, 1943, lost in the shuffle of 12,000
men stumbling aboard beneath the weight of their personal
equipment, the 56th moved into the *Queen*. The concrete
pier seemed to stretch away forever, cold and inhospitable.
One by one 12,000 men dragged forward, listening in the
lonely night to the echo of a weary voice calling out name
after name. And then, everyone was aboard, the last name
had been called, the gangplanks removed, and the mighty
Queen, trembling ever so gently to the power of her great
engines as she backed water, churned the cold oil and
slime of the Hudson into froth, and slid away from the pier
under the gentle nudging of attentive tugboats.

Immense though she was, the *Queen* was as jam-packed
as a small town enjoying a Saturday-night carnival. There

was literally no place on the ship where you could stretch out without knocking someone over. Fourteen of us piled into a cabin marked with a sign of prewar luxury that read, "This cabin accommodates two passengers." Yet our crowding was sheer luxury compared to that of the enlisted men, who were stacked like cordwood in the hold of the ship. Masses of men, laden down with personal equipment, crowded into holds which each night had to be sealed to the outside ocean because of blackout restrictions, gagging in air which became thick and heavy with the odor of perspiration and the cloying stench of vomit. The ocean heaved and thundered as the *Queen* raced her way to Europe, and for the entire five days most of the enlisted men in their "black hole" suffered the curse of prolonged seasickness and the dry heaves.

The first grim touch of the still-distant war came home to me on the night of January ninth. Shivering in the howling wind and sleet that whipped into the bridge, I noticed the darkened form of a ship sliding by the racing *Queen.* Thirty minutes later the radio room crackled with an SOS call from that very same vessel, her holds shattered and her back broken by the crash of torpedoes into her hull. The *Queen* immediately heeled hard over on her side in a straining turn to the south, spurred on by engines thrown to maximum, roaring deeply as the propellers thrashed more rapidly within the water.

The next night the Officer of the Guard lost his footing on the sleet- and snow-covered deck. A muffled scream hung fleetingly on the edge of the ragged wind and vanished, lost as utterly as the dim bundled shape of the man tumbling the distance from the deck, a horrible plunge in darkness and cold. No one could hear the splash above the pounding of engines, the thunder of the *Queen's* bow crashing into the deep swells, or the shriek of wind. The ghost-like wail of *"Man overbooaaard"* sounded helplessly. We didn't stop, we *couldn't* stop. Twelve thousand men were aboard. A quick-thinking crewman flung several life preservers which were swallowed up by blackness, and offered a prayer for the lost soul already far behind the speeding ocean liner.

Our greeting to Europe was a bit raggedy. I was below decks when someone shouted that we were being attacked by enemy planes. The thunder of feet shook the *Queen* as a mob stormed to the rails to see what was going on. The "enemy aircraft" appeared immediately, in the form of several ancient fabric-covered Swordfish biplanes, staggering in and out of a heavy fog to bid us welcome. We were less than enthralled, and the relief at reaching Europe dimmed rapidly with the cold, impersonal, forever-delaying routine of leaving the *Queen*.

The giant liner slipped her anchors into the waters near Glasgow, Scotland. On the afternoon of January 12, 1943, the 56th Group lurched a precarious path beneath duffel and B-4 bags to squeeze onto a tender rolling in sickening fashion in the inlet. Hours later we disembarked at Gourock. It was still cold, even wetter than had been the Hudson River pier, and equally dismal. No one seemed to care that we had just arrived in Europe, not even a single soul to grind out a bagpipe wail. Still, we were made to feel at home through the necessity of standing impatiently for hours in the cold mist until our train arrived. By ten in the evening we had managed to achieve normal confusion, and the Group had jammed its way into the mechanical disaster the English identify as a railroad train.

At our new station in England we discovered that the dire warnings of older veterans were all too well founded.

Breakfast, if I may be flexible with the term, consisted of Brussels sprouts, powdered eggs and an eerie liquid which with unbounded imagination the English called coffee. We unloaded our gear in the barracks, scrubbed the dirt of our ocean crossing off our bodies with freezing water, and began a local tour to see our new home. Unfortunately, the weather thwarted our curiosity, since visibility was held down to barely more than a hundred feet, and it is damaging to one's ego to become thoroughly lost only fifty yards from one's own barracks!

By morning the fog had lifted, and we lost no time in walking to the airfield. Here I saw my first British fighters, the sleek and sensitive Spitfire. The differences between our Thunderbolt and the Spitfire were amazing. The P-47 was a giant, a massive weapon with a tremendous roar and dynamite in each wing. Not so the English fighter, much smaller than the Thunderbolt, sleeker, almost like a lightweight fighter with the agility to dart in and out of battle with lithe, rapid movements. The Spitfires on the field were unlike the Thunderbolt in yet another fashion. The fighters we flew at Bradley Field and at Bridgeport were spanking new, clean, and tested only to the limits of our ability to hurl them about in the air. The fighters in front of us were veterans, their guns seared and scarred from firing, their paint unshiny and in places marked with the repairs of bullet holes and tears from exploding cannon shells. They were veterans; the Thunderbolts were as yet unproven in battle.

In the days that followed the foul British weather and our lack of airplanes kept us on the ground. We filled our time with prosaic duties, enlivened only when we could talk to the combat veterans of our bombers, or when we met a fighter pilot of the Royal Air Force, upon whose every word we hung with intense concentration. Nearly three months had passed since our last time in the air, and to say that we were impatient to fly again would be grossly underestimating the intensity of our feelings. Every day British fighters and bombers passed overhead, sometimes hedgehopping over the trees and buildings to stay below the fog. And then one noon at mess, we heard an aircraft engine, not the particular roar of the British planes, but a sound so familiar. . . .

"Hey!" someone shouted, "that's a forty-seven!" Chairs and benches went flying as the pilots streamed to the windows and doors. Sure enough, there she was! The familiar shape of the Thunderbolt, a single fighter moaning low over the field in a high-speed pass. It was the first P-47 we'd seen since watching our own fighters being towed away at Bridgeport. At least we knew the airplanes were in England.

My first visit to London began shortly after midnight, which, I soon discovered, was a grave timing error. All London lay hidden beneath a rigidly enforced blackout, a pall of darkness which the British seemed to have in great abundance. I wanted to reach a hotel recommended by a British pilot, but I lacked even the faintest idea of how to begin my search. This, I was sure, would present little problem, but I discovered that the English spoken in the United States and that spoken in England are languages foreign to each other. I knew that the hotel was only a fifteen-minute walk from Liverpool Street Station, but after receiving as answer to my queries for directions no more than incomprehensible jumbles of words, I walked blindly, hoping by sheer good luck to run into the hotel.

I ran into everything else. I groped my way blindly through Hyde Park, embracing an untotalled number of

trees, park benches and thorny bushes. Finally I staggered
back to the streets. I'd walk until I crashed into the side of
a building. Then I'd turn, and feel my way down another
street. I was lucky; I found an English policeman who
spoke in a barely identifiable tongue, and he steered me in
what I hoped was the right direction. It required three
hours to reach a hotel only fifteen minutes' walking distance
from the train station.

London provided unique hospitality. Barely had I fallen
asleep when a series of shattering explosions hurled me
from the bed. In a few seconds I was able to distinguish
the roaring blasts as the firing of an antiaircraft gun. This
was too good to miss! I jerked aside the blackout curtains,
to be stabbed in the eyes with the savage glare from the
gun's muzzle blast—thirty feet from my window! What a
wonderful place to sleep!

The performance was brilliantly played, and I hung out
of the window, fascinated by the sights and sounds of my
first air raid. Arcing high over the city were multicolored
blobs of light, tracers weaving their way from the ground
into the blackness, curving and swinging in strange hues
and patterns. Vivid bursts of light appeared magically in
the sky, and vanished, an endless succession of antiaircraft
shells exploding in pursuit of unseen raiders. From utter
darkness the skies over London became transformed into
an incredible pyrotechnic display of searchlights and tracers,
of bursting shells and ghostly white and yellow flares.

And then came the assault against the nocturnal raiders
from the rocket batteries, a fantastic brushwork of fire
streaks against the night, splitting darkness asunder with
blinding lances of light. I felt almost hypnotized by their
searing eruption and tortured, unearthly shriek of flame.
Suddenly the tremendous gun beneath my window ceased

firing, halting its cry with a stunning crash of silence. Dimly, ears still ringing, I heard the faint booming echoes of the distant antiaircraft batteries pursuing the German planes as they fled northward along the coast. Silence again, and that unbelievable maw of blackness returning to swallow the vast city. I fell into bed and slept like a log until morning.

I took every opportunity, then and on later occasions, to tour this heart of British history. I consider a visit to Westminster Abbey one of the great moments of my life. All around me were the tombs of those people who had been the strength of England for all her many centuries. Simply standing in the Abbey to gaze upon the tombs along the walls meant that my feet rested on a grave with the location of each tomb beneath the floor marked in lettering on the worn stone. I knew that all the kings and queens of England were buried here at Westminster Abbey, but I never saw their resting places. Thick piles of sandbags completely covered and sealed off their tombs to protect them against German bombs. Prior to my visit the Abbey had been struck heavily by a single bomb, with more damage inflicted upon the nerves of the living occupants than upon the Abbey's solid construction.

An old monk told me of the incident which started a fire that threatened to sweep through the historic structure and gut it to its four lofty walls. The monk wasted no time with fire officials, but placed a call directly to the King. He told me that, on this one occasion, he ignored protocol and fairly shouted to the King of England: "If you want your Abbey saved, you'd better get some help over here—and be quick about it!" Fire-fighting teams rushed to the scene and thus averted, with little damage, the blaze that might have destroyed the Abbey.

Late in January the first P-47 fighters and maintenance crews for our Group arrived in England. It had been so long since we'd been close to a Thunderbolt that the pilots fairly hugged the giant fighters. And the latest model "C" fighters at that! At least we had something to do which didn't bore us half to death! Unhappily, the weather stayed just as stinking as it had been for weeks, and we were kept on the ground. This gave us the opportunity to check out our individual fighters with meticulous care, and every pilot lived with his own personal plane, inspecting every nut and bolt of the big Thunderbolt to assure that his fighter was in perfect shape. The way the men crooned and lowed over their own planes, you'd think they were carrying on a personal love affair. Each night when we met either in the barracks or at the club the arguments raged fiercely as to who had the best Thunderbolt in the group.

With our first missions pending, we were taken under the wing of Royal Air Force pilots who were experienced veterans of battles with the Germans. The R.A.F. pilots warned us that the German fliers were excellent, that their fighters were as good or better than anything else flying in Europe. They left no doubts but that the Messerschmitts and Focke-Wulfs could match on an equal basis anything that England or the United States had available—and as tactfully as possible they revealed their impression of the Thunderbolt as a sitting duck in the European air war.

This wasn't the first time that we had listened to doubts as to how the Thunderbolt might acquit itself against the speedy and maneuverable German fighters. Always before, we had passed off the remarks as no more than proof of the speakers' ignorance of the Thunderbolt's tremendous performance. But these pilots were combat veterans; they *knew* the Germans, and what they could do in the air.

"Now, look," one Spitfire pilot told us, "likely the Thunderbolt is a fine machine. But it's too big and it's too heavy to mix it up with the 109's and the 190's. You'd never turn with a Jerry, so don't ever make the mistake of trying to get away with it. The second you go into a tight turn with a 190, he'll cut right inside and get you dead to rights."

Oh, wonderful! Just the news we needed most to hear. We argued vehemently with the British pilots; an argument which, we hoped, would result in a less dire forecast of the Thunderbolt's failure in combat. To no avail. "Look, fellows," another pilot said. "We're flying the Spit Mark Five. She's a beautiful fighter, and an angel at the controls. But the truth is that the Focke-Wulf 190 has been running us ragged. The 190 can outclimb us, and can dive faster. It packs a heavier wallop than the Spit; after all, the Jerry has four cannon and two heavy guns on his side. The only thing the Jerry can't do is to turn inside us, but in every other respect the 190 has it all over the Five. When we get the new Spit Nine, we'll have a much better airplane, but right now, believe you me, we're having quite a go of it."

This shook us up. Our confidence in the Thunderbolt had been absolutely uncompromising. Now, experienced fighter pilots, the very men whom we looked upon virtually as idols, were telling us that the Thunderbolt was no match for the German fighters, and that to survive the air war we would have to "play it safe."

Soon after our instruction in tactics from the Royal Air Force, two battle-scarred Spitfires landed at our base, flown by American pilots from the Eagle Squadron. Both men had seen considerable combat, and we dragged them to the side to fire questions at them. Again we received the same discouraging answers. The Thunderbolt was too big. The Thunderbolt was too heavy; it couldn't climb; it couldn't turn. The only way to fly combat in the Thunderbolt was to stay at extremely high altitude, at least 25,000 feet and above, in order to take advantage of the P-47's excellent supercharger. The German fighters, we were warned, would outclimb, turn inside, and fly circles around us.

All the veteran combat pilots warned us to be especially wary of any Focke-Wulf 190's marked with yellow noses. "Those are Goering's personal pets," we were told, "and they're probably the best pilots in the whole German air force. They're tough and they're terrific fliers. If you get bounced by those people, don't play the hero. Run for it, and go like bloody blazes for home."

Everywhere we turned, it seemed, we heard only ominous warnings of the Thunderbolt's future. We had the highest respect for the advice and the help of these pilots, but dammit! the Thunderbolt was a lot more airplane than they realized. The net result of our enlightening instruction was to instill in us a tremendous respect for both the German pilot and his fighter, but never once did we lose faith in our own fighters. Well, we'd know soon enough.

By now some months had passed since our last flight. I felt as if I had forgotten how to fly, and I was almost sick to get back into the air. I'd been assigned a spanking new Thunderbolt and with my ground crew tended the fighter with meticulous care. We sandpapered the metal skin, rubbed on wax, and then buffed it until the P-47 gleamed like a new car. Every time I saw the airplane, I strutted around like a new father. If the weather would only break so that I could fly!

The excitement of preparing our fighters for flight began to pall before the everlasting mist and drizzle that blanketed the airfield. After all, you can inspect every hydraulic line, nut, wire, bolt, gun and mechanical device just so many times. As the mist continued to sweep across the field, we went on with our increasingly boring everyday life, whiling away the time in billiards, poker, craps, writing letters, arguing with one another—anything! Even the quiet British towns with their foreign language and warm beer acquired a growing appeal, and when evening came from four to a dozen of us squeezed into a jeep and rode off.

It was bad enough to be dangerously overloaded and unbalanced on an American road; tearing along the winding, narrow British roads was absolutely perilous. Half of England seemed perpetually to be riding on bicycles, and our mechanical monstrosity wove a precarious path among the high-wheeled obstacles. Never to be forgotten was the sight of a seven-foot Englishman, dressed severely in black tails and a high top hat, who loomed out of the English mist like a giant chimney wheeling through the foggy night. Each evening, when the local pubs closed down, we squeezed back into the jeep and huddled together on the return trip to ward off the freezing drizzle.

Then, we were scheduled to fly the morning of February eighth, but the mist and fog rolled down onto the field like a thick mass, blotting out all visibility. Disgusted, virtually the entire group piled into jeeps and trucks to visit Peterborough and other towns. By that time we had seen every stage show in theaters for miles around, and I'm convinced that in those months of waiting for our first flights I saw just about every trained dog in England.

The long-awaited miracle came the morning of February tenth. At dawn the sun rose and bathed the airfield in golden light. No fog, or drizzle, or mist! Awakening pilots gazed upon this rarity of English weather and with loud whoops dragged their fellows from bed. They acted like a bunch of kids on the last day of school, and wolfed down their breakfasts to get to the flight line. I fairly burst with enthusiasm, and with helmet, flight jacket, and parachute raced down to my plane.

Fate tapped me severely on the shoulder. I was scheduled this morning as Duty Pilot. On the *ground*. I had no choice but to bemoan my sad fate as I watched the Thunderbolts charge down the runway and storm into the air. I could almost feel the joy of the other pilots as they horsed the big fighters off the runway. That afternoon our airfield knew no peace. The Thunderbolts screamed low in mock strafing attacks, buzzing hangars, barracks, the tower, everything in sight. Each fighter howling earthward, hurtling at breakneck speed over the buildings, and then the sudden zoom, and the big P-47 soaring up, up, ever higher, rolling freely. I muttered under my breath, fully convinced that our respite from the fog would be gone by the next day. Sometimes I wondered how the Germans ever found England.

But wonder of wonders, the morning of the eleventh greeted us with broken clouds and sunshine! My ground crew had the Thunderbolt ready and primed for flight, metal skin glistening under the wax coat. She even seemed anxious to be airborne, and I ran quickly through the cockpit check. After close to three months of being grounded, I stood poised at the end of the runway, finally to receive the welcome words from the tower to *roll!*

Throttle forward, the cry of tremendous power, the forward surge of the great fighter. For the next hour, boring through clouds, rolling and turning, plunging for earth, feeling the clutch of inertia in steep turns and pullouts, I had myself a ball. If anything, such a long time on the ground had made me more sensitive to the eccentricities of flight, to the fleeting air loads of gusts, the sensing of sliding and skidding through the skies.

That night we celebrated, singing uproariously in the club. We felt, all of us, as though the Great Emancipation had come. We were flying again! And for several days in succession, the miracle of clear skies and sunshine was repeated, permitting us to race from the ground into the Thunderbolt's natural realm. We sought out every ship we could find, hurling our fighters against the unsuspecting planes in mock but realistic attacks. Several times we slipped through broken clouds to scream down against our heavy bombers, hauling the Thunderbolts around in perfect pursuit curves, scaring the daylights out of the startled bomber crews.

Once we caught a formation of Royal Air Force Hurricanes, and stormed into the middle of them. Faster by nearly eighty miles per hour than the older British fighters, we broke our own formation and swarmed down from the sky in a loose bunch. The British pilots accepted the challenge, but were left flat-footed when we ripped through their scattering planes, hauled the Thunderbolts upward in zoom climbs and burst away. We had no inhibitions and went after everything in the air and on the ground, buzzing ships, trains, trucks, anything that moved. Since we had more pilots available than there were fighters, the standbys took turns flying. Joe Curtis had a forced landing in *my* Thunderbolt; I felt as if someone had shot at me and hit!

On February twentieth we threw our first Group Party, and the wild celebration of the evening nearly wrecked the base and the nerves of the nearby citizens. The Group sent a big truck into town, with pilots leaning out of the windows and shouting, "Hey, we're having a party! Anybody wants to come to Kingscliff Airdrome for a party—jump in!" Down the streets the truck roared, stopping whenever passing girls waved in answer. The truck returned to the field, nearly bursting at the seams with local pulchritude.

It was a wonderful party. Some of the boys became a bit overwhelmed with the spirit of the moment and we watched some old-fashioned knockdown pier brawls, fists flying. No hard feelings ensued, but there were sure some beautiful black eyes!

One lieutenant saturated himself internally with Scotch, braced himself against the wall, and announced that he would give a "marvellus demonshraeshun of bycerkill ridin'." We followed him outside where he grabbed a bicycle and rushed off in a rapid, rolling drunken gait, preparing to leap aboard the moment he felt he had enough speed. He couldn't have seen that bike if it had been a bright, sunny day. After a wild hundred-foot dash, he gave a mighty leap, soared high in the air and cleared the bike by at least four feet. He thudded into the ground in a perfect one-point landing, flush on his cheek, scraping the skin wide open.

We thought he was dead; his body lay crumpled. When we reached him, he was giggling hysterically, absolutely undaunted. We dragged him to his feet, and he broke loose to make another try with the bike. This time he did get on. He pedalled furiously out of sight in the evening mist. A few moments later his shrieks announced his return. He burst out of the mist, tore through the scattering crowd at about 30 miles per hour, and plunged head-on into a brick wall, demolishing the bike and doing no little damage to his face. We dragged him, still giggling, back to the barracks.

Once our training for combat formations and tactics began in earnest, the only occasions we found to break loose and to bounce other aircraft came after we had completed long hours of work in the air. Every time the weather permitted, we went aloft to work out the best formations for patrol, escort and attack missions.

On March 10, 1943, the first selection of pilots from the 56th Fighter Group flew to Llanbedr for gunnery instruction. Not only were we not yet in combat, we were just reporting to school for gunnery! I ferried a Thunderbolt to Llanbedr, and with three other pilots returned by C-47 transport to Kingscliff.

The next morning we were able to let off some steam. Gabreski, Allison, Jim Carter and I flew at 35,000 feet, and then tore at each other in a wild dogfight. For twenty minutes we attacked each other in mock combat, punishing the fighters and ourselves in wicked turns and wild maneuvers. We celebrated on the way home by having a rat race, every man diving at full speed for the ground and then racing for the field at absolute minimum altitude, scaring hell out of every human being unfortunate enough to be caught beneath our roaring fighters. It was the last time. The hapless people of the surrounding countryside were up in arms at being forced to hug the earth while Thunderbolts ripped overhead in succession, jangling nerves and sending livestock into a frenzy. Their complaints became so vehement and were received in such number that Group headquarters finally forbade all future buzzing.

Our good luck with the weather vanished, and fretful boredom returned. I reported to Llanbedr for gunnery instruction, and for fourteen days we sat on the ground socked in, cursing the fog and mist, unable to fly. Two whole weeks on the ground, the Thunderbolts idle and the pilots slowly losing their patience with one another. Finally, on March twenty-seventh, we flew a gunnery mission. It wasn't a success. A thick haze hung over the land, and we were afraid that we'd hit the Lysander towing our target sleeve. We never had the chance to find out; the Lysander's engine quit and the plane plunged straight down. Both pilot and target operator bailed out, but the latter became snarled in his chute and was killed upon impact with the ground. The fatality shook up the British target crews badly, and cancelled out further flights.

Then back to Kingscliff for more training in maneuvers and formation flying. Practice, and more practice, until we felt we could fly our formations with eyes closed. One morning an emergency phone call shattered the normal routine. Waiting in the operations shack with several of us pilots for a training flight, Gabreski was ordered to intercept a bogey, an unidentified German aircraft, in our area. A German! The four of us tore out of the building and raced for our fighters, with Gabreski leading the flight, under the direction of ground radio, vectoring on a course to intercept the enemy plane.

Good old English weather! We flew for more than two hours and saw nothing but blinding haze. Finally we became completely lost, somewhere over London, groping in the thick murk. Disgusted, Gabreski asked for radio homing to Kingscliff, and we turned for our home base. The haze had settled, and I didn't appreciate gliding at 120 miles per hour in the Thunderbolt toward a runway which I couldn't even see. Not until the fighter whistled over the edge of the field could I see the airstrip, and gratefully we dropped the P-47's to earth.

Just in time. No sooner did we taxi to the flight line than

a vicious storm whipped in from the coast, blanketing the field with snow, driven by the force of the wind almost horizontally across the runways. Another flight was still up, and running dangerously low on fuel. Several pilots attempted to grope their way in to land, while the others headed for alternate fields still free of the snow. Dick Allison averted disaster by a hair. On a long final approach to the runway, he spotted a huge cloud bearing down from the north, the wind blowing sheets of snow before it, parallel to the ground. Dick had just flared out and was settling the fighter to the runway when the storm hit him full blast. Seven tons of fighter were flung fifty feet to the side, with a frantic Allison shoving the throttle all the way forward and yanking up his gear to regain flying speed. Buffeted by the wind, he staggered over the trees and climbed out. The moment the cloud passed Dick dropped his gear and slipped the P-47 into the field.

On April fourth, the entire Fighter Group took to the air, and slid into a giant 48-plane formation. This was moving day, a transfer to our new base at Horsham St. Faith, near Norwich. In perfect flying weather the mass of Thunderbolts roared high over the English countryside to reach our new field. We were greeted with the sight of dozens of barrage balloons drifting idly at their cables near the airstrip, just the thing to make a Thunderbolt pilot happy. At least the deep grass of our new home was a pleasure; the Thunderbolt seemed to be rolling on a layer of cotton when I set her down. More good news later that day, when we discovered that the Norwich base was almost like a miniature Randolph Field. Brick buildings for quarters, showers with warm water, large hangars, and some of the best equipment in England!

Early the next morning we were routed from our beds,

with orders for the 61st Squadron to report at once to our commanding officer, Major McCollom. The major was not at all happy. "It seems we have children in our midst," he stormed, "who like to tear up things. Let's get right down to business. Some of you men, for whatever strange reasons of your own, have been shooting up the barracks back at Kingscliff. I learned this morning that the ceilings of the barracks have been shot full of holes. I know some of the men who are responsible"—he called out their names—"and now I want to know who the rest are. Anybody want to volunteer their names?"

The major looked fit to burst. It was all we could do to keep from laughing out loud. Discretion came to our aid, however, and we kept straight faces as the major's face assumed a strange, purple hue. Finally he turned to Joe Curtis. "Lieutenant, you know who these men are. I want you to give me their names."

"Sir!" Curtis hedged, "I'd rather not say."

The purplish color deepening, the major turned to me with the same request.

"Sir, if you don't mind I'd rather the guys owned up to it themselves. I shot a few of those holes myself."

The purple turned to red, and I've never seen a man so mad! He shoved his face directly against mine and shouted, "Johnson, tell me the names of the officers who fired in your room! That's an order!"

Oh, well! It had to come out in the wash, and I had no choice but to name two other pilots. Brown, my roommate, volunteered the information that he'd fired his Colt .45 at least *once*. The major ordered the seven officers responsible confined to the field for two weeks. That night, discussing the major's wrath and our confinement, we all agreed the punishment worth every moment back at Kingscliff.

It had all begun with Dick Allison, who had a penchant for firing his .45 at every opportunity. Dick devised a rather hellish way of saying good night. Every evening, when we were either in bed or preparing to sack in, Dick would burst into the room, flash on the lights, shout "Good night!" and then empty his automatic into the ceiling. Doc Hornig was terrified of Dick whenever his eyes gleamed and he pulled out the .45; he literally begged Allison one night to put the gun away. Dick grinned and let loose a volley into the ceiling.

We decided that Dick needed some of his own medicine, and one night we set an ambush. We would wait in my room, the lights out, until Dick in his usual manner kicked the door open. Then, with a total of seven Colt .45's and an old Army rifle, we'd blast away and cure him once and for all of his habit. Only on this night, Allison was late. To keep from being bored, one of us every few minutes fired a blast into the ceiling, or we'd join together and fire a salvo. The rest of the men in the barracks locked themselves in their rooms, fearful of encountering stray bullets. Allison was shrewd. He waited until we ran out of ammunition. Several minutes later he stormed into the room, shouted "Good night, all!" and emptied his gun into the ceiling.

On April 8, 1943, four pilots of the 56th flew the Group's first operational mission. Major McCollom, Captains Eby and Renwick, and Lieutenant Les Smith of my squadron received assignment for a mission with the ex-Eagle Squadron pilots of the 4th Fighter Group to gain experience in combat tactics. It was a Circus mission, fighters accompanying bombers, the latter sent along to decoy enemy fighters into making an interception flight. Enviously, we watched them take off to join the planes of the 4th Group for the flight at high altitude to St. Omer, just across the French border. Our pilots failed to engage enemy planes, but received a sharp lesson in the quality of the German pilots. They saw two Spitfires plunge in flames. The German pilots broke off the battle without loss to their own force.

Early on the morning of April thirteenth, the teletype in headquarters rattled off the field order that committed the 56th to its first official combat mission. Twelve pilots from the 56th took off to join a large force of British Spitfires on a Rodeo (fighter sweep) to the Calais area, directly into the home grounds of the Abbeville Boys, the famed and, by many a pilot, feared yellow-nosed Focke-Wulf 190 fighters. The VIII Fighter Command still flew under the protecting wing of the Royal Air Force, and the twelve Thunderbolts of our Group were joined by twenty-four other fighters from the 4th Group, based at Debden, and the 78th, flying from Duxford.

Shepherding the Thunderbolts, the large Spitfire force crossed the French coast at an altitude of 31,000 feet. Still prevalent was the belief that the greater the altitude, the better the Thunderbolt's performance. Even the most confident American pilot had been taught to stay high, that below 25,000 feet meant trouble in a battle, and that to be caught at 15,000 feet or below with a German fighter was suicide.

It proved to be an uneventful mission. The fighters passed over St. Omer, greeted by light and inaccurate antiaircraft fire. Over Dunkirk, on the way home after their brief penetration, they were still at 31,000 feet, and ignored entirely by the Germans. The entire mission would have been without any excitement except that over Dunkirk, the engine of Captain Dyar's fighter stopped. No warning; one second he was in formation, and next he was gliding downward, the only sound that of the wind whistling past his cockpit.

His altitude brought him home. Feeling out his airplane carefully, Dyar trimmed the heavy Thunderbolt for her best gliding angle, and kept the ship airborne in a long, sloping descent. He passed over the English coast, just below 1,000 feet, and was fired upon immediately by British antiaircraft batteries, who mistook the P-47 for a German fighter attempting to sneak over the coastline. That night we welcomed Dyar back with more than usual enthusiasm, for the British 12th Group reported with misgivings that they had shot down a P-47 at 300 feet. Actually, Dyar had passed from view of the British gunners, and slipped the Thunderbolt into an empty field in a perfect forced landing.

Two days later the 56th went out for another mission. I stayed home, moaning with the rest of the pilots ordered to remain on the ground. Again the Group missed action, although a swarm of Focke-Wulfs gave the 4th Fighter Group a hot reception. The 4th came out on the losing end, with three of their fighters shot down. They claimed two kills.

And again one of our own pilots missed disaster by the narrowest of margins. In formation at high altitude, Conger's Thunderbolt ran out of fuel. Before the startled pilot could switch his tanks he fell far behind and below the rest of the Group. After jiggling his fuel-selector valve, Conger restarted his engine and slammed the throttle all the way to the firewall, trying desperately to rejoin the Group. He was in the worst possible position, entirely alone, smack in the lair of Germany's hottest fighter pilots. And he was scared silly, hammering at the throttle in an attempt to make the Thunderbolt fly faster. Abruptly a Focke-Wulf came into view, miles away, but passing in front of Conger. Startled, he squeezed the trigger and kept hammering at the throttle, trying to get more speed out of his overtaxed plane. The German ignored his fighter, and a happy Conger came home without further incident.

April seventeenth. A beautiful day, and the day long in waiting. My name was posted to the board for a fighter sweep. First combat!

10

It looked good. At the briefing I learned we were scheduled for a fighter sweep over Walcheren, the largest of the Dutch Islands. The long pointer slid along the map of the briefing room, tracing a flight of 105 miles over the North Sea to show our intended position over Walcheren. We were to be eased into the mission. We'd cross the enemy land at 31,000 feet, and at that altitude and speed the Thunderbolts would spend exactly two minutes over Walcheren.

There were other things to remember, and I paid close attention to the details. Expected fighter opposition was questionable. The Germans might be annoyed at us, and come up for a scrap. Or, as they had done often with the Spitfires, they would ignore us as unworthy of their attention. The long pointer stopped at red splotches, indicating the antiaircraft gun emplacements. All along the French border I saw the red splotches, a jagged but unbroken line indicating battery after battery of guns.

The speaker gave our course figures, altitudes, speeds to be flown. With the other pilots assigned to today's Rodeo to the Dutch Islands, I marked the figures on the back of my hand with a fountain pen. Always available to study, and easy to lick off with my tongue if I were shot down and survived. Strange, this curious detachment at the thought of failure in battle; but then, I never expected to fail, I never accepted the fact that I might be shot down. I was absolutely confident.

Call for a time check; a calibration of watches. "When I call out it will be"—the man in front of the map studies his own watch—"exactly 1001." He waits. "Now." Everyone's watch reads exactly one minute past ten. Weather data. It's going to be cold upstairs. At 31,000 feet it will be 60 degrees below zero. Really cold! Even with the flying suit and the heated cockpit, some of the boys are going to be shivering.

The last man has his say. Words of advice; serious words. Orders to keep in formation. Don't stray off. If the Jerries get you alone, you've had it. Don't play the hero. If you're in trouble get *out*—you've got a fast airplane, use your speed, go for home.

Time to go. I'm pleased with myself. Excited—naturally! Excited about my first combat mission, excited to realize that at long last, all those years of flying, all the skill passed on to me by instructors who wanted me to be able to fly well, to fly better than anyone else, would now be put to the test. It wasn't a war of such personal weight, of course, yet to me it was my own war, a private conflict in which I had to make good, in which I would stand or fall on my own. Everything else became a setting on a vast and intricate chessboard, in which I had to play my own role. But not as a pawn!

The scenes, the smells and sounds, all new to me on the first combat mission, were to become so familiar that finally they would be unnoticed, unseen, like the road you travel on so many times at home that you simply accept its surroundings, but never notice them any more. Today I noticed with remarkable clarity the sounds and feelings of the base, the color of the grass, the way the sun bathed the buildings. I heard and felt the deep rumble of Thunderbolts coming alive in their dispersal areas; knowing that, even as I sat in a briefing room, men were working for me, caring for the Thunderbolt I would fly, imparting to it a mechanical reliability to serve me in the sky, to bring me home.

The distant sound throbbed, deepened in power as crew chiefs sat in cockpits, advancing throttles, studying with meticulous care every dial and instrument. For a pilot's life hung in the balance, and a mistake on the ground could not be rectified in those critical moments when an experienced German flier caught an opponent rendered helpless by the breakdown of his equipment. These factors I had come to realize many years ago; never did I once forget the support and the meaning of the work of those men who serviced my fighter. Outside the briefing room the jeeps waited. We piled our parachutes on the hoods, climbed aboard the stubby vehicles, and were driven to our planes. I glanced at the sky; along the near horizon, haze and smoke. Above, crystal. Good flying weather for the mission.

The sound, roaring and ebbing, flowing in a tumbled stream from the many engines, grows louder as we near our planes. I can look this morning with increased awareness at every inch of the Thunderbolt, listen with greater sensitivity to the smooth pounding of the great engine. My crew grins at me; the big P-47 actually glistens from her waxing and buffing. Not for vanity or pride alone this intensive, gleaming coat, for the smoothness means lessened air resistance and several invaluable, additional miles of speed; enough, perhaps, to place a stream of cannon shells behind a cockpit instead of into a man.

My crew chief, "Pappy" Gould, throttles back the engine and climbs out to the Thunderbolt's wing. He crouches down and grins happily. "She's purring like a kitten, Lieutenant," he shouts above the subdued roar. "Never sounded better!" I smile back; what is there to say?

I toss my parachute onto the wing, climb up. I'm not a big man, but with my bulky flying clothes, boots and parachute even the cockpit of a Thunderbolt becomes crowded. Everything on the instrument panel checks out perfectly, but my crew chief sticks with me until the very last moment. He's leaving nothing to chance, worrying about me. As I taxi along the perimeter he's still on the wing, lying flat, listening to every sound and beat of the engine with—I hope!—only satisfaction. Then I'm at the runway, in a line of fighters, and he slides off the wing, waving. No use calling; the words would be whipped away by the engine roar and the slipstream.

Instructions from the tower. Engine runup; final power

check. "Clear to roll!" And I move the throttle forward, easing off the brake pedals, holding rudder to counteract the torque, letting the fighter have her head, speeding down the runway, faster and faster. The needle moves around, back pressure on the stick, and we're airborne. Gear up; flaps up. Canopy closed and locked.

Engines singing sweetly, we slide into battle formation, alert, careful, flying our best. The Thunderbolts climb, the altimeter needle keeps winding, and soon the big fighter has a different feel, due to the fading resistance of the air as we soar away from the earth. I make every move with practiced ease, and yet I am particularly careful. "This is your first combat mission," I tell myself, "don't foul up things now."

And then we're at 31,000 feet, six miles above the earth, seeing England, the Channel and enemy-held land lying before us, a map sliding ever so slowly across the horizon, closer to our formation. Then water lies beneath our wings. The order to turn on gun switches, to arm our eight .50-caliber machine guns. I'm tense, expectant, prepared for anything to happen.

The enemy coast is below, and we receive the terse order to ease forward on the stick, to gain speed. Noses down, accelerating rapidly, the Thunderbolt mass cleaves the thin air directly over Walcheren. That's enemy territory below. Enemy guns, enemy troops. Enemy fighter fields; even at that moment, enemy radar operators watching our course, enemy observers with binoculars studying our planes. We hurtle through space; Walcheren flashes below us so fast that we're hardly over the island at all.

The formation swings into a wide turn, a long sweeping bank that flashes sun off wings. Slowly the mass of fighters veers about in the cold air, maintaining the bank. Then, before us, England, jutting from the Atlantic. We're over the Channel, it disappears, green and brown are beneath our wings, and we're over England.

The long preparations, the meticulous care, the burning of untold thousands of gallons of high octane gasoline, the uncounted people who planned and co-ordinated and vectored and controlled and administered for this mission, my first combat mission. The advice and the warnings, the million thoughts as to how I'd react to being shot at, as to what I would do when a German fighter flashed through the sky and sun and went after *me* . . .

And nothing—absolutely nothing, happened! Not a single fighter to oppose us, not even a single puff of smoke from a flak battery. The Germans had totally ignored us. It was a hell of a combat baptism. When the ground crew asked me how things had gone, I felt like an idiot.

But this is how fighter pilots are made. Carefully, with planning to nurture them through the early moments, to bring them to that first critical instant of actual combat with as much help as possible. The combat veteran almost every time can single out the rookie from the old-timers, and a novice usually stands little chance against an experienced flier on the lookout for such easy meat. Thus the very shallow penetrations of enemy territory. To give the novice the feeling of actual combat flying, to show him the land, to allow him to realize that this is for keeps, that the quiet, slumbering countryside could erupt in flame and swarms of black-crossed fighters. Better to go easy at first, better to be as well prepared as possible.

Besides—I was still a novice, still unqualified to fly the Thunderbolt in battle. The realization galled me, but it failed to alter the facts. That same afternoon, on our return to base, the anticlimax of my first combat mission was an order for me to report with four other pilots to gunnery school. A fine combat pilot I was. Officially, I shouldn't have been in the Thunderbolt, and neither should Barron, Conger, Carter, or Foster. All five of us had been trained in flying school as bomber pilots. We had never qualified for fighters, and to that very day neither I nor the others had ever fired a machine gun! All my time at Llanbedr had proven fruitless; rotten weather and the mishap with the Lysander had prevented the opportunity to fire either at ground targets or at the tow sleeves.

We flew to the Goxhill gunnery range for our instruction, but our hearts weren't in it. Goxhill was an abominably filthy place, rundown and slovenly, and with an appalling layer of thick coal dust covering everything, including our mess tables and our beds. Every time we taxied along the runway our propellers flailed clouds of the choking stuff into the air. If we left our canopies open during taxiing, we emerged from the fighters looking like coal miners, and had on our hands an airplane with a dust-filled cockpit.

The weather held and all five of us went aloft with an instructor to work over a tow sleeve. The target plane flew a long way off, trailing on a thin cable a fabric-covered sleeve that would show clearly the impact of our bullets as they struck—*if* they struck. On this first day I swung around in perfect pursuit curves, holding constant airspeed and bank, correcting properly, considering all the shooting rules of lead and deflection and wind and gravity. I did everything by the book, exactly as I was supposed to do.

I couldn't hit a thing, and probably I scared the daylights out of the towplane crew. I learned quickly that the rules of firing a rifle from a steady position differ vastly from the complications of jockeying 14,000 pounds of fighter airplane in a constant curve. I was taught, in devastating fashion, that there exists a somewhat different sensation in firing a rifle, its butt comfortable in your shoulder, and releasing the energy pent up in two of the Thunderbolt's eight guns on a gunnery training flight.

Disgusted with myself, I joined the other pilots that night in a trip to Grimsby, where we choked in a movie theater to see an old and scratchy film of Tarzan thumping his chest and stabbing crocodiles with monotonous regularity. The next morning back we went to the coal dust and the tow sleeve. Again I failed even to register a single hit! My tracers flashed all over the sky, sailing everywhere but on the target. My self-disgust increased, and our collective mood didn't fare any better when Barron pulled the most idiotic of pilot errors and landed Conger's plane with the wheels still tucked neatly in the wings. That meant rotation of fighters in order to get the necessary gunnery time in the air, extending each day's firing.

On our last assigned day at Goxhill I began to hit the target sleeve. Most of the errors plaguing me seemed to vanish as suddenly my bullets flew in the general area of the sleeve and, strangely, even struck the target. At the end of our gunnery session I had scored a 4.5 percentage; since a minimum of 5. was required to pass gunnery school—I never qualified as a combat pilot.

April 29, 1943, was the Big Day, the first occasion on which the 56th Fighter Group, out in strength, slugged it out with German fighters. We came out on the losing side. All things considered, however, especially the experience and skill of the Germans, things could have been worse. All three P-47 groups went out on the mission (I stayed home and moaned), and the 56th was assigned to send out three squadrons of twelve fighters each to sweep over the Hague-

Woensdrecht-Blankenberghe area, arriving at an altitude of 28,000 feet.

Major Schilling led the group, and sent the 61st Squadron to 30,000 feet to act as cover for the 62nd and 63rd, flying at the assigned altitude of 28,000 feet. The Germans hit the lower squadrons hard, Me-109's and FW-190's attacking in pairs. The Luftwaffe boys were hot. They screamed in from dead ahead, working perfectly as teams, throwing their bullets and cannon shells expertly into the evading Thunderbolts.

When it was all over, Lieutenant Bill Garth, Schilling's wingman, struggled homeward, his engine crippled by 20-mm. cannon shells. Over Holland the engine ran wild, and Garth bailed out. Captain Johnny McClure went down unseen during the melee and was listed as missing in action (a year later we learned he was a prisoner). Schilling and Charley Harrison got worked over thoroughly and came home with their Thunderbolts badly shot up. Johnny Eaves, from Edmond, Oklahoma, who had joined the Air Force with me and had been with me all the way through training, was also caught in the German meat grinder and came home with his P-47 badly mauled.

Two Thunderbolts lost, two pilots lost, and three returning Thunderbolts shot up. Without any losses on their side, I'd say the Jerries had trounced us pretty badly.

I went on a fighter sweep on May third. Our force was big enough to raise hell with any opposition. More than two hundred Spitfires and Thunderbolts in the air, spoiling for trouble under the leadership of the British. The Jerries refused to accept the bait, and lolled on the ground, comfortable beneath a thick mantle of clouds. I never even saw Europe beneath the thick front.

We rolled out of our sacks at five thirty A.M. on May fifth for my first bomber-escort mission. Today's flight looked promising, for where the Germans might ignore our fighters, they went after the bombers like tigers. It still wasn't my day, I suppose. Three times we climbed into our Thunderbolts, and three times the weather was so bad the tower ordered us out. When a break in the clouds and fog came, we took off, only to run directly into a wild, towering storm front. Back home; Headquarters scrubbed the mission.

Apparently I wasn't regarded as the most promising of pilots in the Group. On May seventh I flew with the formation as a spare, praying someone would develop engine trouble and be forced to go home—so I could slip into his place. No such luck, and over the Channel I received orders to return to base while the formation continued into Europe. Six days later the Group took off on another bomber escort, this time to St. Omer. I sat on the ground, seeking gratification from the news that the Abbeville Boys had ignored both the Fortresses and our escorting fighters. I was getting nowhere fast.

That night my luck changed. I saw my name posted on the board for an escort mission for the following morning. It looked promising; a Ramrod—a bomber-escort mission—to Antwerp, a nest the Germans liked to defend.

11

The briefing was music. "Your chances of encountering enemy fighters are very high," the man with the long wooden pointer said. "Jerry usually defends Antwerp fiercely, and he's concentrated some of his best pilots in this area. It looks as if he'll go after the bombers with everything he has." What could be better? The way things had been going, the war would be over before I ever fired a shot.

Horsham St. Faith rocked to the cry of the 56th's Thunderbolts. Sixteen fighters from each of the three squadrons, forty-eight Thunderbolts howling down the grass runway into the air, forming quickly, sliding wings into formation slots, and climbing for altitude. A big show, with a maximum force from all three P-47 fighter groups. We flew the lead position, paving the way for the 4th and 78th Groups, all of us shepherding a force of about thirty Flying Fortresses. The "Big Friends" flew a staggered box formation, their guns unlimbered and poking into the slipstream.

England's coast and Channel water below; Europe dead ahead. At 31,000 feet Colonel "Hub" Zemke called for battle formation. Five miles from the European coast, six miles into space, the squadron slid apart, Thunderbolts fanning out and moving into line-abreast position, a giant swath of heavy fighters each some 100 yards apart. Wing to wing, the sixteen Thunderbolts bared a massed total of 128 .50-caliber machine guns.

Gun switch: on. Zemke's call for more power, each man easing the black throttle knob forward, the engines turning propellers faster, adding power and speed to the sweeping line of fighters. The Dutch Islands below, and dirty grey flak blossoming. Several times the smoke appeared at our altitude, dark flashes of flame, greasy smoke blossoming out. Not enough to bother with, not enough even to rock our wings.

But the bombers! The sky had come alive with savage energy. A continuous magic appearance of angry flame, sudden flashes of light from exploding shells. Thicker and thicker became the flak bursts, until finally the Fortresses were slogging their way through a thick mass of exploding flame and smoke, driving through a rain of steel splinters and jagged hunks of metal. The flak was too dense, too accurate, for the bombers to escape. Down there steel crashed into wings and engines, tore into bodies.

Someone was on the radio. "Fighters, low at eleven o'clock. Climbing fast." More voices, unknown voices.

Robert S. Johnson shortly after his return to the United States in the summer of 1944, when he was officially recognized as the nation's leading ace with 28 confirmed air-to-air kills. On his return to active flying duty, Johnson traveled to many air bases in the country, lecturing on combat tactics in Europe and demonstrating the techniques he learned so well in air battle over Germany.

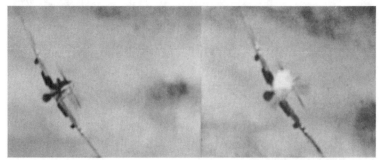

Air Force Photo

In less than one year of actual combat flying, Bob Johnson destroyed in aerial combat 28 German fighters, of which 24 were deadly single-engine Me-109 and FW-190 aircraft. Here is one of Johnson's kills of a Messerschmitt Me-109, which his guns exploded and burned on November 5th, 1943. *At left*, Johnson's Thunderbolt closes for the kill. *At right*, the Me-109 has just exploded in flames.

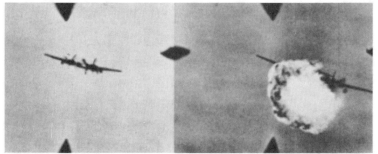

Air Force Photo

Fighter pilots loved to catch the German Messerschmitt Me-110 twin-engine fighters. Once the terror of European skies, they were called "meat on the table" by the wild-flying Thunderbolt pilots. On October 8, 1943, Bob Johnson caught this Me-110 attacking bombers. *At left*, his bullets are chopping up the airplane, and one landing-gear leg has dropped. *At right*–a blast, and *finis*.

Air Force Photo

Air Force Photo

Air Force Photo

At 18 years of age, Bob Johnson was an able athlete, skilled in football, wrestling, and boxing. Already a proficient private pilot, he enlisted in the Air Cadets and began flight training at Sikeston, Missouri, where he is pictured in front of a PT-18 primary trainer. Stubborn, a fierce and determined flier he went on to become the deadliest air killer in Europe. Johnson attributes much of prowess in the air as a fighter pilot to the personal attention and assistance of many of his flight instructors, who imparted to him their own combined vast experience in the skies. In combat, he was an aggressive fighter pilot, a "killer" whose one overriding goal was to engage the enemy wherever he could be found, at any odds and under all conditions.

Messerschmitt Me-109G was a swift, extremely maneuverable fighter with two guns, three cannon. Considered far superior to the P-47, the Me-109 was heavily scored against by Thunderbolts.

Considered deadliest German fighter of the war, Focke-Wulf FW-190 was swift, heavily armed, highly maneuverable at all altitudes. Thunderbolts scored heavily against this ship.

Air Force Photo

The two leading air killers of the ETO *(above)* were Bob Johnson *(at the left)* and Lt. Colonel Francis Gabreski. Picture was taken on May 11th, 1944. "Gabby" scored a total of 31 air kills in ETO, scored 6½ more kills in Korea. *(below)* Bob Johnson waits to be called for mission, discusses tactics with fellow pilots.

Air Force Photo

(Left to right, above): Joe Powers, Sam Hamilton, Bob Johnson, Stauss, and Joe Perry, all of the 56th Fighter Group. These men often flew together in combat.

At left is Francis Gabreski, considered by Johnson as one of the greatest combat pilots who ever flew. As Gabreski's wingman, Johnson scored many of his kills, then went on to command his own flight in Gabreski's squadron.

Air Force Photo

The terrible damage suffered by Bob Johnson's Thunderbolt in a wild fight which almost cost him his life is shown in these two pictures. The P-47 was shot apart by cannon shells and hundreds of bullets. The canopy was jammed closed *(above)*, and the rudder shot to pieces by 20-mm. direct hits.

Air Force Photo

"Without the tremendous support and the skill of my crewchief, Sgt. 'Pappy' Gould," claims Johnson, "my record of air kills would have been impossible." Gould kept Johnson's fighter in excellent shape; the P-47 never failed him.

It was impossible to protect the "Big Friends" at all times over Europe, and even when the German fighters were held at bay, enemy flak scored heavily. All too often Johnson saw bombers town apart, all men lost, as flak made direct hits.

Robert S. Johnson with his close friend, Walker Mahurin *(above)* of the 56th Fighter Group. At one time the leading ace of the ETO, Bud Mahurin was a fearless, highly skilled pilot who was shot down by enemy flak. Mahurin fled enemy troops, returned to England.

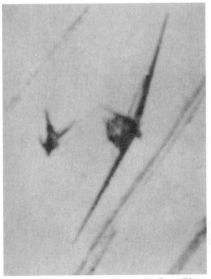

Sometimes German pilots bracketed by Thunderbolt guns were lucky like this FW-190 pilot *(left)* bailing out of his fighter. Major James Dalglish of 354th Fighter Group made kill.

Streaking to the attack through the icy sub-stratosphere, Thunderbolt fighters are revealed by long condensation trails. Pilots disliked vapor trails which gave away their positions to German fighters. Bob Johnson, *(below* in Sept., 1943, with one of the 56th Fighter Group's lucky mascots–a black and friendly crow.

This is Bob Johnson's favorite photo . . . taken in 1944 on his return to the United States. Flanking General Henry "Hap" Arnold, the Air Force "chief" are Johnson *(left)* and America's all-time Ace of Aces, Major Richard I. Bong *(right)*. Flying a P-38 Lightning in the Pacific, Dick Bong shot down 40 Japanese aircraft.

With 28 air kills to his credit, Bob Johnson meets two of the most famous old-time fighter pilots of the AAF–General James H. Doolittle *(left)* and General Carl Spaatz *(center)*. Both men considered Johnson "one of AAF's greatest pilots."

"Two bandits, coming in level, twelve o'clock." "Look out for those four, five o'clock high." The bomber crews, calling for help, announcing the expected arrival of the black-crossed Messerschmitts and Focke-Wulfs, the latter with yellow and red noses, with white wings, the mark of the Abbeville Boys, Goering's finest.

I flew the Tailend Charlie slot, the last man in the formation in Zemke's flight. Ours was the most vulnerable position, the perfect spot to receive a bounce from the Germans. More radio calls, and another voice, calling to us. "Four bandits at two o'clock, low." Zemke had them spotted, rattled off their positions, and I watched his Thunderbolt sliding off on its wing, the formation following in the diving attack.

Here we go! Zemke's fighter plunged, the three of us glued to his tail and wing position. I looked for the fighters he called. Nothing. Empty space, not a black cross in sight. Let him worry about those; from the calls coming in I knew the Jerries had ripped through the bombers, done their damage, and were now arcing swiftly up to meet our challenge. No lack of fight in these people!

My head swiveled from left to right, turning constantly. That was my job. Keep looking, keep looking, spot any other fighters diving after us, gunning for our blind stern position. My job was main cover, to keep the air space behind us observed, to warn the formations below of attackers coming from the heights. Once Zemke committed himself to the diving attack, he ignored what went on behind him. That was my responsibility, to keep him protected. And there they were, in loose formation, diving with full power, ripping down from high altitude.

"White Leader from White Four!" I called. "Eight bandits coming down on us from seven o'clock." Even as I called out the position of the diving Germans, Zemke's

Thunderbolt lifted its nose. Watching his every move, we followed, Thunderbolts wheeling around in a punishing pullout and climb, swinging sharply to the left and up. The Thunderbolt had dynamite in her wings; Zemke brought his formation wheeling about to meet the enemy attack head-on. The *only* way to fight—strike hard.

The Germans flew masterfully and without fear. Four Focke-Wulfs, yellow noses gleaming, ripped directly before Zemke's plane, flashing past his guns in the barest fraction of a second. The second four made their move deliberately, slicing between my element leader and myself, an attempt to break up our formation and make us scatter.

One yellow-nosed Focke-Wulf tore through space not fifty yards in front of my plane, rolling slowly as he flashed by. I was so excited I forgot the rules of air gunnery and simply hammered a burst directly at the German, instead of leading the target. A stream of bullets flashed away from the roaring Thunderbolt, whistling harmlessly through empty air. All I received for my pains was some clear camera footage of the Jerry as he dove. I released trigger pressure and—trouble!

The guns kept firing, a staccato hammering draining my ammunition. I pounded on the trigger and flicked the arming switch several times, trying to cut them off, all the time still climbing in a high, sweeping turn to the right. Two more FW-190's, charging right into the Thunderbolts, spoiling for a fight. I stared at the enemy fighters as they passed less than fifty yards away—directly through the stream of bullets pouring from my eight guns. Pieces of metal ripped away from both diving fighters as they flashed by—two enemy aircraft damaged, while I pounded on the gun trigger trying to *stop* the guns. A moment later they ceased.

The sudden zoom pulled me above and away from the

fight, a climb so steep and sustained that the Thunderbolt buffeted on the edge of a stall, threatening to drop off on her wing and plummet. I kicked left rudder and dropped the nose, skidding into level flight, trying to see what was happening around me. My element leader, Bob Wetherby, had snapped out a quick burst at the four fighters who dove past Zemke's plane, and then continued with Zemke and his wingman. Being Tailend Charlie, I had attempted to get at least one Focke-Wulf and, abruptly, I found myself alone in the sky over Antwerp, a position fairly screaming danger.

I wasn't exactly alone; I could see the bombers forging their way through the thick mass of antiaircraft explosions, and at least forty enemy fighters, sweeping through the bomber ranks and reforming for additional passes. I realized the seriousness of my solo position; we'd been warned time and again never to be caught alone. Besides, I was, in view of my novice status, almost helpless.

I didn't feel I was helpless, not with a Thunderbolt and eight guns under my hands. I should have been scared; I suppose I should have been absolutely cowed by what was going on. Somehow, I didn't experience fear. Perhaps I was too busy, too intent on what I should do, or perhaps I even ignored what might happen to me if I were boxed in. There wasn't anything to gain by pondering the situation. I was in an airplane, and that meant to fly.

My stalling position hadn't helped. The Thunderbolt had dropped almost two miles and a glance at the altimeter showed a height of 20,000 feet—according to all the rules, absolute suicide for the P-47. To blazes with all the warnings. I rammed the throttle forward, gaining speed, and swiveled my head in an attempt to sight some other Thunderbolts.

There they were, about eight fighters, some twenty miles to the west. I kicked stick and rudder and turned toward the protection of the Thunderbolts, flying at maximum speed to catch up with the flight. Right then and there I realized I needed some more aircraft identification; the Thunderbolts turned out to be Focke-Wulfs. They still hadn't seen me, and I banged on the throttle, trying to squeeze extra speed out of the big fighter as I turned and fled.

I never saw another P-47 over Antwerp. At full throttle I left Europe and ran for home. Over the Channel I dropped the Thunderbolt's nose and let her run wild, fast enough to elude any German fighter that might have been tailing me. The airfield never looked so good. As I dropped flaps and gear, and slipped in for a perfect landing, my ground crew stared at me with slack jaws and round eyes. "My God!" the crew chief burst out. "He's alive! Hey, Johnson's back!"

Their astonishment was justified; I had been reported as Missing in Action, and believed shot down by the diving German fighters. The way Zemke laced into me, perhaps I should have been shot down. But with all the foolish things I'd done—or was supposed to have done—including climbing right up through the middle of the diving German fighters, only two of the Focke-Wulfs actually made a pass at my Thunderbolt. They came straight down, diving with tremendous speed. In the climb I was moving so slowly that all I had to do was to kick the P-47 sideways and they tore past me without firing and, more important, unable to fire. Possibly the German pilots felt I was a booby trap and wanted no part of me; the slowly climbing fighter was a ruse they often used themselves.

I don't know what the exact explanation is, and the other pilots had a dozen reasons all neatly worked out, each in conflict with the other. It was my first aerial combat, and so far as I'm concerned the reason I came home that day depended on a great deal more than my skill or the thoughts of the Germans. God was with me, as He was many times after that. That is the way I felt, and I couldn't have cared less for the intricate explanations showered upon me.

Whatever the outcome in the air, the episode started my reputation for being a wild flier. The other pilots joked about the incident, and in a more serious vein several of them wagered that I would be the next man to be shot out of the air. For a while things got real tight; I didn't appreciate their sense of humor.

I flew two more missions which, for me, passed without any excitement. On a sweep to the Cherbourg Peninsula, Gabby Gabreski, Mudge, Biales and McCollom tore after a pack of Focke-Wulfs and scored hits on several. But they couldn't stay with the elusive German pilots, who used their excellent maneuverability to escape from their dangerous positions. Joe Curtis was McCollom's wingman and got caught right in the middle of the scrap; and as happened to many of us, Curtis banged the throttle all the way forward and ran for home, engine wide open, screaming for help over the radio. Several of the boys peeled off and tried to get to his side, but to no avail. They couldn't even catch him, and the last they saw of Curtis during that fight was his Thunderbolt hurtling for England.

On May nineteenth it was my turn to run, and my flight to England seemed to set some sort of unofficial speed record over Europe. The assigned mission was a Circus. In early 1943 the Thunderbolt lacked the range to escort our bombers the full distance to their targets, and thus all deep penetrations by the heavies were made without escort. The Circus was intended as a feint to draw off German interceptors. As the main striking force flew to the primary target, a smaller group of bombers with fighter escort attacked a diversionary target.

The heavy bombers roared unescorted to Kiel and Flensburg, while the fighters shepherded the Circus force of forty Flying Fortresses to The Hague. Our escort route took us, with fighters from the 4th and 78th Groups, on a sweep from Ijmuiden to south of The Hague, and return. The decoy bomber force suddenly changed course, and we never rendezvoused with them. Instead, we made a wide, high-altitude fighter sweep, the kind of a mission in which we were free to look for trouble.

Everything went fine until we had turned and were nearly over the Dutch coast on our way home. Again I was Tailend Charlie and the last fighter over the mainland. Barron, the second man in my flight, broke radio silence. "Two bandits, six o'clock, in the sun." I looked around and saw the two German fighters, far above and a long distance behind our formation. Too far, I estimated, ever to catch us. For the next several minutes I held formation, turning my head only occasionally to check the two reported fighters.

They were decoys, and I was too green to recognize the fact. Once I had spotted the two planes, still high and far behind, I concentrated on flying my formation slot. My head should have been on a swivel, and it wasn't. I never saw the four black shapes hurtling from high altitude. I knew something was in the air when white flashes appeared magically all around my fighter, uncomfortably close. I was so green that I thought the flashes to be light flak, never considering that light antiaircraft guns don't throw shells to 30,000 feet.

To evade what I still thought were antiaircraft shells, I skidded the Thunderbolt sharply to the left and right and changed altitude in a broken line of flight to keep any shrapnel from falling onto me after the shells had exploded. No one had said a word since Barron's warning. I decided to have a look, and cocked the Thunderbolt on its side, to the right of the flight, and glanced back.

"Blue Flight—break!" I yelled, and then almost exploded into action. My heart jammed into my throat, and in a blur of arms and legs my left hand slammed the throttle all the way forward, my right hand jerked the stick hard to the right, my right foot jammed down on the rudder pedal. The Thunderbolt whipped over on her back as I threw the fighter into the start of a split-S. The moment I was inverted I glanced down and saw the enemy coast. "Oh, no, Johnson!" I told myself. "That's Jerry's hunting grounds. Let's go home!"

I held the straining fighter upside down, streaking earthward in a 45-degree dive, and ran for it. The inverted Thunderbolt raced for the sea while I kicked the rudder pedals, slamming the fighter from side to side to present a poor target for any pursuers. My finger poised over the Mayday button, for at the first sign that my fighter might be hit, and that I would have to bail out into the drink, I wanted to be certain that Air-Sea Rescue would be on its way to fish me out of the Channel.

I didn't realize then that my decision to race for home probably saved my life. The moment the lead German pilot saw my wing go up and over, he immediately started to roll his own fighter, snapping around and down into his own split-S maneuver, nicely co-ordinated to bring him out of the diving half-loop smack on my tail—with a perfect setup shot. I never identified the enemy planes; seeing the black wings alive with the sparkling flame from their cannon was enough for me!

The Jerries were masters at the art of cutting up enemy fighters. When the lead plane rolled and arced over in the split-S, his wingman continued straight ahead, snapping out bursts of cannon shells as he closed the distance between our two planes. High above the pursuit one of our squadron leaders, "Pappy" Craig, burst into laughter as he watched my Thunderbolt fairly leap ahead. We were permitted to race our engines to a reading of 52 inches manifold pressure and my instrument read 57 inches, with me pounding at the throttle in an attempt to squeeze even more speed out of the plunging fighter. By the time I reached 25,000 feet, the Thunderbolt was running wild and had streaked away from the pursuing German. I don't know how fast I was going. I was so scared that I don't even remember remaining upside down and kicking rudder back and forth at that terrific speed. At 15,000 feet I rolled the P-47 right side up, leveled out and took a careful look behind me. Not an airplane in the sky. Whew—what relief! Now for home!

Little by little I cut my combat teeth. We flew sweep missions into France and Holland, and on several of these escorted our Big Friends to coastal targets while they dumped their bombs. On several occasions we saw nothing but a layer of white, fleecy clouds stretching to the horizon, blotting out any sight of Europe. The 56th didn't see much action during those missions, but the 4th Fighter Group tangled several times and, unhappily, had come out the loser. Each time they ran into the skilled and veteran Abbeville Boys, the Jerries administered a shellacking to the Thunderbolts.

We lost one of our best-liked pilots in a fatal accident.

Dick Allison, he of the flaming .45, took off on a cross-country flight to England's west coast to visit friends. During the flight low clouds swept in from the ocean and obscured the ground. Flying in clear sunlight above the cloud layer, by instruments, Dick confirmed his arrival over his destination by radio, peeled off, and eased his way into the clouds. Something happened. Almost certainly Dick was affected by vertigo in the grey mist and lost control of his ship. The Thunderbolt whipped into a spin, continuing its uncontrolled plunge to smash into the earth, instantly killing its pilot.

We had a red-letter day on June twelfth, when the 56th Fighter Group scored its first combat victory. First blood! We had flown in combat since our initiation on April thirteenth. In those two months of continuing missions and several dogfights, German pilots shot down several of our people, but not a single enemy fighter went down before our guns.

The 56th took off for a high-altitude sweep at 20,000 feet of the Blankenberghe-Calais area, and was cruising over Ostend, northeast of Ypres, when an excited voice burst out, "Twelve bandits, and they're right below us. Let's go!" Blue Flight peeled off in a diving attack, running for the Focke-Wulfs. The hoped-for advantage of surprise vanished as a sharp-eyed German flier shouted of the P-47's to his formation. Immediately eight Focke-Wulfs nosed down and dove away while the other four whipped around in a sharp, 180-degree turn.

What started out to be a perfect bounce turned into a riot. Captain Walt Cook, leading Yellow Flight, grabbed the golden opportunity. As the Focke-Wulfs wheeled around, Cook led his flight directly out of the sun, which blinded the Germans. And Cook wasn't going to miss. He skidded in to the tail of the last FW-190, rammed home the throttle, and closed to 300 yards. Eight guns roared, and a mass of heavy bullets tore into the Focke-Wulf's fuselage and left wing. Smoke blossomed and a large piece of the wing flipped away in space. The Focke-Wulf tumbled crazily, out of control, toward the earth. Score one for us!

That night another pilot and I thrashed out the events of the day. I was disgusted. Once before we'd been in position for a perfect bounce and an excellent chance for a kill. He and I had flown together since our first meeting in advanced training at Kelly Field. By assignment we alternated between leader or wingman positions. Sometimes he led and I flew his wing; then we changed. After losing out on what seemed a sure kill we decided not to let that happen again. "Bob," he said, "the next time you see any bandits below us, don't wait. Just go on and bounce the nearest son of a bitch. Never mind who's leading. If you're flying wing and you see them first, call 'em out and *go*, and I'll cover your wing. I'll do the same. Whoever gets first crack will be covered by the other guy. Okay?" It sounded good to me. We grinned and shook hands on our new agreement.

The next day we passed over twelve Focke-Wulfs in tight formation. My cohort held the Number Three position in Gabreski's flight, and I flew the Number Four slot, protecting his wing. We were top cover for the day, but I couldn't have cared less. There were fighters below us. "Twelve bandits," I shouted, "right below us!" I kicked rudder and banged the stick over, diving after the Germans. "Come on!" I called, "Let's get 'em!" I didn't need to look back; that's why my buddy was there. I knew he'd be glued to my wing, protecting me against any stern attacks.

The Thunderbolt fell through and streaked earthward.

Everything was fitting into place as the Focke-Wulf expanded in size, as details of the wings and fuselage came into view. The German attack formation loomed larger every second—and still they hadn't moved, still they hadn't seen us! Now they had—look at them go! Black-crossed fighters breaking in all directions, flashing away from the plummeting Thunderbolt that now was so close. I wanted the leader, the Number One man, and I wasn't going to lose him today. I lifted the wing, slid the P-47 through a gentle curve in her dive and lunged for the Focke-Wulf.

Closer, closer, the square wings, big, black crosses in the sights, growing larger, clearer. Everything seemed to be so familiar! Was this combat, or another mock battle with a friend? I did everything as I always had, flying exactly as I had in the wild friendly dogfights over Connecticut and over England, following the same procedures learned through practice. I didn't think that this was a Focke-Wulf, or that the man inside was a German, or that if he managed to whirl that black-crossed airplane around, then four cannon and two heavy guns would be hurling steel and explosives at me.

I talked to myself. "Nope, you're too low. Pick her nose up just a little. That's it, just a little higher. There, hold that for a second . . . hold it . . . *now!*" Trigger squeeze, stick steady, the lead is exactly right, he'll fly into the bullets, hold it down. . . . *Crash!* Something's hit me! The Thunderbolt trembled so violently my finger flew from the trigger—and the explosion stopped! My own guns—all that noise and vibration, the flame and smoke, had come from the eight heavy .50 calibers blasting away. I was so scared I nearly jumped out of my seat and . . .

. . . violent flame, a sudden mushrooming flower of bright fire, jagged pieces of metal twisting crazily, black smoke—there goes the Focke-Wulf, torn into pieces from my first burst! First kill; I'd made it! The Thunderbolt flashed through a spinning torrent of fire, smoke and debris, the remains of the disintegrating FW-190. Instinctively I jerked the stick hard over to the left, rolling rapidly, and then shoved the throttle forward as I hauled back on the stick. The Thunderbolt howled and went for altitude, bursting away from any pursuers that might have charged after me.

I was alone. I kicked the rudder pedals, swinging my head about, searching for my wingman. Where the blazes was he? This wasn't any joke. I had made a grave error by taking a bounce by myself. Back at the field I discovered through the almost violent anger of my commanding officer exactly what he thought of my little maneuver. I got chewed up, but thoroughly. My "friend" was no help. No sooner did we land than he was in the colonel's office, complaining bitterly that I had abandoned him in the middle of the dogfight just because I wanted a kill.

The only kill I wanted at that moment was to have that guy's neck in my hands. He'd never even been in a fight. He never even broke formation! Naturally, he denied any part of our conversation the previous evening, about our covering each other during a bounce.

It was a good day for the 56th, even if I was forced to walk a tightrope back at the base and to suffer being chewed out again and again. "Hub" Zemke had gunned down two of the Focke-Wulfs and my kill made three for the day, which put the outfit in business. Oh, well, despite my being racked by Zemke and the rest, it was worth it. I tried to justify my action to myself; I just couldn't keep from going after the Jerries. After all, we were there to fight! My new flight leader, Gerald W. Johnson, was especially sour about my actions of the day. He congratulated

me on the kill, and then nearly tore my ears off with a
beautiful chewing out!

Two days later I learned that Zemke at least felt I could
fly. As new replacements came in, I was assigned to take
them up to high altitude and shake them out. Two new
lieutenants, Horton and Grosvenor, climbed with me to
34,000 feet. For twenty minutes we wrung out ourselves
and the fighters in a wild rat race. The boys were good. I
radioed for them to take up formation off each wing and
then to fall back a fair distance. Then—stick back and over
to the side, throttle all the way forward, hard rudder—and
go! Straight down, faster and faster, everything the Thunderbolts had to give, plummeting with incredible speed.
The scream of our racing motors could be heard for miles
and miles, a shrieking crescendo that made everyone around
stop and look up, searching for the tiny black shapes
plunging from the sky. Then the pullout, made at minimum
altitude, the shriek deepening to a terrible roar as we shot
over the ground, shaking buildings and sending people
diving for earth. A wonderful way to let off steam.

I received confirmation of my first official victory, and a
joyous occasion that was! I'd made a vow that I would try
to flame a Jerry for every one of my close friends shot down
over Europe. And I fully intended to do just that. The moment of the confirmation, however, was one for celebration.
Doc Hornig and others burst into my room with a bottle of
Scotch sent by General Carl A. "Tooey" Spaatz just for this
occasion. Everyone in the outfit signed their names on the
label and that became the most treasured Scotch in all of
England. I still have the bottle and the general's personal
note.

I didn't suspect then that several days later I'd be in a
frame of mind to sit back and pour the contents of that

bottle right down my throat. On June twenty-sixth the 56th Fighter Group flew its most important mission to date, a maximum-effort Ramrod with forty-eight Thunderbolts to Villacoublay. The VIII Air Force was starting to flex its growing sinew, and on this date they dispatched one hundred Fortresses to take out an aircraft factory near Paris. Eight full P-47 squadrons were to escort the Big Friends while, at the same time, eight Spitfire squadrons would shepherd still another one hundred heavy bombers to strike the marshalling yard at Le Mans. To support these two heavy raids, fifty Fortresses with Spitfire escort went out to smash the Tricqueville airdrome, and twelve R.A.F. Boston light bombers with escorting Spitfires went in at low altitude to shake up the home airfield of the Abbeville Boys. The intention of the diversionary raids was to permit the two main strikes to be made with the minimum possible fighter resistance en route to their targets. Unhappily, the Luftwaffe wasn't in a co-operative mood.

Early in the morning of June twenty-sixth I took off from Horsham St. Faith with forty-eight other Thunderbolts for a cross-country flight to our advanced base at Manston, just north of Dover. We flew on the deck all the way, roaring low over the Thames Estuary before swinging around for our long approaches to Manston. On the ground we lined the Thunderbolts along the airfield perimeter and then left the fighters to ground crews, who checked over the airplanes and refilled fuel tanks.

With most of the other pilots I walked to the Royal Air Force messhall for tea and crumpets, and then went outside for a welcome rest on the grass. The pilots had collected in groups, relaxing and discussing with each other the details of the Ramrod mission. I was still in the doghouse and, I suppose, rightfully so. Blue Flight's leader, Jerry Johnson, left no doubts as to his opinion of my antics in combat. Somehow I had on several occasions ended up alone in our fights with the Germans. I'd damaged several more enemy fighters, but my flight leader, and Zemke as well, were irritated because of their conviction that I was playing the role of the lone wolf. And it wasn't that at all! The only way to fight was to get in there and *fight*—and before I knew it, I'd be a lone Thunderbolt in the middle of black-crossed planes.

That morning I had discussed with Ralph A. Johnson the mission we were to fly. Ralph had been with me through flying school, and we flew many of our combat missions together. "R.A.," I said, "I'm getting sick of being low man on the colonel's totem pole. Every time we get into a scrap with the Jerries, it seems I do the wrong thing and end up coming home alone." He grinned at me and refused to comment. "Well, boy," I continued, "not today. I'm going to stick with Blue Flight all the way through. I swear that if I separate from the flight, it won't be voluntary. The Krauts are going to have to shoot me out of formation."

12

More than fifteen years have passed since I flew that mission. Fifteen years since the most critical moments of my life, eternal seconds of flight, of roaring guns and searing flame, the horrifying sound of cannon shells and bullets flashing, seeking—me. A tumbling stream of emotions, exultation, pain and despair, the grip of terror and Death anxious and expectant. Fifteen years past, and yet every moment is still alive, still painted vividly in my mind. It is easy, so easy, to turn back the years to that warm and sunny morning at Manston . . .

. . . into the Manston briefing hut, walls clouded with

maps and charts, with recognition sheets and colored symbols, the travel posters of a fighter group. This morning especially I am attentive. The words are the same as other briefings, and yet they are different. Details are vital; details of what to expect can save your life, prepare you for the worst: ". . . to be a maximum effort . . . expect heavy and determined opposition." More words on clouds and winds aloft and rendezvous points with the Big Friends: ". . . protect the bombers, at all costs." The latest intelligence reports on escape and evasion tactics, on contacting the underground, how to wiggle past tens of thousands of Nazi troops, how to work your way down to Spain. *If* you're shot down, and *if* you remain alive. No one wants or expects to be shot down, to tumble unsuspectingly before a Focke-Wulf's or a Messerschmitt's guns. But we all check, carefully, our maps, chart courses, vital data, our knives and guns and escape kits.

This isn't an ordinary mission. Too much preparation. Too much careful planning. Details usually accepted as a matter of routine are studied exhaustively; nothing is taken for granted. The Thunderbolts roar sweetly, alive and tense, seemingly as taut as their pilots for a mission everyone knows is our most important to date. There is a feeling in the air, a tenseness that crackles invisibly among the pilots, that is transferred to our ground crews. There's little joking this morning; the usual levity is replaced by somber self-reflection.

We are tense, excited, thinking of the imminent battle miles above the ground when the Germans race after the bombers. No doubt today of a maximum interception. The black-crossed planes will be out in force, and as always flown by skillful and courageous pilots, flying fighter planes the match of those anywhere in the world. I love the Thunderbolt, glory in its power and strength, in its incredible, unsurpassed durability and its tremendous armament—but I am not so foolish as to lack a keen appreciation of the flashing speed and agility of the opposition. And they are rugged, those boys out there!

I run through the fighter's cockpit check almost by instinct, my eyes and hands and feet moving in response to habit drilled into me. I forget nothing, miss nothing, but it is almost rote. I cannot keep my mind off the mission. I know that, more so than on previous Ramrods, I am excited and tense. I wonder what will happen today, and I wonder if I will come home. That quivery feeling. Scared? I try to be honest with myself, and yet I'm not sure! Can I distinguish between the slight tremors of excitement and those of fright? I'm not certain; yet, I am aware, as are the other pilots, that this is the ultimate test. We have been warned so many times and with such emphasis of the opposition today that we are expecting half the Luftwaffe to scream at us. There is no question that we must fly our best—or many of us will not come home today.

This quiver of excitement, the anticipation, I had experienced before. The trembling of knees, the undue clarity of vision and of mind. I remember back even further into the years: clad in boxing trunks, taped fists clenched and taut within the leather gloves, waiting the eternity of seconds before the bell rings, waiting to shuffle forward, to have my head rocked back by a stinging jab, waiting for the fear to leave me, for the opponent's blow to wash my fear away, until I could rush into him, swinging, alive with the moments of the fight. I can never explain these feelings better. I knew them more intimately after this mission, and with every succeeding flight against the Luftwaffe I failed to escape these moments of fear. To deny these feelings, even to myself, would be a lie. Fear was with me as it was with the other men. And it was healthy, a provider of respect and caution, not to be denied, but to be welded into what is described as a fighter pilot's "killer instinct." Fear could also be a friend; it speeded up my reactions.

Thunderbolts moving out from the perimeter, propellers drenched in sun, grass flattened by airblast. Pilots leaning out of cockpits to see beyond those giant engines, weaving their way along, moving into position for takeoff. Orders from the tower, brakes released, throttle forward, go! Hard on the rudder to counteract torque, the needle climbs around, back pressure on the stick. Grass and trees fall away magically beneath my wheels, I work the controls, hydraulics surge in tubes, the gear folds up and inward and tucks away into the Thunderbolt's broad wings.

Left turn, stick and rudder working smoothly, tilting the earth sharply, back on the stick, climb out, and meet in the air. Forty-eight Thunderbolts in formation, sliding and wheeling into neat and precise patterns. No one aborts, no engine fails, the pilot of the forty-ninth Thunderbolt, our standby, mutters unhappily and peels off to return to Horsham St. Faith. We lead today; the 61st Fighter Squadron holds the low and leading position for this mission. I swivel my head. High to my left, bunched together, the sixteen fighters of the 63rd labor for altitude. To my right, slightly higher than my own formation, wings the 62nd. I am Blue 4 in Blue Flight, stuck on the end slot. My element leader is to my left; sliding smoothly through the air to his left ride our flight leader and his wingman.

It is a tight, well-drilled team. Each flight of four Thunderbolts holds tight formation, four finger tips greasing through the air. Manston falls far behind as the forty-eight fighters drone southward, all climbing at an indicated 170 miles per hour. Our throttles are held back, allowing the Thunderbolts to ascend in a shallow, fuel-saving climb.

Dover below, the cliffs melting into the Channel waters. A day of crystal clarity, scattered clouds far below us, miles between the puffy white. There is absolutely no limit to visibility; the earth stretches away forever and forever. A strange world—made for solitary flight, and yet made also, it seems, of three-dimensional movement, the gliding through space of forty-eight fighters, each alone, each linked also by the unseen thread of metallic, radio voices.

Over the Channel, only a mile or so off the French coast. Still climbing, the altimeter winding around slowly, clocking off the hundreds, the thousands, past ten thousand, reaching for twenty. The coastline drifts by, quiet and almost sleepy in the rich sun, unrevealing of gun batteries and listening posts and radar scanners already reporting of our position, number, height and course, data flashed back to German antiaircraft batteries, to fighter fields, to command posts. From this altitude, France slumbers, beautiful and green.

Le Tréport beneath our left wings, the mouth of the Seine River clear and sharp. "Blue Flight, stay sharp. Nine zero degrees. Let's go." Blue Flight wheels, banks and turns in unison with its squadron, the 61st matching flawlessly the wheeling of its two sister squadrons. Below the formation, the Seine River, occupied territory.

"Open up, Blue Flight." Our radio call, orders to the other flights. Move out, separate into combat formation. Pilots work stick and rudder; the Thunderbolts ease away from one another. Now Blue Flight is in its combat position, each Thunderbolt 200 yards apart. Between each flight of four fighters stretches a space of 500 yards and, even further out, holding a distance of 1,500 yards, ride the squadrons.

Almost constantly I turn and look, turn and look, watching the position of my own planes, seeking out strange black specks in the sky, alert for the plunging Focke-Wulfs or Messerschmitts.

Marching in precision, the 63rd Squadron flies to the north, very high, in down-sun position. I turn my head, and see the 62nd Squadron, to our south, and slightly above our own altitude. Other things to check as I divert my attention to the cockpit. Gun switch "On." Gunsight "On." Check the chute harness. Shoulder and leg straps tight, catches secure, the harness fastened. Don't make it easy for the Jerries—check the "elephant trunk." I inspect the oxygen tube, start to count: "3 - 6 - 9 - 12 - 15 - 18 - 21 - 24 - 27 - 30." Oxygen okay; the count by threes to thirty clear and sharp, no faltering. Escape kit secured. If—that big "if"—I go down, I want to be sure of my equipment, my procedures, my position. It's a long walk through France and Spain, *if* luck holds.

The Thunderbolts move into the skies of Europe. A moment to myself. Alone, yet not alone, I pray. If He allows, a moment of thanks on the way home. There won't be time to pray once the black-crossed fighters rush in.

Keep looking, keep looking! It's that moment of carelessness, the second of not paying attention, when the fighters bounce. Occasionally I glance ahead, but I am in the end slot, exposed in the Blue 4 position. At all times my head swivels, my eyes scanning every inch of the sky from my right wingtip, rearward, and above, over my canopy, and down. The silk scarf around my neck isn't a hotrock decoration; without the silk to protect my skin, my neck by now would be raw and bleeding from rubbing against the wool collar of my shirt.

Out of the corner of my eye—a speck. There, far to the

right! I catch my heart with my teeth, swallow, snap my
head to the right. I squint, study the sky. A speck of oil on
the windshield, not a fighter. Gratefully, my heart drops
back where it belongs.

Fifteen miles inland, the Thunderbolt phalanx due north
of Rouen, still over the sparkling Seine. My head continues
to swivel, my roving gaze stops short as I notice a formation of sixteen fighters, directly behind and slightly above
us. They're coming in fast, flying a duplicate of our own
formation. Thunderbolts? I look to the left; the sixteen
fighters of the 62nd Squadron are rock steady. To the right;
there, the sixteen fighters of the 63rd Squadron. Who the
hell are these other people? For several seconds I stare
at their silhouettes—they're Focke-Wulfs!

Slow, Johnson, take it slow, and be clear. I press the
radio mike button on the throttle, and make an effort to
speak slowly and distinctly. "Sixteen bandits, six o'clock,
coming in fast, this is Keyworth Blue 4, Over." No one
replies, no one makes a move. The Thunderbolts drone on,
utterly oblivious of the sixteen fighters streaking in. Am I
the *only* man in the Group who sees these planes? I keep
my eyes glued to the fighters, increasing in size with every
second, trailing thin streaks of black exhaust smoke as they
rush toward us under full power.

"Sixteen bandits, six o'clock, coming in fast—this is
Keyworth Blue 4—*Over!*" Now I see the enemy fighters
clearly—Focke-Wulfs, still closing the gap. Again I call in
—I'm nearly frantic now. My entire body seems to quiver.
I'm shaking; I want to rip the Thunderbolt around and
tear directly into the teeth of the German formation. It's
the only thing to do; break into them. For a moment, a
second of indecision, I lift the P-47 up on one wing and
start the turn—no, dammit! I swore I wouldn't break forma-

tion; I would act only on orders and not on my own. I jab down again on the button, this time fairly shouting the warning of enemy fighters.

What the hell's the matter with them? I glance quickly at the other Thunderbolts, expecting the leader's big fighter to swing around and meet the attack. The P-47 drones on, unconcerned, her pilot apparently oblivious to the enemy. My finger goes down on the button and I call, again: "Sixteen bandits, six o'clock, coming in f——"

A terrific explosion! A split second later, another. And yet another! Crashing, thundering sounds. WHAM! WHAM! WHAM! One after the other, an avalanche smashing into my fighter, heavy boulders hurtling out of nowhere and plunging with devastating force into the airplane. A blinding flash. Before my eyes the canopy glass erupts in an explosion, dissolves in a gleaming shower. Tiny particles of glass rip through the air. The Thunderbolt shudders through her length, bucks wildly as explosions flip her out of control. Still the boulders rain against the fighter, a continuing series of crashing explosions, each roaring, each terrifying. My first instinct is to bail out; I have a frantic urge to leave the airplane.

Concussion smashes my ears, loud, pounding; the blasts dig into my brain. A new sound now, barely noticed over the crashing explosions. A sound of hail, rapid, light, unceasing. Thirty-caliber bullets, pouring in a stream against and into the Thunderbolt. Barely noticed as they tear through metal, flash brilliantly as tracers. The Thunderbolt goes berserk, jarring heavily every time another 20-mm. cannon shell shears metal, tears open the skin, races inside and explodes with steel-ripping force.

Each explosion is a personal blow, a fist thudding into my body. My head rings, my muscles protest as the explosions snap my body into the restraining straps, whip my head back against the rest. I am through! This is it! I'm absolutely helpless, at the mercy of the fighters pouring fire and steel into the Thunderbolt. Squeezed back in my seat against the armor plating—my head snaps right and left as I see the disintegration of my '47. A blow spins my head to the left as a bullet creases my nose. Behind me I can feel the steel being flayed apart by the unending rain of cannon shells.

I notice no pain. I have only a frantic feeling—an explosive urge to get out!

I am not frightened; I am beyond any such gentle emotion. I am terrified, clutched in a constricting terror that engulfs me. Without conscious volition my finger stabs down the radio button and I hear a voice, loud and piercing, screaming, "Mayday! Mayday! Mayday!" The words blur into a continuous stream. The voice goes on and on, shouting the distress call, and not until I have shrieked for help six times or more do I recognize my own voice.

I have no time to think, almost no time to act. Moving by sheer force of habit, by practice become instinct, my hands fly over my body. Without conscious thought, without even realizing what I am doing, I wriggle free of the shoulder harness and jerk open the seat belt.

Another explosion. A hand smashes me against the side of the cockpit; for a moment acceleration pins me helplessly. The Thunderbolt breaks away completely from my control. Earth and sky whirl crazily. I'm suddenly aware that the fighter has been thrown nose down, plunging out of control. The smashing explosions, the staccato beating of the bullets, blurs into a continuous din. A sudden lunge, the fighter snaps to the right, nose almost vertical. The Thunderbolt's wild motions flip me back and forth in the cockpit. . . .

Fire! A gleaming tongue of flame licks my forehead. It

flickers, disappears. Instantly it is here again, this time a searing fire sheet, erupting into the cockpit. The fire dances and swirls, disappears within a thick, choking cloud of smoke. Intense, blinding, sucked through the shattered canopy. The draft is terror. The draft of air is Death, carrying the fire from the bottom of the cockpit, over me, crackling before my face, leaping up and out through the smashed canopy.

The terror is eternity. Burn to death!

GET OUT!

I grab the canopy bar, gasping for breath, jerk it back with maniacal strength. The canopy jerks open, slides back six inches, and jams.

Trapped! The fire blossoms, roars ominously. Frantic, I reach up with both hands, pulling with every bit of strength I can command. The canopy won't budge.

Realization. The fighter burning. Flames and smoke in the cockpit. Oxygen flow cut off. Out of control, plunging. Fighters behind. Helpless.

New sounds. Grinding, rumbling noises. In front of me, the engine. Thumping, banging. Bullets, cannon shells in the engine; maybe it's on fire!

I can't see. I rub my eyes. No good. Then I notice the oil, spraying out from the damaged engine, a sheet of oil robbing me of sight, covering the front windscreen, cutting off my vision. I look to the side, barely able to look out.

Great, dark shapes. Reeling, rushing past me. No! The Thunderbolt plunges, flips crazily earthward. The shapes—the bombers! The bomber formations, unable to evade my hurtling fighter. How did I miss them? The shapes disappear as the Thunderbolt, trailing flame and smoke, tumbles through the bombers, escaping total disaster by scant feet. Maybe less!

GET OUT!

I try, oh God, how I try! Both feet against the instrument panel, brace myself, grasp the canopy bar with both hands. Pull—pull harder! Useless. It won't budge.

Still falling. Got to pull out of the dive. I drop my hands to the stick, my feet to the rudders. Left rudder to level the wings, back pressure on the stick to bring her out of the dive. There is still wind bursting with explosive force through the shattered canopy, but it is less demoniacal with the fighter level, flying at less speed.

Still the flame. Now the fire touches, sears. I have become snared in a trap hurtling through space, a trap of vicious flames and choking smoke! I release the controls. Feet firmly against the instruments, both hands grasping the canopy bar. It won't move. *Pull harder!*

The Thunderbolt rears wildly, engine thumping. Smoke inside, oil spewing from the battered engine, a spray whipping back, almost blinding me to the outside world. It doesn't matter. The world is nothingness, only space, forever and ever down to the earth below. Up here, fire, smoke.

I've got to get out! Terror and choking increases, becomes frenzied desperation. Several times I jerk the Thunderbolt from her careening drops toward the earth, several more times I kick against the panel, pull with both hands. The canopy will not move. Six inches. Not a fraction more. I can't get out!

A miracle. Somehow, incredibly, flame disappears. The fire . . . *the fire's out!* Smoke boils into the cockpit, swirls around before it answers the shrieking call of wind through the shattered glass. But there is no flame to knife into flesh, no flame. . . . Settle down! *Think!* I'm *still* alive!

The terror ebbs, then vanishes. At one moment I am beset

with fear and frenzy, with the uncontrollable urge to hurl my body through the restraining metal, anything, just to escape the fire. Terror grips me, chokes my breathing and thinking and, in an instant, a moment of wonder, it is banished. I no longer think of other aircraft—enemy or friendly. My mind races over my predicament; what I must do. I begin to relax.

The cessation of struggle, physically and within the mind, is so incredibly absolute that for long seconds I ponder. I do not comprehend this amazing self-control. It may be simply that I am overwhelmed by the miracle of still being alive. Perhaps it is the loss of oxygen at five miles above the earth. The precious seconds of relief flee all too quickly. I must still get out of the stricken airplane if I am to live.

Feet on the instrument panel, hands on the bar. Pull. I pull with all my strength until I am fairly blue in the face. I feel my muscles knotting with the strength of desperation, my body quivers with the effort. Not even this renewed struggle avails me. Cannon shells have burst against the canopy, twisted and curled metal.

The fighter heels sickeningly over on her side, skids through the air, flips for earth. I barely pay attention to the controls; my feet and hands move almost of their own accord, co-ordinating smoothly, easing the airplane from her plunge. Out of the dive again, the desire to survive becoming more intense.

I *must* get out. I hunch up in the cockpit, desperation once again rising about me like a flood. The canopy, the canopy. Life or death imbedded within that blackened, twisted metal. C'mon, you sonofabitch! I hunch my shoulder, lunge at the metal. Again, and again! Hard blows that hurt. Steel slams into my shoulder, hard, unyielding. I cry out in frustration, a wordless profanity. My hands ball into fists and I beat at the canopy, throwing punches, hard, strong blows. But I am not in the ring, not striking at flesh and bone. The steel mocks me, unyielding, triumphant. I sit back for a moment, level the P-47 and wonder.

There is another way out. The canopy is shattered, atop me, to both sides. I stand up in the seat, poke my head and shoulders through the broken canopy. I hardly notice the heavy force of the wind and cold. I ignore it. My shoulders are through, I stand to my waist—I can get out!

Despair floods my mind. The parachute snags against the ripped canopy. It can't clear; there's not enough space between the shattered cockpit for both my body and the chute. I'm not going without it! I crawl back to the seat, right the spiraling airplane, and think.

All through the struggle to escape the fighter, I have been talking to myself. Over and over again I have been repeating, "You can get out, you can. If you have to, you can get out!" Again and again the words formed, until finally reality ruled. And after each attempt: "You just must not have to."

I settle back in the seat, the terror and desperation vanished, caught by the wind shrieking through the cockpit, whisked away and scattered forever. I relax, a deliberate move to enable me to think clearly, to study my problem and to seek the solutions. My mind is clear, my thoughts spinning through my brain. I think of everything, a torrent of thoughts that refuse to be clouded, thoughts of everything imaginable.

I am absolutely unconcerned at the moment about enemy aircraft. I know the sky about me is filled with the black-crossed fighters, with pilots eager to find so helpless a target as a crippled Thunderbolt, trailing a greasy plume of smoke as it struggles through the sky, descending. There is no fear of death or of capture. The terror and desperation which so recently assailed me have been born of fire, of the horror of being burned alive. Now the fire is gone, the terror flung away with its disappearance. Solve the problems, Johnson, find the answers. You can't bail out.

A sound of danger snaps me back to full awareness. The engine is running very rough. Any moment, it seems, the giant power plant will tear itself free of its mounts to tumble through space, trapping me in an airplane unbalanced and uncontrollable. I turn my attention fully to flying, realizing that the Thunderbolt is badly crippled, almost on the verge of falling out of my control. Oil still bursts from the holes and tears in the cowling, a thin spray smearing itself against the windscreen, making vision forward almost impossible.

I cannot get out; I must ride this potential bomb to the very ground. My left hand moves almost automatically, easing the throttle back, a move made to keep the engine from exploding. Again—good fortune! The grinding, throbbing noise subsides; much smoother now. My chances are getting better.

I keep thinking of all the intelligence lectures we have sat through, buttocks sore on benches, about how to avoid capture, how to escape to Spain, to return to England. Intelligence officers, reading reports, after a while dull with repetition. Then the actual escapees, pilots who bailed out or crashed, who hid and ran and survived by their wits, who *did* walk out of France, aided by the underground to reach Spain and, eventually, to return to England. It could be done; it had been done. I could do it as well as any. My mind wanders; strangely, I seem to be looking forward to

the challenge. It is a thought wholly ridiculous; to antici-
pate and savor the struggle to escape a land swarming with
quick-fingered troops.

One entire B-17 crew had been shot down and lost not
a moment in hustling their way out through France and
into Spain. In just three weeks from the moment they bailed
out of their burning Fortress and fell into space, they
were in England. A record. *I* can do that—three weeks and
I'll be back. Each time I dwell on the matter my mind
tricks me, returns to me pictures of Barbara and my family.

What am I doing! I have been flying toward England,
an instinctive move to fly toward the Channel. I remember
words, lectures. "If you're going down, if you can't make
the Channel, far out into the Channel, turn south. The
coast is thick with Germans, and you won't have a chance
if you go down there. Head south, head south, south . . ."

The words flash by in my mind. Obediently, I work the
controls, change my course. I look down. Twenty thousand feet to the earth. There—I can see them. They're so
clear and sharp. In my oxygen-starved brain, I *see* the
Germans. They are like ants, hordes of ants, each carrying
a gun and a sharp, glittering bayonet. For twenty miles inland the horde is thick, impenetrable, inescapable. I can't
land *there;* I can *see* the German soldiers.

The Thunderbolt turns, heads for Paris. I will fly over
the sprawling city, continue flying south, try to get as close
as possible to the Spanish border.

This means a crash landing, evasion, escape. I think
about procedures once I am on the ground, the Thunderbolt
stopped. My plans are clear—I'll belly the crippled Thunderbolt in, slide the fighter wheels up along an open field. I
will land as far south in France as the crippled airplane
will take me in the continuing descent. I plan to make the

walk through Spain as short as possible, to get out quickly.
I will *not* be captured. I'll evade them; others have—*I will!*
The thought races through my mind; it stays with me
through all the moments of considering the crash, the evasion, the escape back to England.

There, clipped to the right side of the cockpit near my
knee, an incendiary grenade. Check it! Procedure! Words
and method are habit by now. I hold the bomb, grip it
tightly. This is the way you do it. The moment the ship
stops its sliding across the ground . . . get out. Fling the
bomb into the cockpit. Turn the fighter into flames and
smoke and ashes.

My mind begins to wander; there is still clarity, but now
there is less concentration. The thoughts flit in and out,
they appear and flee of their own volition. One instant I
think of escape procedures, then my mind dwells on the
pilots after they return to Manston. I picture them in my
mind, talking about my missing airplane, listing me as missing, probably dead, victim of the sudden bounce by the
sixteen determined German fliers. I think about Dick Allison, victim of a fatal crash caused by vertigo. Dick was
married, and my thoughts hover about his wife. I remember
her, pretty, wonderful; I think of her holding their new-
born child. I think of her, never again seeing Dick; the child
never to know the father.

I cannot escape the thoughts. Dick's face looms before
me, a face dissolving into a Thunderbolt spinning through
clouds, a gout of flame, mushrooming smoke. His widow,
the child. Then it disappears, the pictures are gone. Barbara. Thoughts only of her. That last sight of my wife,
tearful, trying so bravely to smile as the train carried her
away. How many months since I've seen Barbara? Seen
home? Barbara back home, at Lawton, learning that I was

missing. She knew enough of fighters, knew enough to realize the odds were that I would not survive.

In brief seconds the pictures flash into being, a kaleidoscope of people and thoughts and emotions, a world marching in accelerated time before my vision. I can't do this to them; I can't go down. I've *got* to get back!

My mind reels drunkenly; for several moments I think of the Thunderbolt burning while I flee. I do not realize the truth. Hypoxia is upon me. My body and brain clamor for oxygen; desire, covet the life-giving substance. The hypoxia becomes worse as I stagger through the air, thin and cold at 19,000 feet. The symptoms are drunkenness, a hypoxic intoxication, giddy in its effects, lethal if it is sustained. And yet, through this dangerous moment, I plan with all seriousness my crash landing, plan to shed the parachute and escape through the shattered canopy.

Barbara. My folks. Again I think of them. Again their presence invades the fog of hypoxia, struggles to the fore. Visions of loved ones; my concern for them forcing upward through the mists, the false sense of confidence. Again the thoughts are safety, are mental clarity, are the key to survival. The thoughts of their pain, their anguish. Sharp, clear. I *can't* go down.

My head is clearing. The fog is breaking up, dissolving. All this time I have been convinced that the fighter is incapable of flight, that it can only glide. I have been flying in a shallow glide, descending gently, losing altitude, at 170 miles per hour. Go for the Channel. Fly over the water, far enough out from the French coast to avoid detection by the Germans. Fly as close as possible to England, ditch the ship in the water, crawl through the hole. Air-Sea Rescue will pick me up, will race out to the scene of the ditching in boats or in planes, to rescue me, bring me back to England. Barbara and the folks may never even know that I've been in trouble.

Stick and rudder, still descending gently. The fighter wheels around in a graceful turn, almost ludicrous for a smoking, badly shot-up machine. But the Thunderbolt is still true, still responsive. She obeys my commands. I head for England, a goal, a place to fly, a home to return to.

I stare at the instrument panel. A shambles. Smashed glass, many of the instruments broken. The Thunderbolt descends, nose slightly down, settling gradually, at about 170 miles per hour. I have no airspeed indicator, but I know this fighter, know her feel.

My mask seems to choke me. Strapped to my face, it had been, unknown to me, useless, unable to supply oxygen from a source shot away. I bank the fighter, stare down. At a height I estimate to be ten thousand feet, I unhook the mask from one side of my face, suck deeply the good clean air, air now richer with oxygen, oxygen to clear my head, to return to me my full senses.

With the newly returned clarity comes soberness, a critical evaluation of my predicament. I am in trouble, in serious, dangerous difficulty. Not until this moment do I realize that I have been flying almost blinded. My eyes burn, a stinging sensation that increases every moment in pain.

I touch my face with my hands. No goggles, and memory comes to me. Yesterday I broke a lens, I turned the goggles in for repair. This morning I took off on the only combat mission I ever flew or was to fly without goggles. It was a foolish move, and now, over occupied France in a crippled, smoking fighter, I am paying the penalty for my own stupidity.

In the opening moments of attack a 20-mm. cannon shell had ripped through the left side of the cockpit, exploded with a deafening roar near my left hand, and wreaked havoc with the hydraulic system. The blast sheared the flap handle and severed the hydraulic lines. Since that moment the fluid had poured into the cockpit. Then several more shells exploded, blasted apart the canopy. Wind entered at tremendous speed and, without respite, whipped the fluid into a fine, stinging spray.

Now the wind continues its devastating work. The fluid sprays into my eyes, burning and stinging. I fail to realize during the flight through thin air the effect on my eyes of the fluid.

My hand raises to my face, and I flinch. The pain is real, the source is evident. My eyes are swollen, puffed. Around them the skin is raised, almost as if I have been beaten with fists. It's hard to see. Not until now, not until this moment, do I realize that I am seeing through slits, that if my face swells any more, the skin will close over my eyes.

The moment this happens, I am finished. Half the time I fly with my eyes closed, feeling out the struggling, crippled fighter. It is now that my sense of balance, my sense of flight, comes to my aid. I can *feel* the Thunderbolt when she begins to skid, to slip through the air. I can feel a wing lowering, feel the sudden change of wind draft in the cockpit. I listen carefully, strain with eyes closed to note labor in the engine, to hear the increase in propeller revolutions, in engine tone, when the nose drops. This is how I fly, half blinded, eyes burning.

When I open my eyes to see, I must stick my head through the hole in the cockpit in order to look ahead. For the windscreen is obscured by oil. I do this several times. The wind stabs my eyes with ice picks, and the pain soars.

My attempts to clean my face, to rub away the fluid from my eyes, are pitifully hopeless. I pull a handkerchief from a pocket, wipe at my burning eyes. The first time I find relief. But the cockpit is filled with spray. My hands, my face, my clothes, are bathed, soaked in hydraulic fluid. In a moment the handkerchief too is drenched. Each time I rub my eyes I rub blood from my nose and the fluid deeper into my skin, irritating the eyes.

And yet, incredibly, I am calm and resolved. A succession of miracles has kept me alive, and I am not about to fret anxiously when only calmness will continue my survival. The pain in my eyes is nothing to the pain I have felt; certainly nothing against the past few minutes. Each time I open my eyes to check my flight, I scan the entire sky. My head swivels, I stare through burning eyes all about me. I am over enemy territory, heavily defended country, alone, in a crippled, smoking airplane, half blind. I have no company, and I do not savor the sight of other aircraft. I wish only to be left alone, to continue my slow, plodding pace through the air. I've got to get as far out over that Channel as possible.

Again I look around. My head freezes, I stare. My heart again is in my throat. A fighter, alone. I am close to the Channel, so close, as I stare at the approaching machine. Slightly behind the Thunderbolt, closing from four o'clock at about 8,000 feet, the fighter closes in. I squint my eyes, trying to make out details. The fighter slides still closer.

Never have I seen so beautiful an airplane. A rich, dappled blue, from a dark, threatening thunderstorm to a light sky blue. The cowling is a brilliant, gleaming yellow. Beautiful, and Death on the wing. A Focke-Wulf 190, one of Goering's Boys on the prowl after the raging air battle from which I have been blasted, and slicing through the air—at me. I stare at the airplane, noting the wax coating gleaming on the wings and body.

What can I do? I think of waving my handkerchief at him, then realize the absurdity of such a move. That's silly! I'll rock my wings. But what good will this do? I'm at a loss as to my next move—for I don't dare to fight in the disabled Thunderbolt. I've got to get out over the Channel, continue my flight toward the water and a chance at safety and survival.

I simply stare at the Focke-Wulf. My eyes follow the yellow nose as it closes the distance. The moment the nose swings on a line that points ahead of the Thunderbolt—all hell will break loose. That can only be the German's move to lead my fighter with his guns—the moment before he fires.

All I can do is to sit, and watch. Closer and closer slides the sleek fighter. I begin to fidget, waiting for the yellow flashes to appear from his guns and cannon. Nothing. The guns remain silent, dark. The Focke-Wulf nose is glued on a line to the Thunderbolt. Damn—I'll bet he's taking pictures of me! Rare photographs of a crippled American fighter completely at his mercy.

The yellow-and-blue fighter glides in, still closer. I wonder what he has in mind, even as the Focke-Wulf comes to barely 50 yards away. I think of what *I* have always wanted to do, to close in to point-blank range, to stick my four right guns almost in his cockpit and the four left guns against his tail—and fire. That would really scatter him! And that's just what this bastard wants to do—to *me!*

He's too close. I shove the stick forward and to the right, swerving the Thunderbolt beneath the Focke-Wulf. I've got to get to the Channel; every move, every maneuver leads to that destination—the Channel water. As the fighter drops earthward, I bank and turn back to my left, heading directly out toward the coast. I glance up as the Focke-Wulf passes over me to my left, swings beautifully in an easy curve, and slides on my tail.

Thoughts race through my mind. I know he's going to work me over, just the second he feels he is in perfect position. I can't stop him, I can't fight in the crippled Thunderbolt; I don't even know if the airplane will stay together through any maneuvers. Every moment of flight since I was shot up has been in a long and gradual descent, a glide, easy enough even for a disabled airplane. But now . . . I can't slug it out with this Focke-Wulf.

I look the Thunderbolt over. For the first time I realize just how severe a battering the airplane has sustained. The fighter is a flying wreck, a sieve. Let the bastard shoot! He can't hurt me any more than I've been hurt!

I push back in the seat, hunching my shoulders, bringing my arms in close to my body. I pull the seat adjustor, dropping the seat to the full protection of the armor plate. And here I wait.

The German takes his time. He's having a ball, with a helpless pigeon lined up before his guns. When will he shoot? C'mon, let's have it! He waits. I don't dare move away from the armor plating. The solid metal behind me is my only chance for life.

Pellets stinging against the wings, the fuselage, thudding into the armor plate. A steady, pelting rain of hailstones. *And* he's not missing! The .30-caliber bullets pour out in a stream, a rain of lead splashing all over the Thunderbolt. And all I can do is to sit there, crouched behind the armor plating, helpless, taking everything the Kraut has to dish out.

For several seconds the incredible turkey shoot continues,

my Thunderbolt droning sluggishly through the air, a sitting duck for the Focke-Wulf. How the P-47 stays together is a mystery, for the bullets continue to pour into it.

I don't move an inch. I sit, anger building up. The bullets tear metal, rip into spars, grinding away, chopping up the Thunderbolt. My nerves grate as if both hands hold a charge of electricity. Sharp jolts against my back. Less than an inch away, bullets crash against the armor.

To hell with this! My feet kick right and left on the rudder pedals, yawing the P-47 from side to side. The sudden movement slows the fighter to a crawl, and in that second the Focke-Wulf overruns me and bursts ahead.

My turn. I may be almost helpless, but there are bullets in the guns! Damn him—I can't see the Focke-Wulf. I stick my head out of the window, wince from the pain of wind stabbing my swollen eyes. There the bastard is, banking away. I kick right rudder, skid the Thunderbolt, squeeze the trigger in anguish. Eight heavy guns roar; my ship shudders as steel spits through the air. The moment of firing is more gesture than battle, for I cannot use my sights, I can barely see. The bullets flash in his direction, but I hold no hope that the Focke-Wulf will falter.

It doesn't. The sleek fighter circles lazily to the right, out of range. I watch him closely. Blue wings flash, the FW-190 swoops up, sweeps down in a wide turn. He's boss of the situation, and I simply fly straight and level as the German fighter slides into a perfect, tight formation with me! This is ridiculous, but I'm happier with the Jerry playing tag off my wing than sitting behind me and blazing away at the Thunderbolt.

The Focke-Wulf inches in closer, gleaming blue wing sitting over mine, the top so close that I can almost lean out of the cockpit and touch the waxed metal. I stare across the scant feet separating our two planes. Our eyes lock, then his gaze travels over the Thunderbolt, studying the fighter from nose to tail. No need to wonder what he is thinking. He is amazed that my airplane still flies; I know his astonishment that I am in the air. Each time his gaze scans the Thunderbolt he shakes his head, mystified. For at such close range he can see the tears and holes, the blackened and scorched metal from the fire, the oily film covering the nose and windscreen, the shattered canopy.

The Kraut stares directly at me, and lifts his left hand. He waves, his eyes expressionless. A wing lifts, the Focke-Wulf slides away. A long-held breath explodes from my lungs, and relief floods my mind. I watch the yellow-nosed fighter as he turns to fly away. But . . . he doesn't! The German plane keeps turning . . . he's on my tail again! "That son of a bitch!" I duck.

I cower again behind the armor plate. The Focke-Wulf is directly behind me, .30-caliber guns hammering. Still the bullets come, perfectly aimed. He doesn't miss, not a single bullet misses. I *know* they don't! Frantic, I kick rudder, jerk the heavy Thunderbolt from side to side, cutting my speed. The German waits for the maneuver; this time he's not sucked in. He holds back as the P-47 skids from side to side, and then I see the yellow nose drawing closer to me.

He pulls alongside tight to the P-47. Perfect formation, one battered, shot-up Thunderbolt and the gleaming new Focke-Wulf. By now we are down to 4,000 feet, passing directly over Dieppe, our speed still 170 miles per hour. Over Dieppe! The realization makes me shudder, for below my wings lie the most intense antiaircraft concentrations along the entire coast.

They don't fire! Of course! The Focke-Wulf pilot is saving

my life! *He* doesn't see Dieppe as a horror of flack. This is, to him, friendly territory, an area over which to fly with impunity. Unknowingly, he gives me yet another lease on life, is the unwitting party to the succession of miracles which, through one cumulative disaster after the other, are keeping me alive. Even his presence, his attacks, are in a way miraculous. For the German has laced me over with his .30-caliber guns, and it is only the smile of fortune that he found me after his four heavy cannon had expended their explosive shells.

Water below . . . the Channel beneath my wings! Still in perfect formation, the dappled blue FW-190 glides slowly downward with me. Then we are at 3,000 feet. The coast two miles from me, and hope flares anew. There is a chance now, an excellent chance to make it into the Channel where I can be rescued! I stare at the German pilot. His left hand raises slowly to his forehead in an informal salute; he waves, and his fighter lifts a wing as he slides off to the right.

Relief, the gasp of pent-up breath. Oh, no! Here he comes again! Nothing to do but to crouch within that armor plating. The enemy fighter sits behind me, perfectly in the slot. He's extra careful this time. A series of sharp bursts ripple from his guns. Again the hailstones pelting the tin roof, the bullets smashing into the fighter. Shuddering and helpless, the P-47 takes the punishment, absorbs the terrible beating. I have long given up hope of understanding why this machine continues to stay in the air. The German is whipsawing his bursts, kicking rudder gently as he fires. A stream of bullets, swinging from left to right, from right to left, a buzzsaw flinging bullets from one wingtip across the plane, into the armor plate, straight across. The firing stops.

Here he comes again. The yellow nose inching alongside, the gleaming Focke-Wulf. The German pilot again slides into formation, undesired company in the sky. For several minutes he remains alongside, staring at the wreck I am flying. He shakes his head in wonder. Below my wings the Channel is only a thousand feet away. A blue wing lifts, snaps down. I watch the salute, the rocking of wings. The sleek fighter accelerates suddenly and turns, flying away in a long climbing turn back to the coast.

Free! England ahead, the Channel lifting to meet the crippled P-47. How far, how far can I drag the Thunderbolt with her smashed and laboring engine before she drops into the waves?

All this time I have been so tense that my hand gripped the throttle and held down the mike button, transmitting all the things I had called the Jerry pilot, as well as the gunfire and the smashing of bullets into the Thunderbolt. And again, an inadvertent move comes to my aid. The moment the Focke-Wulf disappears, I release the throttle knob and begin my preparations for ditching. My plan is to belly into the Channel, nose high, tail down. As the fighter slews to a stop in the water, I will crawl out through the shattered canopy, dragging my folded dinghy life raft with me. Then, inflate the raft, move away from the sinking plane, and pray that Air-Sea Rescue will find me before the Jerries do, or before I drift long enough to starve. I am ready for all this, calm and prepared for the impact into the water.

And then . . . a voice! The moment my finger lifts from the mike button, I hear a voice calling urgently. "Climb if you can, you're getting very faint, climb if you can, you're getting very faint!" It's the Air-Sea Rescue radio—homing on me and giving instructions. At this instant I realize that it really is true—I'm still alive! The rugged old 'bolt, she'll *fly*, she'll bring me home yet!

I call back, exultation and laughter in my voice, nearly shouting. "Okay, out there! I'll try. I'll do everything I can, but I'm not sure what I can do. I'm down to less than a thousand feet now." And finally I discover that the battered and crippled Thunderbolt really *can* fly! I have been in a steady glide, convinced all this time the fighter is on the verge of falling out of control and now—only now—I discover that she'll fly. It is too good to be true, and I shout with glee.

I ease back on the stick. The Thunderbolt answers at once, nose lifting, and hauls upward in a zoom climb. I hold the fighter with her nose high until the speed drops to just above stalling.

Now, level out. Hold it, increase speed to at least 170 miles per hour, back on the stick again. And climb! Again I repeat the maneuver, a crippled series of upward zooms, each bringing me higher and higher. Each zoom—a terrific boost to my morale. Clouds above me, a scattered overcast at 5,000 feet. Just below the cloud deck, nose level, more speed, and back on the stick. She goes! The big fighter rears upward into the clouds. Another levelling out, another zoom, and I'm on top. From less than 1,000 feet to more than 8,000! I'm shouting happily to myself, so cocky and confident and joyous that I'm nearly drunk from the sensation. Everything is wonderful! *Nothing* is going to stop me now! I nurse the fighter, baby the controls, and the crippled airplane responds, slides through the air, closer and closer to safety.

"Blue 4, Blue 4." The voice is clearer, sharper. "We have you loud and clear, Blue 4. Steer three-four-five degrees, Blue 4, steer three-four-five degrees."

"Hello Control, hello Control, this is Blue 4. I can't steer your heading. Most of my instruments are shot out. I have a general idea of my direction, but I cannot follow your exact heading. Direct me either left or right. Direct me either left or right. I will correct in this manner. Over."

Mayday Control stays with me every moment, sending flight corrections. I think the Channel is only forty miles across, but I am far south, and long miles stretch ahead of me. At my laboring speed, it seems I'll never get across the water! The minutes drag. How long can this airplane keep flying? I listen for any change in engine sound, for a faltering of the thunder ahead of me. But the engine sings true, maintaining power, and at 170 miles per hour we drone our way above the clouds, guided by an invisible voice through space, drawn inexorably toward home.

Time drags. Thirty minutes. Below the clouds, only the Channel. Thirty-five minutes, forty minutes. And then, a break in the clouds, the overcast becomes broken white cumulus and there . . . directly below me, the stark white cliffs of Dover! I'm too happy to keep radio silence, I whoop joyously. "Control, this is Blue 4. Those white cliffs sure look wonderful from up here!" No one can imagine just how wonderful they look!

The Controller seems to share my joy. In the next several minutes he guides me unerringly through the clouds and steers me to the Hawkinge air base. I can't find the field. The Controller tells me I am directly over the base, but this doesn't help. My eyes are too swollen, the field too well camouflaged. I pass directly over the hidden airfield, circle the field under the direction of the Mayday Controller, but cannot see a thing.

I check the fuel gauges: about a hundred gallons left. I call the Controller. "Hello, Mayday Control; hello, Mayday Control, this is Keyworth Blue 4. I'm okay now. I'm going to fly to Manston. I'd like to land back at my outfit. Blue 4, Out."

Immediately a call comes back. "Roger, Blue 4. If you're sure you can make it, go to B Channel and give them a call. Mayday Control, Out." He signs off. I switch radio control, and call Manston. The field is less than forty miles away, almost in sight. The Thunderbolt chews up the miles, and soon I begin to descend, heading directly for the field.

"Hello, Manston Tower, this is Keyworth Blue 4, Pancake, Over." The reply comes at once. "Hello, Blue 4, Hello Blue 4, this is Manston, Pancake Number One, zero-six-zero, Over."

"Hello, Manston. Blue 4 here. I'm shot up. I will have to make a belly landing. I do not know the condition of my landing gear. I have no hydraulics for flaps or brakes. Over."

"Blue 4 from Manston. Make a wheels down landing if you possibly can. Repeat, make a wheels down landing if you possibly can. We are very crowded, and have other crippled airplanes coming in. Over."

"Okay, Manston, from Blue 4. I'll try it. Check my wheels as I come over the tower. I cannot bail out, repeat, I cannot bail out. I have no hydraulic system to pull the wheels back up, no brakes, no flaps. Over."

I move the landing gear control to "Down" position. Fate still smiles on me. The wheels drop down, lock into position. With all the holes and gaping tears in the Thunderbolt, the wheels and tires have come through unscathed. I circle the field with my eyes almost closed, at 500 feet and less than 150 miles per hour.

This is it; now or never. I descend, turn into a long gliding turn for the runway so that I can see my point of touchdown. I cannot see through the oil-covered wind-screen. Carefully, carefully, not enough power for an emergency go-around. I fly every inch toward the runway, nursing the Thunderbolt down. Over the very end of the field, just above stalling speed, I chop the throttle, drop the heavy fighter to the grass. It is one of the best landings I have ever made!

The fighter rolls down the hill to the center of the Manston field. On the rough, grassy landing strip I fight to keep her headed straight. Without flaps or brakes the big fighter rolls freely, barely losing speed. In the center of the field the strip slopes upward and the Thunderbolt charges along the grass. Ahead of me is a line of parked Spitfires and Typhoons; if I don't stop I'm going to slam into them!

At the last moment I kick left rudder, letting the ship turn freely with the wind. The wing tilts, the heavy machine slews violently about, slides backward into a slot between two Typhoons almost as if I'd planned it that way.

The Thunderbolt has brought me home. Battered into a flying, wrecked cripple, she fought her way back, brought me home. It's almost too much to believe! I feel a great wonder settling about me. My hand moves of its own accord. Engine off, switches off. My hands move over my body. Chute harness undone, straps free.

I crawl out through the hole in the canopy, dragging my parachute behind me. A grin stretches from ear to ear as I stand on the wing, stretch gratefully.

I jump to the ground, kneel down, and plant a great big kiss on Terra Firma. Oh, how good that solid earth feels!

The meat wagon is on hand, and the medics rush to me. I imagine I'm quite a sight, with blood from my nose smeared over my face, mixed with the hydraulic fluid. The doctor shakes his head in wonder, and I don't blame him.

A .30-caliber bullet has nicked my nose. Splinters from 20-mm. cannon shells are imbedded deeply in both hands. A bullet has shot away the wrist watch from my arm; only the strap and face rim remain. Burns streak the skin on my forehead. My eyes are swollen, burning, and the flesh starting to blister. And on my right thigh they discover two flesh wounds from .30-caliber bullets, that I hadn't even known about.

They insist on taking me to the hospital at once. Not yet; I want to look over the Jug. And this airplane is not a pretty sight. My awe and respect for the fighter increase as I walk around the battered machine.

There are twenty-one gaping holes and jagged tears in the metal from exploding 20-mm. cannon shells. I'm still standing in one place when my count of the bullet holes reaches past a hundred; there's no use even trying to add them all. The Thunderbolt is literally a sieve, holes through the wings, nose, fuselage and tail. Every square foot, it seems, is covered with holes. There are five holes in the propeller. Three 20-mm. cannon shells burst against the armor plate, a scant inch away from my head. Five cannon shell holes in the right wing, four in the left wing. Two cannon shells blasted away the lower half of my rudder. One shell exploded in the cockpit, next to my left hand; this is the blast that ripped away the flap handle. More holes appear along the fuselage and in the tail. Behind the cockpit the metal is twisted and curled; this had jammed the canopy, trapping me inside.

The airplane had done her best. Needless to say, she would never fly again.

The doctors hustle me into the meat wagon, and roar off to the hospital for a thorough checkup and repair job.

They look at me with misgivings, and cannot understand why I am not shaking and quivering. Not any more—all that is behind me! I'm the happiest man on earth, bubbling over with joy. I'm back, *alive*. A dozen times I thought I'd had it, thought the end had come. And now that I am back —with wounds and injuries that will heal quickly—I'm too happy to react physically.

I feel like a man who had been strapped into the electric chair, condemned to die. The switch is thrown, the current surges. Then, miraculously, it stops. Again the switch closes, the current. . . . Then, another reprieve. Several more times the closing of the switch, the imminence of death, and the reprieve, the final freedom.

But not all are reprieved.

Captain Eby is gone. Captain Wetherbee is gone. My close friend, Lieutenant Barron, is gone. Captain Dyar also is never to return. All four men were last seen in the vicinity of Forges. All four men, we learn later, are dead.

Foster comes home with a huge hole in his right wing. Johnny Eaves staggers back to Manston in a Thunderbolt shot to ribbons. Charley Clamp barely manages to reach the field in another battered fighter. Ralph Johnson makes it back with his plane shot up, his hydraulic system gone, his right wing ripped, and one elevator in ribbons. His ship is so badly crippled he cannot land. Zemke orders him to bail out, and Air-Sea Rescue fishes Ralph out of the Channel.

It is not a good day. The 56th Fighter Group loses four men killed. A fifth fighter is abandoned. Mine will never fly again. Many others are badly damaged. We claim only two kills.

Our debt grows larger; we intend to pay in full.

13

Until the very moment he set foot on land, Ralph Johnson never knew whether he would survive his mission. Three Messerschmitt Me-109 fighters chewed up his Thunderbolt with cannon and machine-gun fire, forcing him to split-S out of the three-to-one combat and run for England. For long and anxious moments he struggled to regain control of his airplane. Over the Channel, Lieutenant Brainard's P-47 came alongside to escort Ralph back to Horsham St. Faith. The flight was rough, for one wheel hung awkwardly from the airplane, and the controls got heavier with every passing moment.

As Ralph circled the field, Hub Zemke took off for a close

inspection of the stricken fighter. During his approach to the base and the subsequent flight, a tower operator recorded the radio conversation:

Ground Station: You have only one wheel down.

Johnson: I know it—I'll try to shake it out. I'll buzz the tower once more.

Tower: No. It is not down.

Johnson: I'll take it up and try to get it down if my pills hold out. I do not have any hydraulic fluid. What is your position, Colonel?

Zemke: I am over the field, I'll come over the tower for you.

Johnson: Roger.

Zemke: Let me form on you.

Johnson: Roger.

Zemke: Have you tried to shake it down?

Johnson: Yes.

Zemke: Get way up and try again. If you can't shake it down, you'll have to jump. Be careful. Put your landing gear handle in down position, do a bank on the left wing and snap it over to the right. Let me get a little ahead.

Johnson: Okay.

Zemke: That hasn't done it. Do some violent weaving back and forth.

Johnson: Sir, my landing-gear handle is stuck.

Zemke: Is it stuck down?

Johnson: Yes, sir.

Zemke: Let's go upstairs. Follow me. Do you want to try one wheel?

Johnson: I certainly do, sir.

Zemke: Let me take a good look at you. You don't have any flaps and you'll need plenty of field.

Johnson: Whatever you say, sir.

Zemke: Better bail out. How much gas have you?

Johnson: About thirty gallons. That fellow didn't do a very good job of gunning on me.

Zemke: I'm afraid of a landing.

Johnson: You're not half as scared as I am, sir!

Zemke: It's not so bad. (To station): His plane is in bad shape. I'm going to have him bail out northeast of Norwich. (To Johnson): We'll go up to ten thousand feet. Be sure to hold your legs together when you go over, and count ten. Try shaking it once more.

Johnson: Yes, sir.

Zemke: You don't have to sir me up here. Head her out to sea.

Johnson: Yes, sir. Is it okay now?

Zemke: Open up the canopy.

Johnson: It is open, sir. It's been open for a long time.

Zemke: Okay, now, Ralph, head it out to sea. Roll over and bail out. That's it, now roll over and bail out. Be sure that you have her trimmed nose down.

(The Thunderbolt rolls slowly, a shape falls through space. Ralph Johnson, dropping away from his crippled fighter. Zemke keeps talking, with his pilot in spirit, talking to him almost as if Johnson can hear his every word.)

Zemke: Okay, boy, that's fine. Now pull your ripcord, that's it. Now be careful. Go into the water feet first and don't forget your Mae West. That's swell. Now inflate your dinghy and I'll go get the boat for you.

As Ralph dropped into the sea, Zemke poured the coal to his Thunderbolt and raced for the shore to guide a boat back to his downed flier. But all did not go well with Ralph. As he rolled over to drop, his knee and dinghy jammed against the canopy. For five frantic seconds he fought to free himself. Finally succeeding, he counted to ten, jerked the D-ring, and felt the wind jerked out of him by the chute's opening shock.

Just before dropping into the water, at least a mile off shore, he inflated his Mae West. He misjudged his descent, and before he could release a leg strap he was in, water rushing into his mouth, dragged along by the wind-blown parachute. Choking and gasping, he freed himself from the tangling shrouds, inflated the small rubber life raft and crawled in. Twenty minutes later a British Walrus flying boat landed nearby—and then taxied away! The water was so rough the Walrus received serious damage on landing and the pilot dared not slow down—he gunned his engine and finally beached the airplane on shore.

Then, Ralph's luck returned and held. Three civilians in a dory fished him into their boat, and several minutes later transferred him to an Air-Sea Rescue launch which raced him to Yarmouth Hospital. All in all, Ralph had a lucky day, despite his misfortunes. And these had continued right to the very last moment of his ordeal. On the way out of the Thunderbolt, he sprained his back and leg muscles and bruised his knees from striking the airplane. His chin was bruised from striking the parachute buckle, and a combination of swallowing sea water and bobbing about in the rough Channel made him awfully sick! The important thing, however, was that in several days he was able to fly again.

When all the activities of the day were considered, the 56th Fighter Group, though suffering heavy losses to gain its two confirmed kills, had good reason to settle for the day's score. Our primary mission was to protect the Big Friends, and this we did well. Of 250 heavy bombers attacking the target, three went down to the savage flak, and only two dropped before the guns and cannon of the sixty intercepting enemy fighters.

But while the Group could, in its official reports, look with satisfaction to an escort job well done, we as fighter pilots smarted beneath what we could only view as a solid beating by the Focke-Wulfs and Messerschmitts. As far as we were concerned, the hunt was on, the enemy to be hit every time we could find him. This, we felt, would be easy enough to do, for the Hun was strong in numbers, equipped with superb airplanes, and willing and aggressive to do battle.

Two days after I returned in the shattered Thunderbolt, the Group flew a Ramrod to St. Nazaire. Hopes of mixing it up with the Abbeville Boys faded; not a single German plane appeared. On the twenty-ninth, another escort mission, this time a thrust to Villacoublay, where we took our beating three days before. The enemy didn't show. And for the next month the Germans played the will-o'-the-wisp.

On July first, I flew a promising Ramrod to Romilly-sur-Seine, east of Paris, with a swing over Rotterdam as part of our flight course. No interceptions, only flak blossoming in the sky. Then, near St. Omer—a dream! More than twenty Messerschmitts 5,000 feet below us, unsuspecting of our presence. A perfect bounce! I called them in to my element leader, Jim Carter, but he refused to take the flight down. "We're too low on fuel," he radioed back, "I'm afraid we'd never get home after a mixup."

"But I've got plenty of fuel!" I shouted. "Let me make the bounce myself. I'll bust through them and sail right home." Carter insisted I stay with the flight and, as we argued, the golden opportunity vanished. The Me-109's disappeared, running to catch the bombers. I was heartbroken

—a perfect chance to bounce the Krauts, split them up, take a few down, and we could beat it before the Germans even knew what happened. Jim Carter a year later told me, on reflection, that he was sorry we didn't make that attack.

A Rodeo to Le Touquet on July second. Uneventful. The next day we flew to Biggin Hill for orientation lectures by the Royal Air Force, and a chance to get into London during the evenings. While at Biggin Hill we found a rare opportunity to pull some English legs. We crowded into a briefing hut to hear a lecture on German interception tactics; the speaker fascinated us. He was a tall, slim Englishman with a huge, red mustache. We called him The Spy.

Wearing their normally "fierce scowls," the first five pilots signed the roster, and the sight of the names unnerved the Englishman, who was forever suspicious of anything with a German ring to it. And here, right before his eyes—Zemke, Schilling, Shiltz, Stultz and Goodfleisch. All good German names. Relief flooded The Spy as he warily read the following names; Johnson, Goldstein, Johnson, Gabreski, Carter and the rest. After a while be became confused as the roster filled with a strange variety of Swedish, Polish, Jewish and Irish names, plus a smattering of a dozen more. And he was even more confused as we interrupted his detailed report of how two badly shot-up Thunderbolts had been talked back to England by Mayday Control. We did our best to control our grins, for in a moment we recognized the truth—even as we heckled the speaker. I was one of those Thunderbolt pilots, and Foster was the other.

Later that day I found one of the increasingly rarer opportunities to fly as I had flown back in the States. Aloft to familiarize myself with the local terrain, I spotted a Spitfire 9B flying nearby. This was my first look at the new Spitfire with which the Royal Air Force hoped to regain quali-

tative air superiority from the Focke-Wulf FW-190. We
flew together in formation, and then I decided to see just
what this airplane had to its credit.

I opened the throttle full and the Thunderbolt forged
ahead. A moment later exhaust smoke poured from the Spit
as the pilot came after me. He couldn't make it; the big
Jug had a definite speed advantage. I grinned happily; I'd
heard so much about this airplane that I really wanted to
show off the Thunderbolt to her pilot. The Jug kept pulling
away from the Spitfire; suddenly I hauled back on the stick
and lifted the nose. The Thunderbolt zoomed upward, soaring into the cloud-flecked sky. I looked out and back; the
Spit was straining to match me, and barely able to hold
his position.

But my advantage was only the zoom—once in steady
climb, he had me. I gaped as smoke poured from the exhausts and the Spitfire shot past me as if I were standing
still. Could that plane *climb!* He tore upward in a climb
I couldn't match in the Jug. Now it was his turn; the broad
elliptical wings rolled, swung around, and the Spit screamed
in, hell-bent on chewing me up.

This was going to be fun. I knew he could turn inside the
heavy Thunderbolt; if I attempted to hold a tight turn the
Spitfire would slip right inside me. I knew, also, that he
could easily outclimb my fighter. I stayed out of those
sucker traps. First rule in this kind of a fight: don't fight the
way your opponent fights best. No sharp turns; don't climb;
keep him at your own level.

We were at 5,000 feet, the Spitfire skidding around hard
and coming in on my tail. No use turning; he'd whip right
inside me as if I were a truck loaded with cement, and snap
out in firing position. Well, I had a few tricks, too. The P-47
was faster, and I threw the ship into a roll. Right here I had

him. The Jug could outroll any plane in the air, bar none. With my speed, roll was my only advantage, and I made full use of the manner in which the Thunderbolt could whirl. I kicked the Jug into a wicked left roll, horizon spinning crazily, once, twice, into a third. As he turned to the left to follow, I tramped down on the right rudder, banged the stick over to the right. Around and around we went, left, right, left, right. I could whip through better than two rolls before the Spitfire even completed his first. And this killed his ability to turn inside me. I just refused to turn. Every time he tried to follow me in a roll, I flashed away to the opposite side, opening the gap between our two planes.

Then I played the trump. The Spitfire was clawing wildly through the air, trying to follow me in a roll, when I dropped the nose. The Thunderbolt howled and ran for earth. Barely had the Spitfire started to follow—and I was a long way ahead of him by now—when I jerked back on the stick and threw the Jug into a zoom climb. In a straight or turning climb, the British ship had the advantage. But coming out of a dive, there's not a British or a German fighter that can come close to a Thunderbolt rushing upward in a zoom. Before the Spit pilot knew what had happened, I was high above him, the Thunderbolt hammering around. And that was it—for in the next few moments the Spitfire flier was amazed to see a less maneuverable, slower-climbing Thunderbolt rushing straight at him, eight guns pointed ominously at his cockpit.

The next morning, July sixth, I stayed home as the Group flew a Rodeo to Rotterdam. Just as well I remained at Biggin Hill; the Group burned a lot of gas and saw nothing. I took the opportunity to fly both the Spitfire Mark 5 and the newer Mark 9B. The flights were a revelation. Two fighter planes couldn't have been further apart than my big

Thunderbolt and the agile little Spitfire. The Mark 5 fairly leaped into the air after a short run. With several thousand feet below the wings I hauled the stick back. She just wouldn't stall! I pulled the stick back against my belt, and the little fighter went around and around, hanging on her nose.

When I rolled her over, I nearly passed out. Without warning the engine coughed, and quit! Quickly I snapped over to level flight and dropped the nose—and the engine started again. It was the carburetor, and it seemed like a primitive arrangement to me. Imagine mixing it up with a couple of Focke-Wulfs and, just as you need power, the engine quits because a lousy carburetor isn't designed for inverted flight!

Whatever the Spitfire 5 lacked, the Mark 9B more than made up for it. She was a sweet, agile machine, incredibly responsive in turns and in climbs. But she just couldn't roll, and she couldn't dive worth a nickel. When I dove the Thunderbolt, the bottom dropped out. To dive the Mark 9B, it seemed I had to fly it down—it just floated.

July passed slowly and with little activity. The tally showed a total of sixteen fighter missions, escorts, diversionary raids and fighter sweeps. We saw some flak, but Jerry just wouldn't come up and play. For a solid month we cruised over targets that usually bristled with enemy fighters. We even flew two missions a day, with high hopes of major fights. Not a German airplane in sight, just the flak, the ever-present, angry red flashes and black smoke, hanging in the air until the wind shredded the puffs into dirty scud.

We transferred from Horsham St. Faith to a new base at Halesworth, north of Ipswich, about seven miles from the North Sea. The new field wallowed in mud, a sticky, gooey quagmire that nearly drove us frantic. Our planes, trucks, jeeps, boots and clothes were splattered with mud. Our food tasted like mud. We moved into distasteful little tin huts in the shape of half barrels, cold, uncomfortable and dreary. To reach the showers we slogged across some six hundred feet of sucking mud, then to shiver beneath brackish, incredibly cold water.

General Hoyt visited our charming new hostel, and with Ralph Johnson and Charley Clamp, I received the Purple Heart, the only medal that no one ever wants and, once it is received, cherishes the most. I hoped I'd never have to add any clusters to the purple ribbon.

On July twenty-ninth, more than a month since I had last fired my guns, the Luftwaffe finally intercepted one of our missions. The 56th was almost to the German border when Focke-Wulfs bounced the 62nd Squadron. We heard Carcione shouting on the radio, chattering like mad. Only we couldn't understand a word and, consequently, couldn't go to his aid. Again the 56th came out loser. A Focke-Wulf shot Bob Steel's Thunderbolt into ribbons and he went down out of control. None of the 62nd Squadron pilots even claimed an enemy.

My luck on the thirtieth to fly as spare! The Group flew a full-strength Ramrod to Kassel, providing withdrawal support to three boxes of the Big Friends at 23,000 feet. No one dropped out of the fighter formations as they flew inland, so I didn't go. Sixty fighters, mostly Messerschmitts, went hammer and tongs for the Fortresses, and the 56th swarmed after them, engaging in wild dogfights from 23,000 feet right down to the deck. We did better this day, with three enemy planes confirmed as destroyed, two probably destroyed, and one damaged. We didn't escape without losses; Horton and Stover went down.

But I wasn't on the mission, and it seemed forever since I'd been in combat. I went out on August ninth, hopeful for action, and returned with unfired guns. Three days later, as the Group made their first Ramrod with belly fuel tanks, flying to Gelsenkirchen, my generator failed and I had to abort. The Group mixed it up, but little damage was done to either side.

Not until August seventeenth, nearly two months from the time I returned to England in a crippled Thunderbolt, did I again see action. The Germans made up with a wild fury for their inactivity of the past, dull weeks. They rushed in aggressive, repeated attacks both at the bombers and our escorting Thunderbolts. The day had been long in coming but on this occasion the 56th Fighter Group truly cut its combat teeth.

We flew a Ramrod to Regensburg, an area, we were warned, that would be savagely defended by the enemy. As we neared the coast, Hub Zemke called for battle formation. Marching in precision the Thunderbolts spread out line abreast, gun switches and gunsights on, propeller pitch increased for more power. Beneath each fighter hung a 108-gallon belly tank to increase our range; once we engaged the enemy, we would jettison the tanks and enter battle with a clean airplane and plenty of fuel.

Over the coastline the 56th began to weave a snakelike course to evade the ever-present flak batteries below. The German gunners had fabulous accuracy. They knew our speed, and radar gave them a close reading of altitude. Radar controls fired their guns, and if we didn't turn constantly, weaving about, we'd be bracketed within a minute or less. Then the coastal flak was behind us and ahead, stacked high and broad, appeared the Flying Fortresses, a black mass of destruction pushing its way into Germany.

The Ruhr Valley welcomed us in proper fashion. Far below the earth came alive, sparkling with tiny brilliant flashes, an unceasing fire dance of massed antiaircraft guns blazing away, hurling shells by the thousands into the sky. All around, above, behind, below, ahead, and within the bomber formations the sky came alive with ugly blotches, great sores appearing as an angry red flash, spreading into clouds of black and grey smoke. The flak erupted continuously from the flaming earth, until soon the sky looked like the middle of a raging Oklahoma dust storm.

And then came the cries for help, the radio messages of the black-crossed fighters plunging in, Focke-Wulfs and Messerschmitts screaming straight into the formations, rolling slowly, wings and noses sparkling with yellow fire as cannon and guns raked the Big Friends. I checked my element leader's position; to my left and slightly ahead Jerry Johnson's Thunderbolt cleaved the air. I looked down and blinked. Quickly I checked the oxygen connections; for a moment I was convinced I was suffering from hypoxia.

Directly under our formation and drifting like a ghost toward the bombers was a white airplane, a strange, twin-engined machine without a single marking to mar its glistening surface. From the wingtips there showered long streamers of flame, swirling around slowly as the fire reached out and sped away from the white ghost. For several moments I stared, speechless, until I recognized the airplane for what it was. A twin-engine fighter, lobbing giant rockets into the bombers like an ancient catapult hurling fireballs into a besieged castle. Just about that time I managed to get my tongue back into place.

"Hey, Jerry, there's a twin-engine ship below us! I don't think he belongs there; let's go get it."

Thunderbolt wing up and over, Jerry's fighter plummeting for the target. I hung to his wing position, glanced to the side as Frank McCauley's fighter streaked down, after the same target. From the bombers drifted long streamers of glowing tracers, gunners hammering away at the Messerschmitt Me-110. I rolled over on my back and watched as the tracers from the Fortresses, and the bullets from the sixteen guns of the two Thunderbolts, all converged at the same moment on the white airplane.

Blinding light, a mushrooming pillar of flame, stretching farther and farther from the light. I blinked, unbelieving, at a churning mass of flames fully two thousand feet across. The flame hung in space for a moment, seemed to roll up on itself. For several seconds the German pilot tumbled in mid-air, within the flames, his airplane torn to pieces. I was barely fifty yards away when his parachute snapped open. He looked up, horror in his straining eyes at the fire licking greedily along the edges of his parachute. For a second the flame poised, then leaped. A soundless gasp, and the silk was a fiery streamer. Twenty thousand feet to go without a parachute.

I never had the opportunity to go after a German fighter, but the boys sure were busy this day. The Messerschmitts and Focke-Wulfs flashed through the sky in wild dives and zooms, rolling after the bombers, persistent in their attacks. So were our people; the 56th truly extended its fangs. Our pilots destroyed no less than *seventeen* enemy fighters. Jerry Johnson and Shiltz each shot down three fighters for our first triple victories. In addition to the seventeen confirmed kills, the Group listed one fighter probably destroyed and nine damaged. That night Stultz, Sugas and Day were missing from our mess tables. Seventeen confirmed for three of our own people lost.

Two days later we flew a Ramrod to Gilze Rijen, and

again I flew wing position for Jerry Johnson. We were just inland, nearing Woensdrecht, when I called, "Four bandits, three o'clock high, going one-eight-zero degrees to us. This is Keyworth White 2, Out." Jerry snapped back, "Roger." The enemy planes came around in a wide, sweeping turn, sliding onto our tails for a stern attack. "Let's go!" White Flight lifted up, turned to rush directly into the Germans. Immediately the Messerschmitts rolled in a shallow dive, then jerked up in steep zoom climbs. I hung back, covering Jerry as he raced after the enemy leader. In a flash a second fighter whirled around, streaked after Jerry.

I hit the throttle, giving the P-47 her head. The moment the second Me-109 spotted me coming in, he snapped over in a sharp turn and fled to the north. Jerry was only 90 degrees to him as I swung on to his tail. I closed in rapidly to 150 yards, prepared to fire. Suddenly Jerry kicked rudder and sent a burst into the Me-109. A good boy in that Messerschmitt; he pulled into a terrific turn, kicked his plane into a spin. I rolled and dove, waiting for the Me-109 to make his first full turn. I knew just where he'd be for his second turn, and I opened fire at this spot.

Sure enough! The Messerschmitt spun right into my stream of bullets. Immediately he kicked out of the spin and dove vertically. Oh no, you don't! I rolled the Jug, and from 27,000 feet raced after the fleeing Me-109. The Messerschmitt seemed to crawl as the Thunderbolt fell out of the sky. I lined up directly behind the sleek fighter, squeezed the trigger. Eight heavy guns converged their fire.

My second kill vanished in a blinding explosion that tore the fighter into shreds, an explosion that also saved my own life. The Thunderbolt was diving so fast I had lost all control; a split second after the explosion I flashed through the fireball that had been an enemy airplane. Now began the brutal task of pulling the Jug out of her compressibility dive. Until I reached 15,000 feet the controls remained as rigid as steel imbedded in concrete. I was frightened; the big airplane vibrated terribly, threatening to tear the wings off. About two miles above Germany the controls grabbed the thickening air; I pulled on the stick with all my strength. The nose lifted, gravity clutched me, squeezed harder, harder! At four thousand feet, level flight, then greyness, swirling mists, darker and darker, and then unconsciousness.

When I came to, the Thunderbolt had her nose pointed at the sky. The engine howled as the heavy fighter flung herself into the blue. I don't know how fast I dove the ship, but the severe pullout bent metal and wrinkled the wingtips. I had lost my flight or, rather, they had lost me. Back at the field, Jerry Johnson accused me of leaving the flight again.

"How the blazes could I have left the flight?" I snapped back. "I'm supposed to cover your tail. A Kraut jumps you, and I chase him off. How else can I protect you if I don't cut after him?" Oh, well, who cares. I got the Messerschmitt, I protected Jerry Johnson, so what difference does a little chewing out make? Once in the doghouse, always in the doghouse!

The gang was in a wild and festive mood that night, for the 56th's pilots had shot no less than nine German fighters out of the air, and damaged another three. I had my second kill; Jerry Johnson was the Group's first ace, and a happy occasion that was! We lost one man, Hodges, from the 63rd Squadron. Our tally for the last two missions was impressive: twenty-six confirmed kills for the loss of four of our own people—better than six to one! Not good enough—we shouldn't lose *any*.

We could almost feel the tempo of the air war changing around us. On August twenty-fourth, over Dieppe at 27,000 feet, Gabreski called out bandits below us. Gabby threw his plane wide open, and I'd never seen a fighter dive so fast in my life. His guns spat out bullets; one of four Focke-Wulfs erupted in a flaming blast. A second later Gabby's hurtling Thunderbolt ripped through the smoke and debris, rushing past the remaining fighters as though they were frozen in place. We went wild that day, with the Germans running like crazy, diving for the deck, breaking off combat whenever we closed. We got only three kills, but came back with all our people. That brought the tally for three successive combats to twenty-nine confirmed kills against four losses. Seven to one!

The German fighters struck back on September second. Hannigan went down over Brussels, and Van Abel took some shells that killed his engine. The other pilots watched him belly his ship in the water between two of the Dutch Islands. He ditched perfectly, opened the canopy and stepped out on the wing to inflate his life raft. At that moment the nearby islands blossomed in flame as the Germans blasted away at the helpless pilot with machine guns and light cannon. The Thunderbolts ripped earthward, strafing for ten minutes, killing enemy soldiers by the dozens. We were convinced that Van Abel was dead; months later we received news that he was a prisoner.

For this day we lost two men, claimed no kills. The next morning, September third, we flew a Ramrod to Romilly and, later in the day, a Rodeo to Woensdrecht. The Germans met the 56th in force, and in the ensuing melee one of the Group's favorite men, Hi Bevins, went down. He was last seen near Paris, flashing over the trees. Relief swept through the outfit several days later when we learned that

Bevins survived his attackers and was taken prisoner. The tally sheet climbed. For the loss of Bevins, we shot down four fighters.

For the remainder of September, we flew bomber escorts to a variety of targets in France and in Germany. Most of the missions proved uneventful, for the Luftwaffe had pulled in its fangs, and moved the major fighter bases back from the coast. Our fighter-escorted raids were beginning to hurt the Germans. It was bad enough to get slugged in the air, but it hurt even more to have your airfields, hangars and planes on the ground blasted by hundreds of tons of bombs.

The 56th Fighter Group began to reach deeper and deeper into Germany. No longer were we green and open to the combat tricks of the veteran Kraut pilots. We had proved the Thunderbolt, proved ourselves. Now we were the veterans. From September seventh to the end of the month the frenzy of combat subsided, but still the Group blasted ten German fighters out of the sky, losing only one man.

In five weeks of combat, we shot down and confirmed the destruction of forty-three German fighters in aerial combat, for the loss, during this same period, of eight men killed, missing, or taken prisoner. Things were picking up!

14

Battle performance during the month of October established conclusively that the 56th Fighter Group had matured into an efficient and a deadly fighting force. We were being shaped into what we felt was akin to a wolfpack, a mass of fighters able to run and to fight together as a smoothly coordinated team. When necessary, we could split up into elements and flights to race in pursuit of a scattering enemy. Even the men who became separated in the wild aerial melees learned to fend for themselves. Time and again, however, Zemke and Gabreski (often with a sour look in my direction) hammered home the theme that safety lay in

numbers and the closest co-operation among pilots. The
lone wolf, they warned, was a man destined to become a
ready target for the unseen German bounce.

Unquestionably the keys to success for the 56th lay in
the outstanding leadership we enjoyed, the brilliant tactics
evolved for the Group, the superb qualities and almost unbelievable ruggedness of the Thunderbolt, and in the fierce
desire of our pilots to engage the enemy. A mission completed without battle was an unhappy occasion, indeed.
The very purpose of our existence, sharpened by training
and practice, and by the stinging defeats suffered in the
Group's initiation to battle, was to fight.

There was no questioning the battle experience or the
skill of the German pilots, nor could we find solace in the
outstanding performance of the Focke-Wulf FW-190 and
Messerschmitt Me-109 fighters. But as we sharpened our
own ability to slash and to fight, the German aggressiveness
so predominant in the early days of battle began noticeably
to wane. By no means do I imply that the German pilot was
less dangerous an opponent; once battle was committed,
however, the enemy fliers no longer were so eager to slug
it out with us in a free-for-all. Steadily, we shot down and
killed many of their experienced men. At the same time,
we gained constantly in experience and in our ability to
master battle situations as they erupted. The 56th was well
on its way to acquiring a galaxy of aces; indeed, the very
presence in the sky of our Group forbode ill tidings for the
enemy.

This is no empty phrase. In the early days of fighting,
when more often than not the Germans ended the day by
cuffing us about, our squadron adopted the name of Avengers. Under McCollom's, and later, Gabreski's skillful air
leadership, the Avengers slowly but surely began to cut a

swath through the Abbeville Boys and their compatriots. We had Gabreski, myself, Bob Lamb, Jimmy Stewart, Jerry Johnson, Joe Powers, Frank McCauley and Don Smith, among others. All of us became aces, and a celebration was in order when we became the first squadron in England to score a confirmed kill of one hundred German planes—*all of them German fighters shot down in aerial combat.*

In the five weeks of combat prior to October of 1943, the 56th first flexed its muscles. Yet even the tremendous score racked up—forty-three Krauts for eight of our own men—was but an indication of what lay in store for us. The Group in October slugged it out on seven separate occasions with the German fighters. During the month we lost only one man, Fleming, from the 63rd Squadron. Our tally was somewhat better. We confirmed thirty-nine planes shot down, and for dessert added five probably destroyed as well as twelve damaged. But the kill department encouraged us—thirty-nine to one!

Everything was fine except that *I* wasn't doing well. On October fourth I was in Felistowe on a two-day pass and missed a Ramrod to Frankfurt. Just my luck! The Group ran into a mass of twin-engine Messerschmitt Me-110's and scrambled fifteen fighters. Piece of cake! And I missed it! Bud Mahurin and Ludwig of the 63rd went wild over Frankfurt, and each man flamed three fighters—two triple victories for the day!

I went out on the eighth for a Ramrod to Bremen, and this time the Krauts obliged us with a stiff interception. Jerry Johnson rolled over and ran for a German fighter below him, my own fighter behind and to the right in covering wing position. Jerry made his pass and we broke up. I swung into a wide climbing turn to rejoin in a position seven o'clock to the bombers. Directly beneath me, at eleven o'clock, a

Focke-Wulf streaked for the bombers. Hard after him came a Thunderbolt, firing in short bursts, but sliding back and forth as though the pilot had gone crazy. Sure enough—behind the Thunderbolt came another Focke-Wulf, hammering away at the P-47. One—two—three—all of them either being shot at or doing the shooting.

Smoke boiled suddenly from the Thunderbolt as the trailing Focke-Wulf pilot found the range. The P-47 refused to break; it kept sliding back and forth, its pilot grimly determined to get his target. I snapped the stick over and dove, sliding in a long, curving dive after the Kraut. He never saw me. I waited until he filled the sights, squeezed, and watched the slugs tearing apart his cockpit and right wing. A sudden blast, and the wing ripped away. The fighter tumbled crazily, trapping its pilot inside. Far ahead, a thin smear appeared from the engine of the first FW-190, blossomed into flame. Seconds later the crippled P-47 slid into formation with me. It was Nick Dauphin, chortling happily.

Two days later, on October tenth, the Group was assigned to provide withdrawal support for 132 heavy bombers attacking the marshalling yards at Münster. Again I found myself in a crippled airplane, in a sky swarming with German fighters. Our briefing took place at six in the morning, when we learned that we would pick up the bombers just as they swung away from the targets, the most likely time for a massed fighter attack.

The Germans didn't miss a trick. We sighted the Big Friends west of the smoking city, suffering badly from a savage mauling by a great number of single and twin-engine fighters. The moment the Fortresses hove into view we jettisoned our belly tanks. Someone shouted, "Forty bandits! Seven o'clock to the bombers, same level! Shaker

Three, Out." A swarm of German fighters raced at the Big Friends, noses and wings flaming as their cannon and machine guns tore into the Fortresses.

Not a second to waste! Jerry Johnson's fighter rolled, dove under full power. This time it was *our* turn to bounce. At 30,000 feet, the sun directly behind us, we plunged from on high in a perfect attack, hidden from the Krauts, who could see only the glaring sun instead of our planes. Unknown to me, Bill Grosvenor, my wingman, no longer covered me. Something happened to his plane; he lost power and was forced to abort the mission. Only I never heard his radio call as he turned and left formation in his crippled plane— which meant my diving into battle, convinced I was being covered by a wingman who was no longer there!

October 10, 1943; fifteen years ago. Again it is possible to slip back into time, to remember the moments of combat as if they were only yesterday, beginning with a Thunderbolt wing lifting up, rolling, gleaming in the sun, diving . . . g-forces pulling the skin tightly across my body.

Jerry Johnson rips after a Focke-Wulf, smoke streaming from each wing as his guns rip out short bursts. Bullets flashing through the air, magic leaps across space as they seek out the black crosses. Immediately a second FW-190 tears in, skidding into firing position. A wingman, frantic to protect his pilot. I turn into the fighter, throttle, rudder, stick controls moving almost by themselves. This German has no heart for a fight; the Focke-Wulf flicks like a sunburst, rolls into a dive and plunges for earth. The sky is filled with German fighters—targets everywhere! I forget the FW-190 running for safety, pull the Thunderbolt back up and around. Where the devil is Jerry Johnson? I swivel my head; he's nowhere in sight. But the sky swarms with German fighters. Got to hit 'em—take them off the bombers. There, to my left—a Messerschmitt Me-110, escorted by two Focke-Wulfs. All three planes in a long, shallow dive for the bombers, waiting to get into range for the Me-110 to lob its rockets.

Got to break them up, get in there fast. I kick rudder, my left hand shoves the throttle to the firewall as I select one of the Focke-Wulfs. Both escort fighters see me; their pilots jerk up suddenly, whip the agile Focke-Wulfs into steep climbs. To hell with them. I line up on the Messerschmitt, fat and juicy in the sights. He tries to evade, twists and turns; my bullets flash into the big twin-engine fighter. I kick rudder, the eight fifties whipsaw back and forth across the fleeing airplane. The rear canopy dissolves in a spray of glass and metal, the gunner flings up his arms, collapses like a rag doll.

Hits all over the airplane; I know what the feeling is like! The pilot is desperate. He flings the airplane about, suddenly snaps the Messerschmitt hard over to the left. No good! My foot slams down on the rudder, easy on the stick, and the Thunderbolt skids cleanly. Now—roll! The P-47 responds like a thoroughbred, flicks around. Controls back, a sharp turn and the eight guns loom broadside to the target. One short burst, eight streams of bullets converge, and the Me-110 tears apart. I am so close the Thunderbolt shakes from the violent explosion. I hear sharp banging noises, the thud of pieces of metal striking my airplane. Debris from the Me-110, a cloud of smoke, flame and shattered airplane through which I plunge.

I haul back on the stick, throttle forward, trying for altitude. And only now do I notice that big empty space to my right and behind me—no wingman. At least I'm not *alone*. German fighters and rocket-launchers fill the sky. Everywhere I look I see Focke-Wulf FW-190's, Messerschmitt Me-109's, Me-110's, the new Me-210's, and small groups of Junkers Ju-88's. They attack the bombers in a constant stream, diving, rolling slowly through the formations, disdainful of the hail of tracers flashing at them. Their own guns and cannon sparkle almost constantly; every few seconds long gouts of flame leap ahead of the twin-engine airplanes as rockets spin for the formations. It is a macabre sight, for there is other flame in the sky. Splashes of fire twisting and dropping to earth, fighters and bombers torn apart. Parachutes blossoming into being, tiny and white against the blue sky smeared with fire and whirling black dots and long, ugly streamers of smoke. Fighters everywhere; a half-dozen flights dive past me on my left, lunging for the harassed bombers. Not a man sights me; they look intently to their rear, alert for another bounce of Thunderbolts from the sun.

Three Focke-Wulfs, closer, coming in hard and fast. I spot them rushing for the rear of the bomber formations, several thousand feet below. I am the only fighter between them and the Big Friends. Good enough! I apply hard left stick, work easily on the left rudder. The Jug winds up like a banshee and hurtles to intercept the three enemy fighters. At our tremendous closing speed, I have little hope of scoring any hits, but I can break up their attack, keep them away from the Fortresses.

These boys want to fight! The Thunderbolt drops in a steep dive when one of the Focke-Wulfs breaks formation. The swift fighter zooms up in a steep, climbing turn, racing to intercept me, to leave the other two FW-190's free to press their attack. I watch him from the corner of my eye. For some silly reason I am convinced that he can't hit me in the dive. I continue pushing forward on the stick, steepening the dive. Eighty degrees, then 90, full vertical! Still I keep the stick moving forward, pushing over as in an outside loop while I open fire. The nose dips under the vertical; I want to keep my stream of bullets far enough ahead to hit the leader. It is almost a 90-degree deflection shot.

I make every move carefully, quickly, increasing the lead, just the right lead, the gentle trigger squeeze. The guns thunder, chatter, roar, all sounds at once. The wings flash scarlet and orange and fire. White flashes appear all over the German fighter, dancing motes of brilliance; the cockpit shatters, and then the intense glare, the beginning of the explosion as the fuel tanks shred, begin their eruption into flame.

No time to watch! An explosion smashes at the Thunderbolt, the diving fighter lurches. That climbing fighter . . . four cannon hammering. The Focke-Wulf rushes in. A 20-mm. cannon shell tears through the metal tail as if it were butter, snaps the rudder cable. In the dive I almost stand on left rudder. The Thunderbolt fights to roll. A flash before my face; not ten feet from the cockpit, mushrooming fire, the jerky motion of a body exploding outward. My target, the lead Focke-Wulf; vanished.

I grip the stick, my forearm tightening as I apply back pressure. The heavy fighter resists the command, mushes, sags down through sky and space and, finally, yields. Nose coming around and up, still higher, pointing straight up. The Thunderbolt leaps for altitude. Gravity washes away the speed, the wild zoom eases off and I push the stick forward, regain level flight.

Not fifty yards away, slightly to my left, a grey Me-110 rushes at my own plane, nose aflame with four guns and two cannon. Wasted ammunition, tracers streaking harmlessly by me. I kick left rudder, finger around the trigger.

Get 'em! A head-on burst from the Jug's eight guns and there'll be no more Messerschmitt.

It is the queerest feeling I have ever known. The rudder pedal swings beneath my feet. And stays there as . . . nothing else happens! No rudder! In front of me the Messerschmitt pilot grasps the opportunity and I wince as the wings and nose of the big fighter turn magically into searing incandescence. Everything the airplane carries is turned loose. Cannon and machine gun tracers flash by, and I duck instinctively as the Messerschmitt's wings vanish, obscured by dark, angry flame. Rockets! The black shapes, blurred, burst over my head. Too close for comfort! I bang the throttle and try to bend it over the forward end of the throttle quadrant, stick forward, down and out of his fire. Once again my heart is in my throat. I think the Jug feels the same way; she leaps forward as if we've been kicked. Then I pull up and level out about 30,000 feet. The heart of the battle has drifted away; the hornets lunge at each other miles to my right. Most of the enemy planes are away, and below me.

I have a personal problem to worry about now.

I'm in trouble, really serious trouble. I try to analyze the Jug's condition. With the controls damaged the Thunderbolt could whip into a maneuver from which I might not be able to recover. I might not be able to get out of the airplane. That's enough for *me*. I pull back the canopy, release my belt and shoulder straps. The wind slams hard against my face and shoulders. I lift my leg, start to climb out, just as calmly as I sit down to breakfast. I'm strangely more elated about getting Number Five than I am worried about my plight.

Suddenly I come to my senses. "Uh-uh, that's Germany below me," I tell myself. I climb back into the cockpit, and start to think. I'm amazed; fear didn't bring me back in the airplane. I'd thought: "Well, Bob, you've had it. Get out." And the moment these words come to mind, I am on my way over the side. But now . . . I still have the chute, and at the first sign of serious control difficulty I can still bail out. Why not try to work my way at least to one of the occupied countries, instead of Germany itself? I'm convinced that I'll have to abandon the Jug; but the more I study the situation the more willing I am to stick with the airplane.

I think of two months before when a Thunderbolt a lot worse off than this one brought me home. I decide to ride the Jug as far as she'll take me. I remember a bomber pilot whose plane was shot to pieces, and who lost his rudder control. A crewman grasped the broken rudder cable, wrapped it around his hands, helped his pilot fly all the way home. Why not?

So I start hauling in rudder cable. Before I realize what's happening I've got thirty feet or more of cable snarling up the cockpit, and still no control. Disgusted, I coil the cable and jam it against the side of the seat. There's still a chance—the rudder trim tabs. And the Thunderbolt responds! No maneuverability to speak of, but an airplane that will fly and that will answer my controls. We're in business!

I work the stick gently, using aileron control with the rudder trim to bring the fighter around until we're flying toward the west—and England. I start calling for help. Now I'm back in the fighting area, bombers and fighters all over the place. I'm getting scared again; too much black-crossed company in the sky. Right in front of me, and slightly below—a Focke-Wulf, droning along fat and happy. A perfect setup; I drop the nose and ease the throttle forward. The Focke-Wulf doesn't waver an inch. He comes into the sights and I prepare to fire.

A Thunderbolt drops like a rock in front of me. Hits all over the Kraut, and the FW-190 disintegrates into flying wreckage. The P-47 doesn't even slow down, keeps diving, her pilot hot after another target. I have no business here, and I pull back on the stick as I open the Jug all the way, climbing under full power. I'm still going upstairs when two P-47's appear ten o'clock off my wing. I can make out the numbers—they're ours; Ralph Johnson and "Hydro" Ginn from the 62nd.

I call for them to escort me home. Ralph shouts back in exasperation as my fighter streaks past them, running with full power. "Slow that damn thing down, Bob!" Ralph calls. "If you want any help, for chrissakes, slow down!" I throttle back, look gratefully at the two Jugs, one off each wing of my own crippled ship. On the way home two German fighters bounce our formation. Ralph and "Hydro" pull up to meet the enemy head on. Suddenly the Krauts take a very dim view of the proceedings. Both fighters roll and separate as they break for the deck. I'm glad to see them go.

My troubles aren't over yet. Near the English coast I stare with misgivings at the "North Sea Stratus," our name for the solid overcast that moves in with frightening speed to cover the islands. I am even more dubious now than before. The cloud mass is so low and heavy that radio towers stick above the scud, strange sharp peaks looming out of opaque mist. For twenty minutes we descend in a wide spiral, seeking an opening. And there, to our left—a hole in the stuff.

Of all the miracles, this is really it! Directly under the break in the blinding clouds—the end of a runway! Ralph

Johnson stays with me, circling, as the other Thunderbolt slips in for a landing, calling out the meat wagon and fire trucks to prepare for my attempt. I keep my gliding speed above 120 miles per hour so that I can direct the crippled Thunderbolt down by trim tab. The big fighter streaks down, drops below the cloud layer, rushes to meet the ground. One tire hits hard, both wheels down; at 120 miles per hour I slam on the brakes, holding taut the left rudder cable in my left hand.

The Thunderbolt squeals to a halt, and I kill power. I hear Ralph Johnson's fighter slowing to a halt, and the propeller grinding around to a stop. I know the other two pilots are nearby, for I hear them calling. The break in the cloud is gone. The other airplanes are within twenty feet of my own, invisible to me. The fog has closed in, a dark and sight-robbing mass. I climb down from the wing and grope my way through the murk. Several minutes more in returning to England, and the miracle of the break in the clouds, directly over this runway, would have vanished.

I was an ace! My two kills for the day brought my confirmed score to five enemy planes shot down in aerial combat. It was a great and auspicious moment for me. After all, the boys had selected me as the pilot most likely to be one of the first in the 56th to be blown out of the air, and my rear end had been thoroughly chewed by some of the best in the business. Zemke, Gabreski, Jerry Johnson, to mention but a few, all convinced that I would too quickly become cold turkey for a Focke-Wulf's cannon.

I was overjoyed. After weeks and weeks of inactivity, of missing out on some of the best "killer" missions, I had finally come across the opportunity to mix it up. It had been quite a day; two kills scored for the single mission. I was the fifth man in the European Theater to reach the coveted ace position. Before me—in my own Group—were Jerry Johnson, Hub Zemke, and on this same day, Dave Schilling. Dave made his the hard way; in four successive missions he shot down a German plane. One of the boys from another Thunderbolt group had racked a score of five, but it was to the 56th that the honors went. Five aces in England—and four of them came from our own Group.

My fighter was still undergoing repairs on October fourteenth. When the Thunderbolts returned, we received the news that three German fighters had been flamed without loss for our side. But the men were not jubilant, and they showed little enthusiasm for their victories. It was not difficult to understand why.

The target had been Schweinfurt, and the fighter escort was able to reach only as far inland as Aachen and Düren. The moment the Thunderbolts broke off escort the sky darkened with hundreds of German fighters. Everything the Krauts had capable of carrying armament went after the hapless Fortresses, and an estimated four hundred fighters worked over the 224 bombers that managed to reach the target. Never had the Big Friends suffered such devastating losses. The sky over Schweinfurt turned into a slaughterhouse. The Germans hit the Big Friends with everything— while our fighters were unknowingly returning to base, without the range to move in to break up such attacks.

I remembered a B-17 I had seen go down near Rennes. It wasn't a pretty sight, but at least on that occasion ten parachutes appeared in the sky, the entire crew; a rare moment when all the men were able to abandon their stricken airplane. A big flak shell scored almost a direct hit. In an instant smoke obscured the airplane; a ripping blast hurled it backward from the formation. Then came the dark shapes

of men leaping into space, and the joyful sight of silk opening, of ten men dropping safely. The bomber died slowly,
burning in its death throes. Pilotless, the great aircraft
dropped a wing, fell off and plunged earthward like a flaming meteor. Slowly, answering the trim, the Fortress pulled
up, swooped into a chandelle, trailing geysers of flame and
pieces of burning wreckage. She hung on the top of the
chandelle, slid down and again dove for the ground. Again
the controls, trimmed for flight, brought her up and out.
Several times the bomber plunged and swooped and then
fire reached the tanks. An intense teardrop of light, mushrooming flame, and a fireball more than three thousand feet
across. Tiny pieces hurtled through the air; nothing else was
seen.

And at Schweinfurt *sixty bombers* had died! More than
six hundred men dead, wounded, or captured from these
airplanes! How many more killed, shot to ribbons in the
cripples staggering home? The 56th provided penetration
support for the 2nd Air Task Force from Sas van Ghent to
Düren. Just as they were ordered to break off escort, more
than a dozen Messerschmitt Me-110 fighters were sighted at
15,000 feet, going after the bombers. The 61st Squadron hit
them in a diving attack, shot down three, and pulled up
when the others broke for the deck and ran.

Still the tempo of battle increased. The VIII Fighter Command received more fighters from the States, and all over
England new units were being formed. On November third
we were visited by planes of the 4th Fighter Group, staging
at our field to refuel for a mission. As they came in to land,
two fighters blew their tires. On takeoff another Thunderbolt blew a tire; the airplane tore off the end of the runway,
hurtled upside down and crashed over on its back, burning.
Before the crash wagons could reach the scene, a big Mili-

tary Police officer, Delaney, dashed to the ship and ran directly into the flames. He jerked free the straps trapping the pilot in the cockpit and physically dragged him out of the airplane.

The boy was hysterical. "Go away!" he screamed. "Let me die! Let me die!" The flames had reached him and his clothes were still smoking. Delaney ignored his cries and dragged him away from the fighter, falling on the pilot to protect him just as the Thunderbolt exploded in a terrific blast. We learned later that the youngster lost an eye, but he had survived.

Once the runways were clear, the 56th climbed out for an escort mission to Wilhelmshaven. The Ramrod proved uneventful on the way to target, disappointing for us but pure bliss to the bomber crews. We all flew at high altitude, caught in a layer of air that sent contrails streaming thickly from the bombers. And then, on the way home, I saw a single Messerschmitt Me-109 far to my left and below. The sneaky bastard! He slipped just beneath the contrails, working his way slowly up to the bombers. Just as he moved beneath the cottony swaths, I pulled in fast on his tail. He never saw me as I raced in to his rear. A pigeon—two big rockets beneath his wings, waiting for the moment to cut down a Big Friend. Two hundred yards back I squeezed the trigger; white flashes all over the airplane. The Kraut snapped over in a roll to the left and started to dive. No good to dive against the Jug. I came in so close I almost rammed; I virtually shoved my guns into his cockpit and fired. The Me-109 exploded; I flew through the scattering remains. That made Number Six. A good day for all. The Group hit an enemy formation, flamed four bandits. We lost none on our side. This was the kind of scoring I liked!

We were waiting for Sadie Hawkins' Day; we'd promised

that by this memorable occasion, the 56th would have at least one hundred German fighters tallied. November sixth was the day of promise, and by the morning of the fifth we still lacked the required number. I didn't make the mission, but the boys flew a Ramrod to Münster. Six enemy fighters went down, and George Hall of the 63rd received the honors—he flamed a Messerschmitt Me-210 for the Group's one hundredth kill. All of our people came home. That night we celebrated in royal fashion, for tomorrow was a holiday. Sadie Hawkins' Day, naturally!

Each month now held promise of heavy action, and our tally sheet kept climbing. It was inevitable, even with our newly gained combat skill, with our aggressiveness and the failing zest of the Germans, that we should suffer losses. The Germans still flew excellent fighters and had enough hot pilots to give us a real rough time. On the eleventh the Group escorted bombers to Münster. We scored five planes shot down, but lost Butch O'Conner and Van Meter.

Two days later we picked up the Big Friends at 29,000 feet, just east of the Zuider Zee. They were shot to hell. Many of the bombers lagged with smoking engines, others came back with engines stopped and propellers feathered. It was a terrible sight. The crippled planes staggered along with gaping tears in their wings and fuselage. Every now and then a flare arced brightly, a pyrotechnic cry for an escort to shepherd a dying cripple. We saw no action this day, but there had been plenty. The Lightning escort lost eight of their big fighters, getting only six Germans in return. A new P-47 Group which escorted the Big Friends over the target was shot up badly; they lost four men while the Germans remained untouched. Many of the bombers strayed off course and wandered to Norway. They were so shattered by the German fighters that the Liberators slipped beneath the Flying Fortresses for protection against diving attacks.

We finished November with wild action over the Continent, and furious air battles in which the Germans fought savagely against our attacks. Loren McCollom, who had first greeted me on my arrival at Bridgeport, had transferred to the 353rd Fighter Group. By now he was a colonel, and a full-fledged veteran and most courageous combat leader. On the twenty-fifth McCollom led his fighters in a screaming dive bomb attack against the German airfield at St. Omer. His wingman reported that an antiaircraft shell exploded with a sheet of flame directly under his Thunderbolt, shattering the fighter's belly. The blast sheared away metal, and the wingman gaped as Mac's legs showed clearly through the bottom of the torn airplane. Miraculously, Mac rolled her over and dropped free. We finally received word that he was in a prison camp.

The night of November twenty-sixth I had plenty to moan about. Almost all my missions had been flown as a wingman, with little opportunity to cut loose and run after the Kraut fighters. Now, on a Ramrod to Bremen, I was leader of the 61st Squadron. And just after takeoff I had to abort! My gauges showed fuel pouring away through a leak in the tank. The same thing happened to Morril of the 62nd. Out of gas over Holland, he bailed out and ended the war as a POW.

But what a day to stay home! VIII Bomber Command sent 633 heavy bombers to attack Bremen and Paris, and the Krauts swarmed up in force. And wouldn't you know it, most of them were twin-engine stuff. The 56th went crazy, setting a Group record for kills on a single mission. Bud Mahurin feasted on the Messerschmitt Me-110's, flaming three of the fighters, to score his second triple for a sin-

gle combat, and boosting his score to eleven kills. Dave
Schilling racked up two Focke-Wulf FW-190's, and Gabreski
flamed two Me-110's to bring his total score to five—another
new ace. Craig from the 62nd got an Me-110 and an Me-
210; in the same squadron, Cook blasted two Me-210's to
reach ace status. It was a great day for the 62nd, for Ralph
Johnson got two Me-110's, as did Valenta.

Total score: *twenty-three* enemy fighters shot down, three
probably shot down, and nine damaged. Our losses in
combat—*none!* Still better!

I was still on the ground three days later. Over Bremen
some of the toughest Krauts met in a long time came upstairs to slug it out, and the boys reported a furious scrap.
Gabreski was running strong, bagging two more to bring
his score to seven. For the day the 56th confirmed six kills,
losing Windmayer from the 63rd. The Jerries came out of
the sun to slam into the P-38 escort, and before the Lightning pilots could do much about it, eight of the twin-
boomed fighters had been shot down—without loss to the
Germans.

On the last mission of November, the Germans stayed
on the ground. Fate placed an unkind hand on Bill Grosvenor's shoulder, and at 30,000 feet his engine quit. Bill rode
the Thunderbolt down; at 4,000 feet the engine caught. Since
he was already so low and far behind the formation, he chose
to stay on the deck and hedgehop all the way home. When
a locomotive appeared in front of his speeding fighter, he
just couldn't resist the temptation; he'd never fired his guns
before and figured that now was as good a time as any.

That was a mistake. His bullets exploded the locomotive,
a sight that fascinated Grosvenor. He was so fascinated
that he failed to notice a steel tower just on the other side
of the train. At better than 300 miles per hour the Thunder-

bolt smashed into the tower. The impact tore the big fighter to pieces, flinging it high into the air. And out came Bill, jerking the ripcord the moment he cleared the airplane.

Bill had a hairy time of it. He parachuted into Belgium, and friendly natives hid him from the searching German troops. For nearly a week a woman kept him secreted within a cave beneath a barn. With the search called off, the underground shipped him to Brussels, where he and a bomber pilot huddled in an old woman's apartment. Only, the bomber crewman was a nitwit; he just *had* to visit a friend on the other side of town. German troops picked them up and threw them into prison; they also found the old woman.

For several weeks they tortured her, trying to force from her the location of other American fliers secreted within Brussels. She never revealed any information, but the underground reported that the Germans left her in hideous condition. All because the fool of a bomber pilot couldn't stay hidden for a while!

The Germans did their best with Grosvenor, and because of his refusal to reveal anything but his name, rank and serial number, starved him. In a few weeks Bill was skin and bones, and then was thrown into a tiny, dark cell for thirty days. Here a stroke of luck befell him, for the German guard had been a prisoner in the States in World War I and never forgot the excellent treatment he received from his captors. He brought cigarettes to the imprisoned Americans and did what he could to ease their lot.

Finally, with the invasion a reality and our troops swarming toward Brussels, the Germans herded their prisoners into freight cars to ship them into Germany. The ride, Bill said, was wonderful. Every few hours Thunderbolts chewed up the tracks in dive-bombing attacks, forcing the train to

move back and forth. During one stop the German guards
ran to the rear of the train, and with forty other American
POW's Bill ran for his life. He reached the front lines to
stagger into a British camp.

Grosvenor was our last casualty in November of 1943. In
five major air battles the 56th shot down forty-four German
fighters, claimed five as probably destroyed, and sixteen as
damaged. In those same air battles, we lost four men to the
enemy. Pretty good; a score of eleven to one. We were rolling in high gear.

Except, that is, for me. I hadn't done much since my
sixth kill on November third, and fretted with each passing day as I sat out mission after mission on the ground.
Between repairs to my fighter, and a wicked sinus that
caused the doctor to order me into bed, I felt I was being
left out of the whole fracas. The escort mission flown on
December first to Solingen—while I stayed home—didn't
cheer me any. The Group scored three kills, but ran into
absolute hell. We lost Cleve Brown, Pruden and Ludwig to
what Gabreski described as some awfully rough boys in
the Focke-Wulfs. Gabby came home in a Thunderbolt
really dragging her tail; a Kraut chewed up his engine and
shot away two cylinders. Mudge came back with a shell
through his gas tank, his plane flying on fumes as he
landed. Brooks' propeller ran away over France, and he
was halfway out of the ship before he decided to try to
bring her home. Fats Morril, a big boy weighing in at 250
pounds and one of the best pilots we had, had to belly in
his crippled plane. Things got worse as a stricken B-24
came in to land at Manston; on its final approach a wing
tore off and the bomber exploded, killing instantly the
eleven men aboard. A Fortress overshot Manston and

plunged into the Channel; only a few got out. Not a good beginning for the month.

Five days later, on a Ramrod to Paris, we lost Goldstein. The boys came home glum—not even a German fighter damaged. Not until December eleventh, when we escorted Fortresses to Emden, did we find the opportunity to really cut loose. And then the Wolfpack ran wild.

15

Early on the morning of December 11, 1943, more than six hundred heavy bombers assembled over England. The Big Friends met below and above clouds, slid into formations, creating order out of seeming chaos. Elements, flights, squadrons, groups and wings took their positions. Staggered into boxes, in precise, planned formations, the armada wheeled majestically and thundered toward Germany. Several times I had occasion to witness from above the amazing skill and dexterity with which the bomber pilots handled their tremendous machines.

At our briefing we received instructions to support the

first two boxes of the 3rd Bomb Division to the limit of endurance. The Germans struck early at the Big Friends. We were over the Frisian Islands at 30,000 feet when someone called out eight to twelve fighters, coming in fast from the east at 35,000 feet. Far to the south thundered the Flying Fortresses, tiny black specks, painting a mass of gleaming vapor trails in the substratosphere. The Krauts decided to take us on, and that was an early sign that we might run into some of the older and more aggressive Luftwaffe veterans. No doubt about it; the Germans withheld any attack until they had drawn abreast of our formation, with the sun directly behind their force. And down they came! Two and three fighters grouped together, swinging into the rear of the 62nd Squadron.

It was a familiar trap. We received orders for the 61st and 63rd Squadrons to stay out of the fight, and to continue on course to rendezvous as protection for the bombers. Which is exactly what the Krauts were trying to prevent. They hoped that we would be stupid enough to commit all forty-eight fighters to a brawl with the dozen German airplanes, eliminating the escort our Big Friends needed so desperately. It didn't work; the 61st and 63rd continued on course while the 62nd turned into the enemy fighters. Shortly after, a radio command went out for any 62nd pilots able to disengage to do so and come running to rejoin. Four Thunderbolts broke out, leaving the other twelve to hold the Krauts.

North of Emden, the remaining thirty-six Thunderbolts swung into a wide turn to head for Bremen. We were at 35,000 feet, tiny specks in a sky filled with gigantic cloud formations, many of them towering above us. This didn't make formation flying any easier, since the clouds reflected the intense sunlight.

Sooner or later it had to happen, I suppose. Halfway through the turn two fighters directly ahead of me drew together with alarming speed. Even before I could shout a warning one Thunderbolt sheared a wing, and rammed the splintered metal into the other plane. Steel slashed into fuel tanks and in the next instant both fighters tore apart in a blinding explosion. Two parachutes spilled out into the air, billowed and opened. My feeling of relief was cut short. Only pieces of bodies remained in the chutes.

Just like that, two good men lost. We couldn't help either Larry Strand or Ed Kruer by watching the wreckage fall. There was nothing to do but to hold our course and continue on toward our rendezvous with the bombers. We saw the Big Friends just off Spiekeroog Island. Above and to their rear, forty-plus twin-engine fighters, maneuvering for a mass cannon and rocket attack. And more than sixty single-engine fighters, tearing into the Big Friends in devastating frontal assaults, zooming fast to reach top cover position for the twin-engined stuff.

Gabreski called out the attack and the 61st plunged in loose formation for the enemy; an attack, as Gabby described it later, that "let all hell loose." I picked an Me-110 at least two miles below and ten o'clock to me. The gunner called out my plane, and the Messerschmitt whipped over and dove. By the time I came close to the Me-110, we were just above the ground. I didn't see how the twin-engined ship could come out of her dive, and I pulled up, waiting for him to plow in. At the last moment the airplane flipped right side up, and the pilot poured the coal to the ship. Down I went—and again he rolled over, perilously close to the ground. I pulled up—he rolled out. I grew tired of this nonsense and dove; again he rolled over. Only this time I kept diving. As the Me-110 rolled back into level flight, the airplane filled the sights. Perfect! One short burst knocked the bottom out of *his* bucket! The airplane tore itself apart in mid-air. Number Seven.

My squadron had a field day. Paul Conger, Bob Lamb and Don Smith *each* scored triple kills. Joe Powers and Robill Roberts each flamed two Krauts, and single kills went to Gabreski, myself and Bill Aggers. To add to the party the 62nd Squadron scratched four more. It was heartbreaking to lose Strand and Kruer in the collision, for otherwise the day would have been perfect. We didn't lose a man in the fight.

December was the month I'd been waiting for. On the twenty-second we flew a Ramrod to Osnabrück, picking up the bombers over the Zuider Zee. As we passed Zwolle Holland, a B-17 dropped out of formation and swung into a steep turn; aborting the mission, the pilot was anxious to get out of German air before any fighters caught him alone. Luck was with this Big Friend today. Near the tops of scattered cumulus clouds I sighted what seemed to be two shadows—moving fast. Shadows in the sky come only from airplanes, and I slipped down to look.

Sure enough! Two Messerschmitt Me-109's, greasing their way around a towering cloud, working into position to burst out from behind the cloud cover—right smack on the tail of the Fortress, in a perfect position for a bounce. With Joe Perry riding my wing I turned to go after them. About six miles back and still two miles above them, the pilots spotted me and veered off. I turned to the south as if I had failed to sight the two fighters. Immediately the Messerschmitts hauled around in a 180-degree turn and poured on the coal to reach the lone bomber.

It worked! With Joe Perry hugging my wing, we rolled out of the sun and dove. Intent only on the Fortress the

Kraut pilots never even saw us coming. As they neared a towering cloud the fighters split up, streaking around the cumulus so that they would come out prepared to hit the Big Friend from left and right sides. I came down with tremendous speed and ran for the Me-109 on the left, diving slightly below. I pulled out in a climb with great speed and closed in rapidly to 150 yards. Just as I squeezed the trigger, the 109 banked slightly to the left and the pilot looked back. My first stream of bullets smashed into his canopy and tore away his face. Perry was still glued to my wing as I hauled back on the stick, looking for the Kraut's pal. He had lost his zest for fight, and we watched him dive into a cloud, far below. That made eight.

On December thirtieth I failed to gain a confirmed kill, but I know of one German fighter that never flew again. We picked up a group of Liberators swinging away from Ludwigshafen. The Big Friends had done a good job. A river of flames danced in the city, sending up mountains of thick, black smoke. The Luftwaffe didn't want to play, and except for the heavy flak things were quiet. Until we reached Nancy, just easy of Strasbourg. We saw two German fighters at eleven o'clock to us and more than a mile above our flight. They were something new; they looked like Focke-Wulf FW-190's until we identified the long, pointed noses of in-line engines.

I'd heard about them. New Focke-Wulf FW-290's, reported to be hot as hornets. At the moment the two Krauts were having a ball, swinging around in wide barrel loops, almost as if they were teasing us, daring us to come up. That's just what we did. As we climbed, the FW-290's split. One raced straight ahead and the second swung into a climbing left turn. This one for me; the Thunderbolt climbed beautifully and at 27,000 feet I moved in quickly to his tail. He saw me coming, and racked the FW-290 over in a steep left turn. I jerked the stick hard over to the right and added left rudder. The Thunderbolt clawed around beautifully, rolling inside the Focke-Wulf.

Still in the turn, I fired. I could barely see the Kraut because of the sun in my eyes, but in a moment smoke trailed behind the Focke-Wulf. That boy was *good;* the FW-290's nose snapped down, and he ran for dirt in a wide-open power dive. These characters all had to learn for themselves that they couldn't outdive the Thunderbolt!

I closed to firing distance and squeezed out a burst. Still diving, the pilot threw his airplane about in violent maneuvers, twisting and jerking so violently I could never keep my guns to bear for more than a fraction of a second. I fired and missed; cursing, I fired again. My feet danced on the rudders and the stick never stopped moving for a second. A dozen times I squeezed out bursts, and a dozen times he weaved through the bullets. At 10,000 feet the needle indicated over 450 miles per hour. That was enough for me; I hauled back on the stick, pulling with all my strength. A low overcast with its top cover at 4,000 feet obscured the rough terrain and steep hills immediately below the clouds. Still accelerating in the vertical dive, the Focke-Wulf plunged into the mist. I know that he didn't pull out; he *couldn't.* But since I didn't see a parachute, or actually witness the airplane striking the ground, all I could claim was one Focke-Wulf damaged.

The next morning we flew a Ramrod to Kerlin-Bastard. The bombers kept going out every time the weather permitted, hammering relentlessly at German targets. For the last two months we had gone aloft every time the bombers went out, and the only justification for remaining on the ground was either a damaged fighter requiring repairs, or grounding orders from the doctor. No one complained; in fact, our gripes were loudest when we couldn't fly. Our target of Kerlin-Bastard the morning of the thirty-first called for refueling at our advanced base of Exeter on England's south coast. Over the Jersey Islands, the hand of Fate came down again on one of our pilots. A fighter to my left pulled up, rolled slowly and peeled off, accelerating rapidly in a power dive. Barnum screamed on the radio, "Gello, pull out, boy, *pull out!*" It was Marangello, unconscious from lack of oxygen. His Thunderbolt aileron-rolled over the two planes to his left and suddenly ran away, Marangello unconscious and helpless in the cockpit. Barnum called to him all the way down, begging him to pull out of the dive. The Thunderbolt plummeted into the water and rocks, disappearing in a scarlet blast.

That started the day out tragically, and again we mixed it up with the Germans with our only loss being a man who had died without being shot down. On the return trip, almost to Nantes, we ran into the Krauts: "Bandits attacking the bombers, twelve o'clock to them. This is Keyworth Leader here. Out." I couldn't spot a single German fighter, but from Les Smith's call they had to be directly beneath me. I rolled the Jug and went downstairs. Sure enough—two Focke-Wulfs right below, hell-bent for the bombers.

I looked back—two more. And behind them, another two! I kicked the Thunderbolt into a wide turn, still diving, and pulled up behind the last FW-190, staring at the fighter through the gunsight. The moment before I pressed down on the trigger the sky ahead of us tore open in a dazzling flash of light. The first two Focke-Wulfs; damn them! Their cannon shells exploded two bombers in a terrifying blast. I hauled around in a tight left turn as the Focke-Wulfs screamed through the bomber formation. They ig-

nored the blistering tracers hurled at them from the Fortresses and sailed on through, seemingly unscathed. The
two trailing fighters came around in a wide sweep to the
left for another pass.

Not this time; I closed rapidly. Both fighters swerved
and ran. Twenty men had died in those two heavy bombers; I wanted these Krauts, and I wanted them bad. I
poured the coal to the Thunderbolt and raced after the
fleeing Focke-Wulfs. Luck stayed with me; the Germans
raced for cloud cover far to the east. Picking up great speed
in the dive, the Thunderbolt narrowed the gap. Still at
long range I snapped out a burst, aiming at the trailing
fighter. A blast of fire enveloped the Focke-Wulf; the ship
flicked over in a left roll and raced for the ground, exploding on impact. I skidded to bring the guns to bear on
the next plane. The ship came alive with the white flashes
of my bullets. This one simply headed straight down and
plunged into a hill, erupting in a mass of flames and debris.

Score nine and ten.

New Year's Day. And what a present we received. We
flew to a maintenance depot at Wattisham to have the
Thunderbolts modified. Our engineering officers were making a terrific fuss over a new propeller designed especially
for the Thunderbolt. They insisted that the fat paddle
blades of the new propellers would bring a tremendous
boost in performance, that the increased blade area would
permit the props to make the greatest use of the Thunderbolt's 2,000 horsepower. We listened to their enthusiastic
ramblings with more than a grain of salt—and never were
we more mistaken.

Four days later we flew a Ramrod to Münster, the first
time we went into combat with the paddle-blade propellers.
With four Messerschmitts directly beneath me, I rolled to

my left to pull in behind them. My fighter quivered and began to shake badly, as if partially stalled. The next thing I knew I was in a dive and *wow!* What a dive! I hauled back on the stick, afraid that the engine would tear right out of the mounts. What I didn't realize was that the new propeller was making all the difference. I called to Gabreski, "Get 'em, Gabby! Something's wrong with my ship."

The next morning I took the Jug up and wrung her out. She never flew better. I was disgusted; unaware of how the paddle blades had affected my performance, I had missed an easy kill.

But what a difference these blades made. At 8,000 feet I pulled the Thunderbolt into a steep climb. Normally she'd zoom quickly and then slow down, rapidly approaching a stall. But now—the Jug soared up like she'd gone crazy. Another Thunderbolt was in the air, and I pulled alongside, signalling for a climb. I'm not an engineering officer, and I don't know the exact feet per minute that we climbed. But I left that other fighter behind as if he were standing still. The Jug stood on her tail and howled her way into the sky. Never again did a Focke-Wulf FW-190 or a Messerschmitt Me-109 outclimb me in the Thunderbolt. The new prop was worth 1,000 horsepower more, and then some. Later I had the opportunity to mix it up with a Spitfire 9B, the same model fighter that had flashed past me in a climb. This time the tables were reversed; I was astonished as we both poured the coal to our fighters, and the Thunderbolt just ran away from the Spit.

On January sixth I met one of the Luftwaffe old-timers, one of the toughest pilots I've ever fought. Near Coblenz the Group raced in a dive after fifteen Focke-Wulfs. Gabreski locked onto a Kraut's tail and the German's wingman came hard after Gabby. I saw him swinging in, turned hard, and made a head-on pass. The Focke-Wulf jerked up steeply to the right, turning away. I threw the Jug into a roll and went after him. He put his fighter into a wicked turn, but I kept rolling and firing, sticking like glue to his tail. He steepened the climb, but with the new propeller the Thunderbolt never let go. I kept rolling, squeezing out bursts, scoring hits steadily. He turned, twisting violently to lose me.

I stayed with him, following every move, still firing, still scoring. Abruptly he flicked over and dove, jerking from side to side to avoid my fire. He was terrific, one of the very best. But the dive was his mistake. Again and again the Germans tried to break out of a tough position by diving. Never did they learn! The moment my nose went down the engine and propeller wound up in a scream and narrowed the gap. I went in close, less than fifty yards, and squeezed out a long burst. The bullets tore into his cockpit and left wing root, flaming a fuel tank. The Focke-Wulf tumbled crazily, end over end, and tore apart. Number Eleven.

A New Year's present on January sixteenth—a two-day pass to London. Roberts and I took off the moment the passes were in our hands. We couldn't have received the break at a better time; the same night we left the airbase a thick fog rolled in, and the Group didn't get off the ground for three more days. The train stopped at every little station, groaning and dragging itself along. At one isolated town, soaked in a blinding fog, we sat idly for fifteen minutes.

Crash! Without warning, the train rammed forward violently. Suitcases burst from their racks and spewed into the passengers. For a while everything was pandemonium; a great many people were hurt. Doctors worked their way forward through the cars, attending to the injured, and only then did we learn how lucky we'd been. A second train had stopped directly behind ours. A third train came racing through the fog, smashed into the one behind us, which in turn crashed into our own. Nine people were killed and many seriously injured; we didn't have a scratch.

London was even darker and gloomier than I remembered. Adding to the normal confusion of the blackout was the thick fog, and we were afraid we'd never find our hotel, only three blocks away. I knew things had become desperate when an old Englishman stumbled into us, and in a strained voice inquired if we could bloody well tell him where in the bloody hell he was. This was wonderful—an Englishman asking *me* where he was, in fog, in blackout, and in London! We certainly couldn't tell *him*. He had a few under his belt and was feeling little pain; we heard him staggering and stumbling his way through the dark. His hobnailed shoes echoed clear and sharp through the fog. Every so often he staggered into a curb or lurched into the side of a building. For several minutes after each collision he stood rock-still, bellowing and cursing. He passed us four more times in the three hours it took us to reach the hotel; and he was still cursing.

When we returned to the field, we discovered that Hub Zemke had returned from a temporary duty flight to the States. Dave Schilling had just taken over the job of C.O when Zemke stomped into his office. "*I'm* C.O. of this outfit," he snapped with a grin. "Take off." And so he was. Schilling "took off."

I scored my twelfth kill on January twentieth, and the circumstances were such that I wished I could have prevented the air fight from following through to its bitter conclusion. Over Rouen, Les Smith called in, "Four bandits, two o'clock below. I'm going down into them. Red Leader here." Les rolled over and led his flight into the Focke-Wulfs. Diving with the flight was John Allen Dimmick, out on his first mission. As they lined up behind the Krauts, two of the Germans split off suddenly to the right. With Dimmick flying his wing Smith blasted away at a target. Two more Focke-Wulfs burst out of the clouds and raced onto Dimmick's tail.

I banged the throttle forward and dove, shouting at Smith to break off. "For God's sake, Smith, break! There's a Jerry on your Number Two man. Break! Break, Smith!" Les was too intent on his kill; he never heard my call. I dropped straight down, squeezing all the power and speed the Thunderbolt had. Far out of range I snapped out several bursts, hoping the bullets would scare off the Germans. They ignored my fire; one Focke-Wulf closed in to point-blank range to blast Dimmick with his cannon. Just as his shells exploded along the wingroot of Dimmick's Thunderbolt, I closed in to firing range.

Bullets smashed all over the Focke-Wulf. I didn't even see what was happening to Dimmick. I wanted that German, I wanted to kill him. I've never before been so badly afflicted with the urge to kill as I was at that moment. The Kraut ran for it, diving as he twisted and rolled. I hung grimly to his tail, squeezing out bursts. We plunged into clouds at 4,000 feet, the Thunderbolt hurtling down, on her back, as I caught the Focke-Wulf in my sights and hammered out a long burst. The fighter whipped into a split-S and at tremendous speed plummeted into the ground.

Dimmick had been seen to roll over on his back, flames bursting from the Thunderbolt. He never pulled out, and the burning fighter smashed into the earth. His death shook me up. Dimmick had served in the Artillery at Fort Sill before enlisting as a cadet. For some time he lived with the Gaffords, close friends of mine in Lawton. It was a tough break to lose him, and especially on his first mission.

My thirteenth kill came on the thirtieth of January, during a Ramrod to Bremen. Approaching the target I called out the incoming fighters, "Twelve bandits, nine o'clock below and about fifteen miles west." We were at 27,000 feet, the German fighters slipping through broken clouds a half mile below our formations. We turned in toward the enemy; our position was perfect. We came straight down on them, ripping into their ranks like a flaming avalanche. The moment the Krauts sighted us they broke, running for safety. The scattered clouds messed up what could have been a perfect bounce. Twin-engined fighters ran frantically in all directions. "Powers; cover me!" Joe's fighter slipped onto my wing, and I started down after an Me-410. It was so easy it was ridiculous. The Messerschmitt dove at full speed in a straight line; full speed to him, but a crawl to the old Jug. His gunner must have been daydreaming; I closed to 150 yards and squeezed the trigger. The eight guns tore the Messerschmitt apart.

The 56th was running wild. At one moment I watched at least six German fighters plummeting in flames, and Thunderbolts racing after anything with a black cross on the wings. Three Me-109 fighters skimmed the clouds, and I took Joe Powers down in a bounce. The Jug ran away in the dive, and before I knew what happened I was on top of the Messerschmitt, watching him starting to disintegrate. No time to confirm the kill; I jerked the stick back and skimmed over his canopy, the big paddle blade dragging me into the sky. I never saw what happened to the airplane.

January proved another outstanding month for the Group. Our fight on the thirtieth erased sixteen German fighters to bring the month's tally to thirty-nine Krauts shot down for the loss of one of our men in combat.

I had thirteen confirmed kills with which to begin February, and this particular month was a time of mass air fights over Europe. For everyone, it seemed, except myself. I started the month with a vicious boil on my leg; for a week I'd ignored the pain, afraid that if I reported to Doc Hornig he'd ground me. And things were just too hot and heavy to stay on the ground with a boil!

That was my worst mistake! One morning I limped to the airplane, and just couldn't climb into the cockpit. When I dragged into Hornig's office, and he studied my leg, I thought he'd explode. Doc Hornig climbed up one side of my back and down the other, giving me hell every inch of the way. He threw me into the hospital, and then he went to work on the leg. I stared with no small horror as he stuck a fierce-looking instrument into the boil and jabbed deeply. I'm not sure just what he did there, but I had to hang on to the bed with all my might to keep from belting him. I was one sore cookie for the next week.

In the first weeks of February we lost Langdon and Patton in battle. On the fifth a disgruntled Doc Hornig discharged me from the hospital, and I walked down to the flight line to see the boys taking off through a snowstorm. With the British and our people working together, we put 1,200 fighter planes over Paris, circling above a stream of bombers plodding their way in and out of the target.

A single Messerschmitt Me-109 burst out of the clouds and raced into the 56th Group. The German barreled down in a dive, shot up Keen, tore Jack Patton's plane apart with cannon fire, and disappeared. A week before this mission, Jack and I were standing before the operations shack, checking over his fighter. Heavy clouds hung low over the area;

no flying. Out of the thick fog fluttered a baby seagull. It hovered for a few moments, then came down gently on the tail of Jack's Thunderbolt. Jack picked up the bird, and cared for it for several days. It was a beautiful creature, with a snow-white breast and gray wings. Not once did it resist Jack's hands. Three days later the gull died; three days after that—Jack was shot down.

I flew my only February combat mission when the Group escorted bombers to Leipzig. The Army Air Forces hurled more than three thousand bombers and fighters against Germany, the most tremendous force ever assembled. The mass of planes darkened the skies over Europe. Long trains of bombers, stacked deeply into defensive boxes, rumbled miles over the earth, incredible and unbelievable in their number and furious sound.

I cannot speak for the feelings of the Germans as they sighted the miles and miles of bombers crashing their way through the sky, but at least the Luftwaffe rose to do battle, throwing its weight into the armadas while the bombers threaded a path through the dense flak storms. North of Dummer Lake, Foster called in, "Bandits, seven o'clock low. Keyworth White Three here." Gabreski led the squadron, and I held the lead position for Blue Flight, to Gabby's left. We looked down—thirteen Messerschmitt Me-110's, skimming the tops of broken clouds at 15,000 feet. Everything was shaping up for a perfect bounce.

Gabby led the squadron in a sweeping turn to his left to bring us out ahead of the German formation. The Messerschmitts were in echelon to the right, six in the lead group and seven of the big fighters bringing up the rear. I slid under Gabby to come out on his right, and then cut back under his plane to resume left position. As he turned in behind the enemy in a dive, I cut across again and bingo!

We came in to hit the Krauts with eight Thunderbolts in line abreast formation. All eight of us fired at once—sixty-four heavy machine guns roaring in unison. We hit the first bunch in true Thunderbolt fashion, ripped through their scattering ranks and began to chop up the second echelon.

The Krauts went crazy, jerking their fighters around in all directions, trying to shake us off their tails. We swept on by and when we pulled up in front of their broken ranks and looked back we could see only two fighters. I raced after one in a dive, almost sawing the Messerschmitt in half. Gabby streaked after the other as I dropped to his wing to cover him. That made one apiece. Far below us we spotted two more in a shallow dive, engines trailing thick exhaust smoke as they ran for safety. They went down like wheat before a scythe—one, two and two flaming fighters. The day ended well; I had two confirmed for kills fourteen and fifteen. The Group flamed fourteen without loss.

Our tally for February came to fifty-five German fighters destroyed in aerial combat, for the loss of two of our side. We had come a long way from our early days of combat, when the Germans ran riot over us and sent us home more times than not with several of our people missing and others badly shot up. For the months of October, November, December, January and February, the 56th Fighter Group stormed, like the Thunderbolts we were, against all opposition. In this period we lost ten men in combat—and shot down a confirmed total of 209 German fighters.

16

Early in 1944 the operations of the 56th Fighter Group were "imperilled" by a single fighter pilot. The amazing thing was that he flew in a Thunderbolt instead of fighting against them. So fiercely desperate was Flight Lieutenant Michael Gladych to kill Germans that often we feared for his life as he tore after enemy aircraft. Prior to his "temporary visit" with the 56th, Mike Gladych had flown in combat with the Polish, French, and British air forces.

We did not envy Gladych his past experience. When Mike joined our ranks for temporary flight duty, he had just completed five years of close brushes with death. When

German troops assaulted Poland, Mike flew like a madman in an obsolete PZL-11 fighter and managed to shoot at least five German planes out of the air before his country collapsed. With several other pilots Mike then fled to Rumania, where he was thrown into jail by pro-Nazi police. The Polish fliers escaped and, barely one step ahead of the Gestapo, reached France. But the Gestapo never gave up its quarry that easily, and one night in a dark Lyons alley a trained German killer went after Mike. In a savage hand-to-hand struggle Gladych killed the German, but paid heavily for his victory. He fell unconscious—blind.

He came to in darkness, bound hand and foot, a captive in an insane asylum. For five days and nights the horror-stricken Gladych endured the tormented shrieks of the inmates. He felt he, too, was going mad. Five days after his capture a French doctor explained that his commitment to the asylum had been in error. In his towering anger Mike felt pain stabbing his blinded eyes.

"Go ahead!" the doctor shouted. "Open them; *open them!*" And Mike Gladych, miraculously, could see. He owes a tremendous debt to that doctor, who had wisely diagnosed Mike's blindness as acute strain on the optic nerves, which could be cured only by a sudden and great shock.

After his recovery Mike flew obsolete French fighters in a courageous but lost battle against the Luftwaffe. He fled to England and with other Polish exiles joined the Royal Air Force. He was obsessed with the urge to kill Germans, and his fellow pilots predicted that his frenzy for battle to the death with anything of German origin would soon cause Mike's own demise. Over France in a British fighter, Mike lost his squadron and single-handed ripped into three German fighters. In a furious battle he shot down two and then ran out of ammunition. Blazing with anger he rammed the third plane. Pieces of wreckage burst into the canopy, slashing Mike's head and eyes. He set course for home, and fainted.

He returned to consciousness two days later, swathed in bandages in a British hospital. Luck not only rode with Gladych, it hugged him tightly. In a fantastic flight his fighter droned in a gentle glide to England. With Mike unconscious at the controls the airplane touched ground at high speed, in almost level altitude. It tore itself to pieces as it skidded out of control and came to a stop—two hundred yards from the hospital! After repairing his head, which was laid open to the bone, the doctors told Gladych he'd never fly again. Mike just didn't believe them; several months later he was in a Thunderbolt over Berlin.

With Gladych at the 56th was another "visiting" Pole, Colonel Gabsewiez, a close friend of Gabreski. He was a tremendous man to be flying fighters, at least six feet three inches tall, and weighing 240 pounds. He spent ninety minutes checking out in the Thunderbolt, and happily joined the group in a sweep over Germany. Just across the border his belly tank ran dry, and his engine coughed several times. In his excitement Gabsewiez shouted, "Gabby, Gabby, vot I do? Vot I do? My engine, she go poof, poof!" The other pilots nearly choked with laughter.

Several minutes later Gabsewiez and Gladych spotted a single German fighter far below them. They shouted to each other, and before anyone could make a move, their Thunderbolts were gone, racing after the enemy plane. Only, Gabsewiez and Gladych had been flying Spitfires, an airplane that, in comparison to the Thunderbolt, crawls in a dive. In their plunge they tore earthward so fast they couldn't slow up and flashed well below and past the startled German flier. Back at the field that afternoon, Gabsewiez commented with a slow shake of his head, "Whew! The dive! She is *fantastic!*"

On February twenty-sixth the boys went to Happy Valley, our name for that charming area known as the Ruhr, where it seemed possible to step out of your airplane and walk on the flak bursts. I stayed at home and sweated them out, and I mean sweated. Mike Gladych had my airplane, and I was convinced that I'd never see it again, or that Gladych would drag himself home in a wrecked Thunderbolt. Unbelievably, the airplane came home in flyable condition. Mudge and Barnum had flown off Mike's wing; somewhat dazed about the entire event, they related the proceedings.

Mike flew Number Three to Barnum, and they noticed early in the flight that Gladych maintained a perfect position. No one ever worried when they had The Killer with them. Mike could see enemy planes, it seemed, when they were still out of sight. Suddenly, they noticed that Gladych was no longer in formation. Dismayed, they circled, trying to locate the missing Thunderbolt. They were at 18,000 feet, and just east of the Ruhr Valley. And down below, 18,000 feet below, in fact, was a Thunderbolt hell-bent for leather after a Messerschmitt Me-109. Mudge and Barny dove after the two planes; sure enough, it was my fighter, the HV-P lettering standing out clear and sharp.

The book says a Thunderbolt can't hold a turn at low altitude with the Me-109, but Mike never read the book. He clung to the tail of the German fighter, moving in closer and closer. They were right on the deck, actually flying beneath the tops of trees. Mudge and Barny couldn't understand why Gladych didn't cut down the Messerschmitt; he had plenty of lead but refused to fire. When the German pilot saw the other two Thunderbolts, he ran for safety, skimming the trees as he fled down a valley. He had good reason to run, with the three big fighters on his tail. Halfway down the valley was an opening to the right, and several miles further a gap on the left. Mudge took the first turn, and as the Messerschmitt burst out of the valley, snapping to the left, he stared almost into the guns of Mudge's Thunderbolt. He and Barny cut loose at the same time; the Messerschmitt splattered along the ground for several hundred yards in a shower of flame.

Mike throttled back and circled the burning fighter; he wanted to be sure that the pilot was dead. Had that German survived the crash and run from his plane, Mike was prepared to cut him down with his propeller or wingtip. When Mike returned, and I'd heard the tale, I asked him why he didn't fire. He couldn't; the gun switch was broken. Not being able to shoot down the Me-109 so infuriated him that he tried to spin the German in, or run him out of gas. He was actually trying to run the Kraut out of gas over his own home, 350 miles from our base!

On March second we escorted bombers to Frankfurt; some of the boys mixed it up with the Krauts, but my squadron plodded along without seeing action. On the way home Gabreski led the 61st to 10,000 feet, far below our usual escort altitude. You can't see ground details from six miles high, and we were down low hunting for good targets to shoot up. South of Aachen, near the German border, I noticed an airbase and called to Gabreski, "Hey, Gabby; here's one to our left. It looks pretty good, but I don't see any planes. Let's shoot up the hangars."

Gabreski swung into a steep turn and dove, the squadron following. Until this time we had done very little strafing, and were still amateurs at the game. Instead of dropping to the trees several miles from the field and coming in on the deck—to surprise the German flak gunners—we foolishly rolled over at 10,000 feet and dropped straight down. The Krauts waited for us with great anticipation, for we were meat on the table for them. They were good; not a German fired until we were racing over the field.

In the dive my fighter eased ahead of the pack, and I rushed at the field in lead position—the safest place to be when the Germans were biding their time. But I spotted a large hangar to my left and swerved; the squadron tore past me. Now I was in last place—the Number One Sitting Duck, as I soon discovered. Joe Powers took the left end of the hangar, Gabby poured his bullets into the center, and I raced in to shoot up the right side.

I came out of my dive at better than 500 miles per hour. At this speed the ground doesn't merely approach; it leaps upward. As my bullets arced ahead, red flashes appeared magically across the hangar, my bullets smashing through metal and glass. I became so engrossed in the scene that I barely pulled out in time. Germans in panic tried to scatter from the hangar, rushing in all directions like rats fleeing from a sinking ship. Within the building something exploded; a sheet of flame ripped through the roof, setting the structure on fire. I pulled out, the last Thunderbolt in the pack. And now I realized why being Tailend Charlie in a strafing run just wasn't healthy. Every machine gun and cannon on the field turned to fire at *me*.

I flashed over the hangar and started down on the other side. Gabreski's fighter seemed to leap in front of me; I jerked back on the stick to avoid a collision, pulling straight up. Just what the Krauts wanted, a target unconcealed by trees or other obstructions. As the Thunderbolt zoomed in a vertical climb, pieces of red-hot metal appeared magically from beneath the airplane. They were so close I could have been firing them from my own guns. I don't know how many seconds passed before I breathed again, but it seemed as if I couldn't get away from the flak. Still climbing, I frantically slashed the Thunderbolt from side to side. Every moment I peeked around the armor plate.

Still with me! Red fingers of flak soared after me from the right; I kicked the Jug back to the left and stared around. Again the flak, following my every movement. Then the big guns cut loose. Smoke bursts appeared, explosions which I heard over the roar of the engine, bouncing the 'bolt around. Any second I expected to feel the kick from a shell smashing into the Thunderbolt. It was an eerie feeling, almost like running over a bed of hot coals, fearing the moment when the pain would lance through my feet. And then the sky vanished, replaced with wonderful, thick, obscuring clouds. I got out of there in a hurry.

By now the 56th was marching across all Germany. New belly tanks increased our range to such an extent that we flew escort missions all the way to Berlin, seeking out the Luftwaffe eagle right in his own nest. On March sixth we flew the direct route to the German capital. We didn't need a map, for there ran from the North Sea all the way to Berlin the inescapable Flak Highway. Five miles wide and extending from 30,000 feet right down to the deck, a tortured ribbon of deep, angry, exploding flame and thick, acrid smoke. On the sixth even the flak gunners promised to outdo themselves; ahead of us the sky was alive, every few hundred feet of space punctured by the wind-shredded bursts of flak, and more being added every second. I led my outfit to the left of the enormous bomber train; Mike Quirk held his squadron on the right; and Gabby paved the way, over the top and leading the Big Friends. A new man, Herron, flew my wing. This was his first mission, and before the day was over he had ample opportunity to cut his combat teeth.

The fun began shortly after we crossed the German border. Quirk's voice came loud and clear over the radio: "Thirty bandits, three o'clock very low." He didn't wait around for company, but with his eight Thunderbolts tore for the German formations far below us. Gabby and I called after him several times, trying to locate their position. We hadn't mixed it up with the Krauts for weeks and we wanted in on the party. But Quirk's boys were having too good and hot a time to bother speaking to us. We held our escort positions, moaning and cursing because we were missing the show. I didn't know that this was only the prelude. Gabby moved southward, searching for the enemy.

West of Hanover, Dummer Lake hove into view. And so did the biggest mass of German fighters I'd ever seen! A swarm of airplanes rushed in, from the north, two o'clock to my squadron as I orbited to the left, eight o'clock to the lead bombers. For a moment I thought they were Thunderbolts. I sang out, "Watch those monkeys on the right; they . . . Hell, they're Focke-Wulfs!" Barely did I call out their position when we were in the mass. Everywhere I looked I saw wings with their stark, black crosses. Eight of us against this black swarm—and head-on! Everyone hit the trigger— no time for aim; just scatter lead—as we tore through the German formations.

I slammed the throttle forward, kicking rudder and jerking the stick over hard. The squadron whipped around in a tight turn, racing frantically to get on the tails of the German fighters. Then we saw the *other* Krauts! There were at least fifty plus in the first bunch; and now came more than fifty fighters, flying top cover for the lead group; and yet another fifty covering their left flank. We were the only squadron in the area; I had eight planes to meet the German force of between 150 and 200 fighters. This was a beauty!

As we raced after the lead formation, I pressed the radio button and called for friends. Gabby had been far out on the right looking for German fighters, and I had found them on the left. We couldn't wait for Gabby's Thunderbolts to show; with my own planes hugging the space around me, we began to close the distance to the German fighters.

A fantastic sight faced us. Ahead of me were more than 150 German fighters; with our own formation mixed in with them, a wedge of nearly 200 fighter planes rushed at tremendous closing speed to the bombers. Directly ahead of us were sixty of the giant Big Friends, droning along in majestic formation, bombers stacked neatly in their defensive boxes. And behind them more and more four-engine giants. More than twelve hundred heavy bombers sweeping in awesome parade through the German sky, lined up as far as the eye could see back toward England. Solid formations of sixty planes each. More than twelve thousand men in the Big Friends.

And more than thirteen thousand heavy machine guns in that fantastic armada! As the German fighter force screamed in to attack, our Thunderbolts became just so many more Krauts to the bomber gunners—and at the tremendous combat speeds we became equal targets.

And not until that moment did I ever appreciate the guts it took for the German pilots to plunge head-on into such a bomber mass. One moment the sky was filled with only black shapes of airplanes; the next instant all hell broke loose. The heavens came alive with countless motes of light, searing bursts of fire, flame dancing and sparkling, weaving and arcing through the air. The mile-cube of bombers leading the twelve hundred had opened fire. In sixty bombers hundreds of gunners tracked our approach with their .50-caliber machine guns. Nose gunners, top turret gunners, waist gunners, and belly turret gunners, all firing, all spitting blazing fireballs at us. And they all seemed to be firing at *me!* In barely two or three seconds the individual streams of tracers vanished. A violent storm of blazing lead leaped into existence, flung toward our fighters.

The Germans, too, had fired. A mass of flame leaped forward from the wedge; an incredible fire storm. A combined total of more than seven hundred cannon and hundreds of machine guns, hurling untold thousands of tracer bullets and explosive cannon shells toward the bombers. Sudden bursts of familiar dark and angry flames; the rockets shearing away from the Focke-Wulfs, hundreds of rockets, each with terrible power in their black shapes. The 20-mm. cannon shells exploded with brilliant white flashes; in an instant the bombers were struck by thousands of these intense blasts, explosions all about and all too often within the Big Friends. The rockets flamed ahead, weaving an erratic path as they bore inexorably toward the Flying Fortresses, painting strange flame-and-smoke trails in the sky behind them.

Each time a rocket hit—disaster. A spear of flame lashed into a four-engine shape; magically, intense light flared into existence, and within a second the Big Friend and the ten men within had disappeared, replaced by a searing ball of fire, churning angrily as it was born, a monstrous swollen eye of flame nearly a half mile in diameter. In the brief seconds it took for my Thunderbolt to hurtle through the mile-cube of bomber space, I saw German fighters suddenly tumble out of control. Either crippled or with their pilots dead the fighters spun crazily through the air; with so many planes passing within only a cubic mile of space, collisions were inevitable. Sometimes, the black-crossed wings streaked like arrowheads of steel and explosive fuel, utterly incapable of direction, to embrace a Big Friend, unable to evade. Metal clashed, ripped apart. Steel and aluminum shearing in thin layers, spilling flames, wreckage and the bodies of men into the bitter air above Germany.

From each savage collision metal dropped, and metal fluttered, ludicrous, and almost featherlike. Wings or tail surfaces, flip-flopping almost gently as the spume of jagged steel and flame rushed by in the endless plummet to earth. Within the cubic mile of space, within the heart of the more than six hundred American pilots and gunners, the bombardiers and radiomen, streams of cannon shells and bullets and rockets sought and found their quarry. Sometimes the flame appeared as a tiny lance, a creature struggling outward from a rupturing fuel tank, seeking air through a gash in a wing; and then, maddened by its freedom, leaping explosively across the wing, into cockpits, surrounding the crewmen. A Big Friend does not often die quietly, nor does the giant craft yield its throbbing life without pain and terror and, in those who watch, a helpless, sickening feeling of futility.

Few of the Big Friends succumbed without a fierce struggle. Crippled bombers, engines pouring thick smoke, dropped away from the greater safety of the cubic mile, the formation box in the sky. Some gasped as power died in one or two or three engines. Others staggered, many feet of wing or stabilizer or rudder shot away. Pilots covered with their own blood, with steel in their bodies and limbs broken, clung grimly to their controls, coughing blood and fighting to maintain their giant craft on an even keel, to survive in the teeth of the murderous gantlet they must run. They fell out of formation with gaping holes and tears in wings and fuselage, mushing through the sky with gunners hanging lifelessly over their heated weapons, with oxygen systems ablaze, with bombs hung on racks as fire licked at the eggs within the bays. Bombers falling, bombers dying slowly, crewmen refusing to abandon their stricken craft because a buddy was wounded and would die unless a friend remained to administer aid. Pilots died in crippled giants because their men could not bail out, because parachutes were torn by jagged pieces of flak, because men were unconscious from lack of oxygen. They could not, they would not, jump—not while a man lay helpless behind them. And so they all died, meeting their end as fire reached finally to fuel cells or to bombs, or died instantly as the pilot sought to belly in his crippled hulk of a bomber in rough fields or through trees.

Then we were finished, the lead box of Fortresses behind us, the Focke-Wulfs scattering their formations and turning to hunt down the strays and cripples, to pick off each bomber sagging away from the thick defensive formations. They had other targets as well; the helpless man descending within his parachute straps, jerking frantically on shroud lines, trying to lift himself up or to slide down faster through space. Staring in horror as the German fighters clawed around, turned head-on, the wings and nose sparkling.

I tried almost to fling the Thunderbolt at these black-crossed ships, cursing as they flashed out of range of my guns. Herron was still with me, tied to my wing, as much for his own protection as to provide cover for my attacks. Six different times I lined up on a German fighter, the kill almost assured, and six different times, before I could fire, I had to haul the Thunderbolt around to chase a Focke-Wulf off Herron's tail. I was desperate to pour bullets into the enemy planes, but a kill might have meant Herron's loss.

Within minutes the churning mass of planes spread over a vast area. The bombers, their ranks thinned and their surviving members badly bruised, crashed onward through milling fighters and angry flak bursts. All around the bombers the Focke-Wulfs had scattered, some to cut down the cripples, the others to evade the Thunderbolts which plunged with almost reckless abandon against the black-crossed planes. A mile above me a B-17 swooped out of control, flames streaming from the engines and the crew leaping into space. Two Messerschmitt Me-109's circled the falling giant, snapping out machine-gun fire at the men helpless in their parachutes. The Krauts had their fighters wide open, black smoke pouring from the exhausts. I slammed the throttle forward and climbed, the paddle blades hauling me up quickly. The leader of the two German fighters raced straight ahead for safety while his wingman broke to the right. By now I was raging with anger; I was determined to get at least one of the two planes. The lead Messerschmitt suddenly stopped smoking. It was a complete giveaway; I knew that at this instant he'd cut power. I chopped the throttle to prevent overrunning the enemy fighter. I skidded up to my right, half rolled to my left, wings vertical. He turned sharply to the left; perfect! Now—stick hard back, rudder pedals co-ordinating smoothly. The Thunderbolt whirled around, slicing inside the Messerschmitt. I saw the pilot look up behind him, gaping, as the Thunderbolt loomed inside of his turn, both wings flaming with all eight guns.

This boy had never seen a Thunderbolt really roll; he was convinced I'd turned inside him. At once the Me-109 straightened out and dove. They never learned! Now I had him dead to rights; I closed rapidly as the ground rushed toward our two planes, squeezing out short bursts. White flashes leaped all over the fuselage and wings. I was scoring; good hits that were cutting up the Messerschmitt. He didn't give up easily, and racked his fighter around in a wicked left turn. I got another burst into him; some of the slugs tore into his canopy. The fighter belched forth a thick cloud of smoke and seemed almost to stop in the air; then I was overshooting him. I jerked back on the stick, flashing over the smoking airplane. I rolled and looked back; I saw only a flaming mess on the ground.

Two Thunderbolts closed on my own fighter; Sam Hamilton and Joe Perry. "Hey, Sam," I called, "is that him there on the ground?" Sam chuckled. "Hell, yes, that's him." And *that* made me feel better.

I circled the area, and gasped. Right below me was one of the largest and most crowded airfields I'd ever seen. Lined along the hangars were models of every type of Allied airplane the Germans had ever captured, everything from Spitfires to Flying Fortresses. I saw German types I never saw before, or since; Heinkel He-111 twin-engine bombers, the ungainly Junkers Ju-87 Stukas, and others I couldn't identify. Planes were stacked on that field like chessmen onto a board. "I'll be damned!" I shouted. "Look at that airdrome!" I started to call the fighters together for a mass strafing attack when eight Thunderbolts flashed beneath my plane, diving steeply. The pilots tore the field apart; they couldn't miss even if they flew over the field, eyes shut, and squeezing the trigger. Streams of bullets chopped airplanes to pieces; one after the other the ma-

chines began to burn and to smoke heavily. German mechanics dashed frantically in all directions as they sought
cover; dozens fell before the withering fire of the strafers.

The four planes above the attackers rejoined, and we
climbed for altitude. At 15,000 feet I spotted a single Me-
109 dropping in fast, racing directly for Sam Hamilton
and his wingman. "Break, Sam!" I yelled. The Messerschmitt
plummeted between our fighters, and I snapped out a head-
on burst. He skidded, and dove. Another burst into the cockpit, and the Kraut plunged without swerving into the ground.

It was quite a day. I scored kills sixteen and seventeen,
and the Group tallied a confirmed ten fighters destroyed.
Hub Zemke went wild in the midst of the thick German
formations and scored a triple. We lost Stauss from the 61st
squadron; his plane badly shot up, he rode the cripple to
5,000 feet, called, "So long, you guys," and bailed out. The
Big Friends suffered a savage beating. With so great a
distance to fly, they eventually lost more of their number
than had gone down on the devastating Schweinfurt raid.
The cripples were unable to stay aloft during the long
flight home from Berlin, and before the day passed a total
of sixty-eight giant bombers fell. Seven hundred men lost;
it was almost unbelievable.

That night in my combat report I wrote—somewhat vehemently—that we could prevent such massacres of the Big
Friends by improving our escort tactics. I insisted that instead of remaining close to the bombers, the Thunderbolts
should fan out to either side and well ahead of the bomber
formations. We could then hit the Germans as they rushed
in. It mattered little if the sweeping Thunderbolts flew in
strength; the sheer momentum of attack by the Germans
would carry the defenders back some, but even eight
Thunderbolts, moving in aggressively, meant a firepower of

sixty-four heavy guns into the midst of the German ranks, and eventually, we could stop or disrupt their attack. Audacity, aggressiveness, an attack pressed home, could break up and delay the attack against the bombers, and give us time in which to call for assistance from the other patrolling Thunderbolts and other escort fighters. I argued that the only way to protect the bombers was to hit the Germans *before* they could move in close enough to wreak their devastation. On March fifteenth, only a week later, I would have the opportunity to put this argument to the test.

Two days later we again flew the Flak Highway to Berlin. I was in the 2nd group, and we missed the really big scrap which started when the Thunderbolts leading the fighter escort tangled with a mass of Krauts over Dummer Lake. The Germans used the same tactics as on March sixth. In a wild free-for-all, Bud Mahurin of the 63rd Squadron flamed three fighters and emerged from that roaring battle as the leading ace in the theater. Twenty kills confirmed in aerial combat!

Almost as if in celebration, the 56th Group cut a new record in the air over Germany. Bennett of the 61st Squadron shot down three fighters for the second triple, and I had a little excitement of my own. A boy named Smith from the 63rd Squadron dove after a Kraut, and never saw two Messerschmitt Me-109's race in to his own tail. And the Krauts never saw *me*. I came down in a howling dive, killed the pilot of one fighter with a single burst, skidded, and exploded the tanks of the second Me-109. My score kept climbing—that made numbers eighteen and nineteen.

Mike Gladych helped to keep things from getting *too* boring. Mike never quit; he always stayed in the middle of a fight until he figured he had just enough gas to get him home. But not until his fuel reached the critical point would

he even think of ending his one-man war with the Luftwaffe. And sure enough; we had regrouped and were on
the way home and . . . no Mike. Gabreski yelled for him,
"Hello Keyworth White Three, what is your position?" After
three calls and no reply we began to worry. That was a
foolish thing to do with Gladych.

The radio crackled and Mike's voice came back in a monotone, "Hello Gabby, hello Gabby, this is Mike. I'm okay. I
am being escort out by three Focke-Wulfs over Dummer
Lake." Gabby muttered something unintelligible as he
racked his fighter around to try and reach Mike in time to
help. He might as well have saved the fuel. Gladych turned
into the three German fighters, and exploded the leader.
And at that moment his fuel reached the critical stage; if
he fought a minute longer he'd never get back to England.
There's always one way to get home in the Thunderbolt,
and Mike took it, gunning for the deck in a screaming
power dive, the two Focke-Wulfs hot on his tail. Mike
dropped below treetop level, engine howling, trying to shake
his pursuers. As he flashed over a clump of trees, an airbase loomed before him. No one could ever accuse Gladych
of being a slow thinker; he poured a long burst of bullets
into the German planes and crewmen as he thundered
overhead. The first man in a surprise strafing attack hardly
ever gets hit; the ones that follow usually catch all kinds of
hell. Later, a grinning Mike told us, "You know, it's funny
ting, they no bother me after I cross the field." The German
gunners had blasted both Focke-Wulfs out of the sky.

Mike didn't have the fuel to get back to England. In a
solid overcast above the Channel the engine sputtered and
died. At the last possible moment Mike bailed out and
jerked open the chute. Two hundreds yards off shore, he

dropped into the water, shucked his harness, and swam to the beach. That same day he was back at the field.

We set a record for kills on March eighth, but it was a bitter victory. Reeder's Thunderbolt took a burst of flak, and he had to get out of the burning airplane. Just before he rolled over, staring into the face of death, he gave us his last call: "So long, you guys. Tell the rest to bite my butt." He sounded pretty disgusted. Icard, Roy, Carcione and Marcotte failed to come home. It had been a long time since we'd lost five men on a single mission.

17

Back on the Flak Highway! March fifteenth, a bomber escort to Brunswick, but flown along the familiar, flame-and-smoke route chopped out of the sky by the enemy antiaircraft batteries. The German fighter pilots had chosen Dummer Lake as their favorite point to tear into the Big Friends. And with good reason; their past success had littered German soil with the wreckage of many twenty-five-ton bombers.

Leading a squadron of eight fighters, I cruised far to the left of the Fortresses, orbiting wide so that we could break up oncoming German attacks, and still have time to shout for help before the enemy fighters reached the Big Friends. Far to the north, in the direction of Bremen, contrails streamed high above our own level. At least fifty, and by their looks they were Focke-Wulfs. I led the squadron in a fast climb to block their approach, calling for help. Every time the radio channel quieted I called, as slowly and distinctly as possible, "Forty-plus bandits, nine o'clock, high to the lead box of bombers now over Dummer Lake."

Damn, they were high! The Focke-Wulfs rushed toward the lead bomber formation at a height of at least 38,000 feet. They had found their previous attack wedge successful, and were hopeful for a third repeat performance. Fifty fighters and more as top cover at 38,000 feet, and two boxes of fifty-plus Focke-Wulfs, line abreast, at 23,000 feet. At 27,000 feet I turned the squadron and we dove, racing head-on into the fifty fighters directly in front of our own eight airplanes.

Our formation opened wide, the Thunderbolts spreading out, straight in as we accelerated in our downward rush. Every plane's wings flamed, eight heavy guns roaring in short bursts, bullets spilling into the midst of the German fighters. They scattered! We hurtled through the formation. The other fighters glued themselves to me, eight Thunderbolts clawing around at tremendous speed to hammer at the trailing Focke-Wulfs. The Krauts had enough; a dozen fighters snapped over and dove away.

Sucker bait! I looked up—and there they came, the top cover of more than fifty fighters, eager for an easy kill. *If* we had taken the bait and dove. I yelled over the radio, "Okay, pull straight up—*now!* The top cover's coming down." Eight hands jerked back; eight Thunderbolts reared nose high and soared, leaping in vertical climbs. I've never been so close to so many airplanes! We zoomed straight up and the German fighters plunged straight down. I swear that some of us must have grazed the Focke-Wulfs; one pilot stared in horror at me as we flashed by, wings almost colliding. There wasn't room enough for a small butterfly in that area.

But the line-drive attack worked beautifully. The tight formation of Focke-Wulfs fell apart at the seams as the fighters flung themselves about wildly to avoid our zooming wedge. The fight assumed even more incredible proportions —here came the other fifty fighters to help the first group beat off our attack of eight airplanes! We had done to them exactly what they had been doing to our bombers.

Friendly fighters had heard my call. Hard after the diving German top cover came a dense swarm of our planes, a group of twin-boomed Lightnings and several groups of Thunderbolts. I still swear I flew through the tail booms of several P-38's as their pilots screamed down after the Focke-Wulfs! In the time it took us to zoom upward through the German formation, some ninety of our fighters pounced joyously into the fray. For several seconds our eight Thunderbolts separated from the central mass, and I've never seen the like of that fantastic struggle.

A mass of nearly three hundred fighter planes fought savagely in a wild, screaming battle, all with their engines wide open and firing almost steadily. The sky dissolved into a twisting and churning nightmare, planes struggling fiercely from 30,000 feet right down to the very ground, and all within a tight area of five miles square. Tracers flashed through the weaving maelstrom, and I saw flame blossoming, explosions, the white flash of cannon, from both the Focke-Wulfs and the big Lightnings. It was a wild, macabre scene, a duel to the death of agile warriors.

Not four miles to the south rumbled the gigantic train of Big Friends, twelve hundred giant Flying Fortresses, marching resolutely through the flame and smoke of intense flak. Bombers as far as one could see, stretching far to the horizon, and disappearing out of sight. The avalanche of steel and explosives, more than thirteen thousand men at war, miles over the Reich. From the Big Friends the pilots and crews stared gratefully at the savage battle north of their own marching ranks; gratefully, for not a single German fighter broke through our own defensive wall to reach the bombers to wreak carnage like that of a week before. On this day three of the giants went down; two to flak, and a third from an oxygen-system failure. Not one suffered a single bullet hole from a German fighter. Twelve hundred bombers—enjoying a badly needed respite.

There was no time to wonder at their good fortune. I turned and plunged directly into the swarming mass of fighters. I never knew from one moment to the next exactly what was happening. My feet and hands and head and eyes moved constantly within the cockpit, working rudder pedals, stick, throttle, trigger. I skidded and slipped, dove, zoomed, twisted, slewed wildly, turned and rolled, anything to survive and avoid collision with the fantastic mass of twisting fighters. Time and again I missed by bare inches collisions with other airplanes.

One moment I was pulling up in a climb; a Focke-Wulf slid from beneath my fighter, skidding wildly to the left. He wasn't more than fifty yards away. I worked stick and rudder, trying to slide around on his tail. Just as I started the turn another plane skidded under me, a red-nosed Thunderbolt piloted by Flight Officer Klibbe. His wings blazed as he fired steadily at the FW-190, forcing me to snap roll away from his fire. Klibbe really plastered the Kraut, who at that moment looked for all the world like a yellow cur dog running with his tail between his legs.

A second later a Focke-Wulf seemed to jump directly in front of me. I squeezed the trigger and he disintegrated almost at once; I nearly ran into the exploding pieces. Number Twenty! I looked around; there—a Focke-Wulf pouring cannon shells into a P-38, diving steeply. A slight movement of stick and rudder, the proper lead, and a two-second burst. The Focke-Wulf's canopy dissolved into spray. Flame billowed from the tanks. Twenty-one!

And then—they were gone. In a miraculous second, the battle was over, the sky below us smeared with greasy smoke trails, with tumbling and burning airplanes, parachutes drifting gently toward the earth. In the few minutes of intense combat, planes had fallen like flies, far and away the majority of them German planes. Thunderbolts of the 56th Fighter Group cut down twenty-four enemy ships, losing only one man, Kozey, from my squadron.

The Thunderbolts and Lightnings hadn't quit, however. As the Germans dove frantically for safety, racing over the clouds far below, our fighters rushed in pursuit of the whipped enemy force. I searched the sky in vain, seeking one German fighter that didn't have a Thunderbolt or Lightning glued to its tail. I wanted one badly: I'd never scored a triple kill for a mission, and today was the perfect opportunity.

For a moment I thought of my wingman, a young pilot on his very first mission. I thought: "Poor Holtmier! He's probably had it by now." In the melee I hadn't had the chance to look after him as I dodged other fighters. I've never worked harder in my life than I did in those few minutes. I made the Thunderbolt do things that were impossible; no German fighter could stay with me, and I was certain that no one else could, either. With most of the Focke-Wulfs running for their lives, I looked around me.

I gasped. There was Holtmier, tacked onto my tail as if he were glued there! How he did it, I'll never know, but there he was dogging my tail. He later told me that, in his battle to stay with me, he hardly remembered seeing a Focke-Wulf. He said he was afraid to get lost from my wing, and I can understand that. What a battle for a first mission! Holtmier did one of the best jobs that any wingman had ever done.

I waved to him and turned to look for anything that even resembled a target. I had almost given up hope of racking the third kill for the day. Six Thunderbolts far below us had grouped together in a climb for altitude, and I radioed them that I would cover their climb. And there, darting from cloud to cloud below them, came a single Messerschmitt Me-109, trying to sneak up on the six Thunderbolts. That boy had nerve, but now he was mine. I called the other fighters. "Cover me; I'm going down after a 109. He's directly beneath you."

I had nearly a ten-thousand-foot dive on the Messerschmitt; the Thunderbolt wound up like a demon and hurtled earthward. I came whistling in on his tail as he skimmed through the cloud tops, confident that he hadn't been spotted. Just as my finger went down on the trigger—he disappeared, swallowed in a cloud. Damn! Here was a perfect setup for a triple and he was gone. There was still a chance; he might decide to stick his head out of the clouds. I must have grinned from ear to ear. Not only did he burst out of the clouds, but he loomed barely 150 yards in front of me, and, obligingly, directly in the center of the gunsight.

It was awfully nice of him to co-operate, I thought, as

I hit the trigger. The Messerschmitt went to pieces and exploded as it disappeared into the clouds. And there was the triple!

Suddenly it had happened. Less than a year before this mission—an impossibly long time, it seemed—my fellow pilots were convinced that I would be the very next man to be shot out of the sky by a German fighter. And now . . . I was the leading ace of all Europe. I could hardly believe it was true. Twenty-two kills, the highest-scoring American fighter pilot in the European Theater!

18

March fifteenth had been a red-letter day for me,* but that night I discovered that I was close to the end of my combat tour. In less than twenty more hours of combat flight time I'd be through—automatically grounded for transfer back to the States. I didn't want that *now!* Things were happening too quickly over Germany for me to quit at this point. I marched to Hub Zemke's office and requested an extension of twenty-five hours' additional combat time.

* *Three months later, combat evaluation and intelligence credited as a confirmed kill one fighter I had claimed only as damaged, bringing the score for this one mission to four kills.*

Normally, after 200 hours, a pilot was rotated back to the States, but apparently my 200 hours were going to be exhausted just when things were hottest. Colonel Zemke smiled; I think he anticipated my request, and granted it immediately. He also had good news for me; only that day my promotion to captain had come through.

Everything now lay in my favor. I was in excellent physical condition, I knew the tactics of the German fighter pilots, and we were entering a period of expected excellent weather. With some luck I might even rack up five kills within a week to reach the magic figure of twenty-seven kills; one more than scored by Eddie Rickenbacker in World War I. Zemke wanted our Group to have the first pilot to reach this coveted mark; he promised that the moment I reached twenty-seven kills, I would be on my way back to the States. I could even pick my missions; Zemke did everything possible to place the magic score in my grasp. And yet, the so-called magic figure wasn't nearly as important as simply staying in the fight. Even if I had the chance to reach twenty-seven, I didn't want to miss out on the full combat extension. Although I saw nothing wrong in getting another five or even ten kills; that's what I was here for!

The opportunity to flame any more German fighters seemed to vanish. On March sixteenth we flew to Friedrichshafen. A new boy on my wing couldn't shake his belly tank, and I ordered him to run for home. He misunderstood; and the golden opportunity slipped by. In a wild melee I had to protect the rookie and pass up several opportunities. Two days later we went back to the same target. I ached for a solid fight, and got little more for my pains than a hell of a scare from some accurate flak gunners. *Too* accurate! On March twentieth, we took off for Frankfurt. At 24,000 feet we were still in the soup; clouds towered far above us. We gave the flak boys some exercise, but no one in my squadron even got nicked. I logged an instrument training flight in my book.

The mission for March twenty-second held tremendous promise—the Flak Highway all the way to Berlin. And I was to lead the squadron; the perfect position to make the initial bounce of German fighters. *But* . . . Hub Zemke took my place. The Group's luck was more than ill; tragedy struck the 56th. When they failed to encounter enemy fighters, one flight leader took his flight through the clouds, into a terrific storm. Funcheon, Stream, and Mussey plunged out of control. They all went into the North Sea. The leader was the sole survivor, and needless to say, felt terrible. Stream had flown *my* best fighter, "Lucky."

I flew an escort mission the next morning. All we saw on the trip to Osnabrück and return were thick clouds, flames gutting the city, and the inevitable flak. Not a single black-crossed fighter. Early the next day, March twenty-fourth, we climbed into our Thunderbolts for a mission to Brunswick. A storm front closed in, visibility disappeared, and we never got off the ground.

I took a break on the twenty-fifth and visited London. While I was gone the Group escorted the Big Friends to Bordeaux and Chartres. They shot down four fighters and burned another on the ground. I was stunned to learn that while I had relaxed in London, Bud Mahurin, Jerry Johnson, Fields and Everett had been lost! Mahurin and Jerry Johnson; I couldn't believe it!

Fields was the first to go. As he raced over an airfield, flak gunners tore up his fighter. Fields bellied in the crippled airplane and before the Thunderbolt stopped sliding along the ground he was outside and running like a gazelle.

The last the boys saw of Fields, he was clearing fences, ditches, and everything else in his way. Jerry Johnson went down to shoot up the airplane so that the Germans couldn't salvage any equipment. He set the Thunderbolt on fire and decided to go after a train passing nearby. Just as he closed in the sides of the train dropped away and several batteries of flak guns came out blazing. That was all for Jerry; he bellied in and slid across a field in a mountain of dust. Jerry climbed out, shook hands jubilantly with a gaping Frenchman, and headed south for Spain, wide open.

Bud Mahurin bounced a Dornier Do-217 bomber running for safety over the treetops. He screamed in at 200 feet and plastered hell out of the Dornier. At the same time the tail gunner poured a stream of shells into Bud's engine. Mahurin waited until the Dornier exploded, and then he bailed out of his burning Thunderbolt. He was still several feet in the air when his feet began to work up a storm. He hit the ground, already running, and really took off. While the boys circled overhead, Bud kept up his hundred-yard dash for a full three miles, and then fell face first into a ditch.

Everett, bless him, went down to try and pick up Jerry Johnson. The terrain was rough, and the hapless Everett caught his wheels in a tree. With his gear snarled and branches tangled in the wheels, Everett ran for home with a wide-open throttle, landing gear still half-down. The air drag burned up his fuel and over the Channel he ran out of gas. He went down with his Thunderbolt. That evening we made bets that the other three would all pass into Spain at the same time that very same night, if they kept running the way they were when last seen.

I went out the morning of March twenty-eighth, for a milk run to Calais. Nothing but flak. Brunswick, on the twenty-ninth, promised action. We ran into some Messerschmitts, but had little chance to do more than chase them off Schilling's tail. Still no action, and now March had passed. Two weeks, and not a chance to rack up a single German fighter since my triple kill on the fifteenth. When were the Krauts going to come up and fight?

A mission on April first to Strasbourg looked promising, but again the Focke-Wulfs and Messerschmitts played coy. A few made a halfhearted appearance several miles from our formations, but fled when we turned toward them. Jimmy Stewart took his flight down to strafe Lille airdome; it was a trap, and the moment the Thunderbolts came into sight of the field all hell erupted. Owen's fighter took a flak burst in the fuel tanks; Stewart screamed wildly, "Bail out, bail out, *you're on fire!*" A heartbroken Stewart chewed up the field in vicious fashion, running so close to the ground that he smashed into a telephone pole. It was impossible, it *couldn't* happen, but the Thunderbolt sheared the pole in two and Stewart came home with a jagged piece of the pole impaled in his wing.

My disgust with the way things were going mounted steadily. On April fifth the Group went out for a strafing mission to Denmark; we received a recall in flight because of a storm front closing in, and returned to base. Three days later we flew a Ramrod to Hesepe. The bombers charged through the flak, plastered hell out of the town, and came home. The Germans were coy again. Action had become so scarce I was determined to quit combat after I completed the tour extension.

Promise on April ninth—a bomber escort all the way to Tutow and Poznan in Poland. Trouble began soon after takeoff. One flight of four had mechanical troubles. Then my wingman complained of engine roughness. Over the Danish coast I sent him home with the number four man, and that left only Sam Hamilton and myself to cover an area originally assigned to eight Thunderbolts.

Over Denmark the Krauts decided to mix it up—*at last.* Sixteen Focke-Wulf FW-190's dropped from high altitude to slam into a Liberator formation, raising havoc with their cannon as they tore through the surprised bombers. As the German fighters dove past the bomber box they pulled up into a sweeping right turn—all sixteen fighters rushing directly at Sam and myself. Well, this was what I'd been trying to find for weeks. Sam and I went at the Focke-Wulfs head-on, breaking up their formation. We turned sharply to swing onto their tails when they rolled and broke for the deck. Hamilton dropped after them; I had new business. The top cover plummeted down to bounce us, and I turned into them. Sam dove after the others. Two FW-190's locked onto my tail while I fought to jettison my frozen belly tank. I had made several turns with the German fighters, rolling away as they came too close, when Sam called excitedly, "Hey, Bob! Come down here and take these bastards off my tail!"

I was tied up for the moment. "Okay, Sam," I called, "just hold out for a few more minutes and I'll be down. I'm pretty busy right now." I rolled sharply to the right and skidded hard, swinging my guns around. The Focke-Wulf pilots quit right then and there; they rolled and dove away. I looked for Sam and couldn't find him; two more Krauts jumped me even as I fought to get rid of my belly tank. Sam was still calling for help; I rolled the Thunderbolt and came around after the Krauts—they dove out of range. But before I could descend to find Sam, two more bounced me. Things were really getting hot!

I shook these two by forcing them to dive when I swung

onto their tails. I spotted Sam 18,000 feet below me, right on the Baltic Sea. Three fighters whirled around in a tight rat race, the Thunderbolt in front with a Focke-Wulf pressing hard on his tail. White splashes geysered from the water where his cannon shells and bullets struck as they snapped out bursts at the harried Sam. "Hang on, boy!" I shouted, "I'm coming. Hang on!" At 450 miles per hour indicated airspeed, the belly tank still refused to jettison. It cut my speed slightly and didn't do me any good in maneuvering, but I was stuck with it.

At 5,000 feet I shallowed my dive to kill speed. The Krauts really had Sam going; he was in serious trouble as one clung to his tail, dangerously close with its tracers. The second Focke-Wulf hung off and every time Sam came around, he rushed in for a head-on attack. Sam knew that if he straightened out even for a second to take a burst at the fighter coming at him, the pilot on his tail would tear him up. So Sam just kept turning and turning. The book says that on the deck the Focke-Wulf can easily turn inside the Thunderbolt, and that the P-47 pilot who tries to turn with the FW-190 is about to commit suicide. I don't know if Sam read the book, but he kept ahead of the pursuing Focke-Wulf, matching him turn for turn, and even gaining on him!

Then Sam started to think. Every time the second Focke-Wulf jumped him for a head-on pass, his .30-caliber nose guns flashing yellow—why, he became a perfect setup for Sam's own guns, and Sam wouldn't even need to bother with his gunsight. Suddenly the battle assumed proportions more to Sam's liking. The moment Sam noticed the flashing of the enemy guns, he squeezed the trigger. It was a sad mistake on the Kraut's part, because he fired only two popguns against Sam's eight heavy .50-calibers.

And that rang down the curtain. Sam placed a burst

into the Focke-Wulf's engine; flame erupted, a wing tore off, and a stream of slugs ripped into the cockpit. This unnerved the character on Sam's tail; for a second he wavered in his turn as he looked up at me and noticed the belly tank jammed on my fighter. Before he could decide whether or not to jump my plane—an easier mark with the restricting tank—Sam's Thunderbolt screamed around in a wicked turn and locked onto the Kraut's tail, and out across the water they went. Cruising 500 feet above the two fighters, I watched Sam's first kill smash into the water.

Before I settled back to watch the second fighter go down, habit brought my head swiveling around to look behind me. I was just in time to see a Focke-Wulf bouncing, nose twinkling from the .30-calibers. My left hand slammed forward on the throttle, my right hand hauled back and left on the stick, my heart went to the top of my head and the Thunderbolt leaped upward. I racked the Jug into a tight left climbing turn, staying just above and in front of the pursuing Focke-Wulf. Those wonderful paddle blades! To get any strikes on me the Kraut first had to turn inside me, and then haul his nose up steeply to place his bullets ahead of me. The Focke-Wulf just didn't have it. At 8,000 feet he stalled out while the Thunderbolt roared smoothly; I kicked over into a roll and locked onto his tail.

He was coming *at* me! I had slipped into firing position when he whipped around in a 180-degree turn; I've never seen a tighter or quicker turn in a fighter—*any* fighter—in my life. That man was *good!* He didn't even turn, I thought, just suddenly reversed his flight and ran at me. Several times we rushed at each other, and then I started firing inside bursts as he weaved toward the land. It worked. Twice he ran into a stream of my bullets. The Focke-Wulf snapped over in a steep turn and ran for the coastline.

I didn't want this boy to reach home. The canopy leaped into the air as the pilot jerked the release; I pulled around tight to get my bullets into him before he could get out of the airplane. He had one leg outside the cockpit when the slugs smashed him back inside. That's one man who would never sight again on our planes; if I hadn't gotten him, then he certainly would have shot down several of our fighters or bombers. He was as good as I'd ever met.

Number Twenty-three!

The next morning, April tenth, we resumed the hunt with a short mission to Brussels. I didn't relish the mission, for it had been so long since we'd met any opposition over Brussels that we had come to regard the area as friendly. The Luftwaffe kept it that way, too, and we played tag with the flak. A strafing sweep to Oldenburg was the order of the day for April twelfth, but the Krauts greeted us with a terrifying flak barrage. We were half scared to death before we got out of there. On the way home Sam Hamilton and Herron blew hell out of a canal barge and then scouted around for targets. As they approached a canal there appeared suddenly from behind a barn an old German farmer driving a wagon. A little boy hugged his knees in desperate fear as the two red-nosed Thunderbolts howled low over the ground. The farmer was frantic with his own fear, whipping his horses, trying to get the terrified animals to run. The sight of that little boy in such desperate fear shook up the two pilots; they quit their strafing runs and resumed formation.

Not until April thirteenth, on a bomber escort to Munich, did the Krauts come upstairs to mix it up. Three Focke-Wulfs climbed through cloud cover to sneak in a burst at the Big Friends; I spotted their shadows and let the 61st Squadron down for a bounce. My shells streamed into an FW-190 as he disappeared in a cloud; just my luck—a perfect setup and I had to lose him! Only—I didn't! As I rolled in a climb over the top of the cloud, the Focke-Wulf burst out of the mists, almost in formation with me, and exploded. The pilot had bailed out in the safety of the clouds as his ship started to burn. My wingman almost ran into him; the German pulled his shroud lines frantically—convinced he was a target. But my wingman was even more surprised to find the German there!

Number Twenty-four!

From 15,000 feet I noticed a flicker of light, miles to the east and right on the deck, the kind of light that flashes off a canopy. I dropped the nose and angled off to check; sure enough, a Focke-Wulf hedgehopping at high speed, fat and sassy by himself. He never saw my approach, and I closed the distance rapidly between our planes. I wanted a solid burst at 200 yards; too eager, blast it! He'd seen me, and abruptly the Focke-Wulf whipped up in a steep chandelle to the right, neatly eluding my guns. The Kraut decided to slug it out; after all, the advantages were his. The Thunderbolt was strictly a high-altitude fighter, and easy meat when on the deck—or so someone had told him. He came in fast in a head-on attack, and rolled to his left to break. I kicked left rudder, squeezed the trigger and held it down. Perfect; the Focke-Wulf ran directly into my stream of bullets. White bursts of light flashed all over his wing-roots and cockpit. That took all the fight out of him; he raced into a cloud, and I hung to his tail, squeezing out bursts. Then he disappeared into the mists, and I pulled up. I banked steeply to hit him when he came out, but the fight was over. A flaming mass hurtled into the ground and exploded.

Twenty-five!

19

With my twenty-fifth German fighter shot down in aerial combat, good luck fled with the wind. Storm fronts with their towering cloud masses, with fog and cold, a blowing nightmare of rain and sleet, rumbled heavily in from the North Sea to obscure earth, sky and ocean. More than once I took off in the Thunderbolt, only to disappear within the grey and endless mists that robbed all sight. And each time I fought my way back to our base, flying by instruments, staring at the glowing dials and needles in front of me, the world outside the windscreen of the fighter dissolved to a shapeless limbo. "Scratch the mission." There is little sanity in struggling through hundreds of miles of violent storm, of fighting winds and lashing torrents of rain.

I flew on days when the clouds fled, when the stratus and cumulus, and the low, sweeping scud disappeared as if they never had been. All Europe then lay naked to eyes from on high, the coastlines imprisoned by water black and green. On such days the dust and moisture of the air lay captured within the lower heights, and the upper ramparts were swept clean, an arena of crystal clarity and infinite vision, blockaded only by the eventual curvature of the earth. On these days the lower stratosphere was invaded by swift black and silver shapes. Each such creature of steel and whirling propeller blades, of power and beauty, painted its own signature, a cottony swath of vapor in the heavens, streaming magically behind each fighter almost as if the killer airplanes sought in vain to flee from the pursuing condensation. When the bombers massed, wheeled majestically, then the vapor trails became the equal of major meteorological phenomena.

Massive brush strokes in the highest realm, deep and thick and solid, the calling cards of the giants marching in a thunder of thousands of powerful engines, sound waves flung from hurtling blades, chopped out of the cold air to rumble with the giants' footsteps the long miles to earth, beating sonorously, heavily, upon the land. The marching of the city destroyers, a reverberation of warning upon German soil, of unbelievable agony to be flung throughout the cities.

Day after day the finest of Germany, the elite eagles of the Luftwaffe, stayed on the ground rather than storm the aerial phalanx. Before, they had struck with savage fury, spilling blood and steel the length of their land. Now their fighters hesitated, their ranks shorn of numbers by the scythe of our Thunderbolts, the Lightnings and Mustangs. Not a man among us accepted the German as second-rate, or cowardly, or unable to fight; more and more, however, the enemy fighters remained on the ground while thousands of tons of steel and fire and concussion waves maimed the cities which had grown through long hundreds of years, and shattered the factories of a newer age.

And when the Aryan sons did fight, it was my cursed luck to miss the brunt of the action, to be far to the left of the endless bomber stream when the Focke-Wulfs and Messerschmitts hammered at the right. Here I sought battle with all my will, but the struggles raged in wild fury in the air space all about, but never close, to me. My missions came and went. I grew weary in the straps and harness and the tight-fitting mask, restricted within the Thunderbolt's cockpit. When combat was joined, it became my misfortune to meet enemy pilots who had lost their stomach for battle, who fled headlong into clouds to race for safety.

Only the flak failed to disappoint us, only the flak was ever present. Germany was no longer a nation as such; she had become a bristling pit of antiaircraft weapons, a land armed to the teeth with great guns that spewed torrents of steel, smoke and flame into the air. The rivers of flak, tortured and twisting, churning almost as if in pain, convulsed with angry red and black smoke. Without the flak, without the terrible highways, Germany for days on end would have lain defenseless before the assembled might of the bombers. But the flak never slept, never rested, never roared without inflicting agony and losses.

The amazing thing about this war in the high air is that there were so many ways to die. I had read about and for weary hours listened to the defenders of the men who fight across the ground, and those who battle on and within the cold oceans. They prattle that it is the airman who enjoys the easiest role in war, that death when it comes in the air is swift and clean. They say this, and can say it, only because they do not fly, and do not fight in the air. The men who crewed the Big Friends know far better than I—and I do not wish to know—the variety of deaths that can be found in the roaring holocaust of a blazing four-engined bomber.

From the cockpit of my Thunderbolt, I one day witnessed a sight so grisly, so horrifying, that I am glad few men, indeed, can ever have such a scene imbedded in their memories. It occurred during a mission all the way to Berlin, the flight over the familiar Flak Highway to the center of German power. On this day the Luftwaffe rose to do battle, and the fighters clashed by the hundreds.

I hunted for a target, eager for the fight which might bring the victories I had sought in vain for weeks. No luck; everywhere I looked the Thunderbolts, Lightnings and Mustangs raced after their fleeing quarry, determined to run the Germans clear out of their sky. Ten thousand feet below me a silver-blue Mustang streaked after a Messerschmitt Me-109, the enemy plane dodging and twisting, trying to outrun the faster, more maneuverable American fighter. The Messerschmitt was doomed; it was only a matter of seconds before the tracers flashing away from the pursuing Mustang struck home. And even if the German did elude the P-51, I had dropped to a thousand feet above the Mustang, covering his attack. Either the Mustang or my Thunderbolt would make the kill.

The end came, a long burst of tracers into the German wing, white flashes of light dancing across the black cross, walking their way toward the cockpit. More strikes; the Mustang pilot poured it in. A flash, and then dirty black smoke streamed back from the engine, the beginning of disaster. Immediately the canopy flew back, the German pilot threw himself away from his burning airplane. Almost at once I saw his hand jerk toward the D-ring.

But the Mustang was too close! Directly behind the German fighter, rushing in with superior speed to be certain of the kill, the P-51 had closed to minimum distance. The German pilot rushed back through the air, tumbling slowly. Before the parachute began to open, the hurtling form smashed into the Mustang's spinner and whirling propeller blades!

I have never seen a more horrible sight in my life; for interminable seconds time was frozen. Stunned, I seemed to see the ghastly scene unfolding in slow motion. The impact of the pilot's body crushed the large spinner, flattening the heavy metal to a crumpled disc. For an instant the German's midsection hung impaled on this metal, then, following the rush of the limbs and the head, was flung into the grinding propeller blades.

The human form *shredded*. Nothing recognizable emerged from that terrible flashing of blades.

The startled Mustang pilot jerked back his canopy to bail out. To him the impact of the hurtling German flier was the same as a terrible explosion, and there was no time to waste in abandoning his airplane. The damaged propeller blades, plus the distortion of air rumbling past the crushed spinner, imparted to the sleek fighter a seemingly disastrous vibration.

But the airplane could fly. I dropped slightly ahead and to the side of the crippled Mustang, waving for the pilot to remain in his cockpit. Another Thunderbolt dropped off the Mustang's other wing, an escort to try to bring the damaged fighter back to England.

The pilot gave it a try. Crippled and difficult to fly, the Mustang nevertheless remained in the air, shepherded by our fighters. We were lucky; the Germans didn't care to bother us. The Channel slipped beneath our wings, and we began the long descent to the Mustang's home field.

We followed him in closely, staying alongside as his wheels lowered and the flaps dropped down. He didn't bother with the traffic pattern; anxious to rid himself of his bloody machine, the pilot rushed earthward in a straight approach to the runway. His wheels touched, and the plane screeched to a halt as we roared overhead in a steep turn. As we circled and came back, barely fifty feet over the ground, the pilot climbed from the Mustang, staring in horror at his airplane. Unable to control himself, he became violently ill. We poured the coal to the Thunderbolts and turned for home.

Nearly a month had passed since my twenty-fifth kill. When I prepared for a bomber escort to Berlin on the morning of May eighth, I was downhearted to realize that this was to be my last mission. In recent weeks the Germans had virtually abandoned Berlin to a slow death by explosion and fire. Few raids were contested by the Luftwaffe, and May eighth bore no promise of any more action than we'd seen in nearly a month. Our orders were to fly a diversion route to the south of the main bomber stream, to intercept any German fighters that might form in the air for an attack from the south against the Big Friends. The weather report of heavy clouds and poor visibility, with a thick and obscuring ground haze, didn't make matters any more promising.

The bombers rumbled overhead as early as five thirty in the morning, a roar echoed back into the dark sky from the Thunderbolts being revved up for power checks by the crew chiefs. It was a big show, five hundred Flying Fortresses to dump a thousand tons of hell into the heart of Berlin, three hundred Liberators to strike at Brunswick with another eight hundred tons. The 56th Fighter Group split into two forces to disperse effectively its escort strength.

Over the European coastline we kicked our fighters into battle formations, weaving 15 degrees to one side and then back again to evade the ever-alert flak batteries. For several minutes after landfall the flak remained light and sporadic; as we deepened our penetration, every little town and every clump of trees seemed to come alive with the angry muzzle flashes of the heavy batteries. But only flak; no company in the air. We cut into Germany along the northern end of Happy Valley, cursing the clouds that billowed up in thick masses. For a while visibility grew so bad that we flew on instruments, breaking in and out of the blinding clouds. Then we were due south of Brunswick; the formation wheeled and took up a new course to the north and the main bomber stream.

My disgust mounted. I had remaining only five and a half hours of combat time; when the last minute went, I would be finished with the combat tour and the extension. The thought of flying my last mission on a milk run with absolutely nothing happening appalled me. Up to this moment I still had time remaining to break out of formation and run for home; I would land with enough time to fly another mission during which the Luftwaffe might show signs of life. I was so disgusted I tried to find serious fault with the airplane so that I could claim a mechanical failure and abort the mission. As it was, I had a headache, the engine was running rough, and I thought the prop was going to come off. The more I thought about it the worse things became. I could just make it back to the base with perhaps a half hour left to complete my tour; enough to justify another flight into Germany. And that made up my mind; I pressed down the radio button and began my call to Joe Perry to have him take over.

I made one final study of the bombers—a B-17 exploded with a dazzling glare! There they were; fighters diving through the formations. Suddenly my headache was gone and the big Pratt & Whitney purred smoothly. I stabbed my finger down and yelled, "The bombers are being hit— let's go get 'em!"

We turned to the left, throttles wide open as we raced to take the fighters off the Big Friends. As we neared the long line of Fortresses, a Messerschmitt Me-209 burst out of the formations in a screaming dive, passing directly below me. I rolled over and pulled back on the stick; the Thunderbolt clawed around and in a moment I was tacked onto his tail. Almost at once the stream of exhaust smoke stopped; he had cut his throttle and at the same moment pulled his fighter into a tight left turn. The same old mistake! The moment the smoke cut out I chopped power, skidded up to my right, back on the stick, and rolled inside his turn, firing steadily in short bursts. The Kraut glanced back to see a skyful of Thunderbolt wing spitting fire directly at him. I know he thought that I had cut inside of his own turn; he straightened out and the smoke reappeared as he tried to run for safety in a wide-open power dive, rolling steadily as he dropped. They never learn, I suppose.

The Thunderbolt flung herself after the Messerschmitt. My Jug followed his every move, rolling with him every foot of the way, snapping out bursts. The white flashes leaped all over the black-crossed airplane. Suddenly the Thunderbolt's diving speed brought me *too* close; I rolled over the Me-209 just as his left wing tore off and flipped away. I flashed directly over the disintegrating fighter, still upside down. I rolled back to level flight and hauled back on the stick to zoom upstairs, looking for trouble.

I glanced behind me; the entire flight was still there, all three planes in battle formation, covering me while the rest of the Group bounced other German fighters. We reformed our formation and raced for the bombers. My Number Three man called, "Bandits below at three o'clock heading for the clouds." I couldn't see the fighters. "Go after them," I radioed, "I'll cover you." With his wingman tacked tightly behind him, he rolled over and disappeared into the mists. They burst out of the clouds like greased lightning, three Focke-Wulfs on their tails, blazing away with cannon and guns. "Turn tight left and climb!" I shouted. Both Thunderbolts flipped neatly away from the line of fire.

The three Focke-Wulfs raced over in trail, holding a tight left-turning circle. I rushed the lead German, firing in short bursts to force him to break off the pursuit. The Focke-Wulf rolled away, and I swung my nose to bear on the second plane. Hits! All over the wings and wingroots, and there it was. Number Twenty-seven; rolling over slowly, a dead man at the controls, fire flaring from the engine as the ship eased into a dive. The Focke-Wulf hurtled down and exploded as it struck the ground, 4,000 feet below my wing. The third broke for home.

That was it—the fight was over! And just in time; my last mission couldn't have been more perfect.

My fighter was still rolling when "Pappy" Gould and the other crewmen raced toward me, shouting, "How many?" They'd seen the tape missing from my guns and knew at once that we'd been in a scrap. I grinned and held aloft two fingers. *That* did it; they went wild with joy. The moment I taxied the Thunderbolt to the line and climbed out,

Generals Griswold and Auton were on the spot to congratulate me. Apparently a great many people were sweating out this mission! Photographers were waiting for me to land and the moment my fingers gave the sign of two kills they closed in, flash bulbs popping. But the best greeting came from Hub Zemke. Grinning broadly, he grasped my hand and said, "Get the hell out of here, Johnson. You're going home!"

20

From twelve thousand feet the world no longer existed; beneath the wings of the speeding Skymaster transport rolled an unbroken expanse of billowing white clouds, dazzling in their reflection of a glaring sun. Clouds below stretched away forever, infinity above. Through the cockpit glass we seemed barely to move as the endless fairyland drifted slowly beneath us, a strange and unreal suspension between turbulent atmosphere and vacuum. The minutes and hours existed only in the sweep of the chronometer's dial hands, and in the knowledge that even as we seemed to drift in the never-never world of flight, I was actually speeding toward the United States and home.

It had been a strange departure, for only minutes before the pilot moved the black throttle knobs forward and imparted life to the four-engine giant, we received the news flash that the long-awaited invasion had begun. After all these months, the streams of Big Friends marching through the terrifying flak, staggering beneath the savage fury of the German fighters, the lash of cannon shells and bullets and fiery rockets, it had come to pass. This was my only regret about the eagerly sought return home; my realization that the final battle had been joined, that even during those same moments when we droned in isolation over the unseen ocean, my friends were plummeting into the German fighters high over Europe. It was a battle for which I had long waited, and now I would miss the culmination of all our twisting fights against the best the Luftwaffe had to throw against us.

In the days subsequent to my last combat mission, I listened at every opportunity to the short-wave radio that brought to England the voices of my fellow pilots as they hammered down the German fliers who desperately sought to destroy our bomber streams. I could never quite accept the fact that in England I could hear the actual progress of battle over the Continent. And only through this separation from the fight did I come to realize how greatly things had changed since our arrival in England early in 1943.

Four days after my last mission the Group escorted the Big Friends to Frankfurt. The Ramrod proved uneventful, and then the Thunderbolts spread out in the 56th's newest maneuver—the Zemke Fan. In flights of four, the Thunderbolts fanned out over Germany, spoiling for trouble. On this day they found it, and I hung to the edge of my chair with tension as their voices crackled over the airwaves. The

boys were excited, shouting to each other of enemy sight-
ings. Hub Zemke stumbled into the midst of a giant enemy
formation and was calling for help. A Focke-Wulf shot his
wingman to pieces and the remaining three Thunderbolts
were being battered by the overwhelming German force.

Another voice broke in, a flight leader calling to Thunderbolts high over his own four fighters: "Hey, there's four
of us down here on top of sixteen Focke-Wulfs! C'mon down
and help us let loose of 'em! There's plenty for everybody!"

Nothing could top Johnny Eaves that day. Gasping for
breath, panting, his excited voice burst over the radio: "I'm
(gasp) down here (gasp) by myself . . ." He paused
to suck in air: "I'm chasing (gasp) thirty 109's. I'm about
(gasp) to catch 'em!" He nearly choked with excitement:
"You'd (gasp) better hurry up! It's going to be a (gasp)
hell of a fight!"

And he meant exactly what he was saying! Single-
handed, Johnny screamed in a dive into the midst of thirty
Messerschmitt Me-109's, rolling onto the formation, firing
steadily. Two German fighters burst into flames before his
guns and he damaged several others. He had every advantage with him and Johnny went wild, throwing his Thunderbolt in head-on passes at anything that appeared in the
air. He not only shot down two and damaged several others,
but scattered the rest.

As I listened to Johnny Eaves's incredible fight, I recalled
when we had first entered combat. We flew beautiful formation, we were cocky and imbued with the feeling of our
strength. And all two little Focke-Wulfs had to do was to
fly right down the middle of our pretty formation and we
wouldn't know what to do except to sit there and shake!
Now one, just one, of our men didn't hesitate a moment to

plunge into thirty enemy fighters to scatter them all. The changes during our eighteen months in Europe were, to say the least, profound.

Bob Rankin, a little, wiry professional musician, played a lethal tune with his eight guns and shot down *five* fighters in a single, incredible battle. He jumped a German echelon formation, rushing at the end fighter. Guns flaming, he went right down the line, the Thunderbolt's terrible firepower tearing apart the enemy planes. Two more German pilots to Bob's right watched what was happening— and bailed out! Not an American fighter was behind them; but the sight of Bob Rankin having himself a ball was too much for them. The entire Group had a ball. We lost three men, but the 56th shot down eighteen German fighters, and put a new figure of four hundred enemy aircraft destroyed on the scoreboard. The Germans just didn't seem to be the "supermen" that we had first met high over Europe. And I had to miss the gravy that I had helped prepare!

Saying goodbye to these people had been the toughest thing I had ever done. I walked about the airbase, stopping in to see all the men with whom I'd lived on the ground, and fought with as a team in the air. The thoughts of going home, of seeing Barbara and my folks, had me feeling terrific. I waved at the replacements, new pilots to whom I was the old and grizzled veteran. Then I came across Jim Carter and Eastwood, Gabby and Chuck Howard and the rest of the "old" gang. I just fell apart at the seams. I tried to talk, but it was impossible. My throat was choked solid. All I could do was to grasp their hands, turn my head, and run. I couldn't get over the feeling that I was walking out on these guys. They had come to Europe with me, and now I was going home, while they stayed behind.

It had been the same thing all over again with my crew-men, who had sweated and struggled to keep my Thunder-bolt in perfect shape, to bring me back from every mission. These were all men with whom I had lived and fought, not only in combat but in fun in our rooms, at parties. I'd cussed with them and we'd gotten drunk together. Several had saved my life. My eyes were more than a little damp. It was too much; I got away from the field as quickly as I could.

And then I boarded the big Skymaster, grateful for the invitation from the pilots to join them in the cockpit to fly the airplane. For five hours I brushed aside my personal thoughts and flew the four-engined transport, wrapped in the beauty of the endless clouds and the serenity of the long, undisturbed flight. We landed for fuel at a West Ice-land base, a wicked landing in the teeth of a raging gale. Take off, and climb into blinding mist, a ceaseless wind that shrieked and hammered at the giant transport. For ten hours we struggled through the blinding storm, jolted se-verely, the two pilots up front flying strictly on intruments, blind men with electronic eyes, a magic seeking of the flight path. Long hours of shaking, thundering flight, and finally a breakout, the four engines pulling up higher and higher until finally, the Skymaster found calmer air, a layer of visibility between the storm below and high clouds above.

Approaching Greenland, we faced a towering thunder-storm, a true giant that reared more than ten miles above the ocean. We veered from our course, grateful for the sud-den spaces that split the storm front below, that showed the glaciers and giant crevices in ice. The sun broke through above us, and the ice became a dazzling panorama of sparkling jewels, with vivid green and blue lakes caught on mountainsides or isolated within the long rivers of ice.

Darkness came, bringing overhead the familiar cover of stars. A sudden and wonderful transformation, the storms far behind us, peace and solitude within an air ocean incredibly at rest. Touchdown at Newfoundland and another wonder awaiting—the first real ham, real eggs, real coffee, and the first white bread I had seen in more than a year and a half! We *were* getting close to home.

The minutes began to drag. We were so close! In the darkness of another night the coastline began to change. Canada below, and then the four engines rushed us toward the United States, toward New York, where Barbara waited. The minutes dragged on and on, the engines droned quietly, a soothing and gentle sound. I fell asleep.

When I awoke, we were letting down, losing altitude slowly as we headed for LaGuardia Airport in New York. I nearly fell out of the airplane when I looked outside. *Lights!* Lights on the ground! It was fantastic; I hadn't seen the lights of buildings or cities from the air, or even from the ground, for more than eighteen months. I stared and stared; another world lay below me. The sight was dazzling, the ribbons and rows and whorls of lights, red and yellow and white and green and blue and amber—all the colors, twinkling, staring, glowing across an earth that I had nearly forgotten existed. Below our wings were scattered clouds; I strained to see through the mists and breaks to study that wonderful, wonderful sight. We flew south of LaGuardia to drop below the clouds, then turned, sweeping low over the city, resplendent and dazzling and utterly marvelous in its brilliant sheen. The broad wings lifted, banked, and we glided to earth. Water below, the big lights in the wings bringing the propellers into stark relief.

I flew every inch of that approach. Not in the cockpit, but still just as much up front as if I sat in the pilot's seat. I felt the nose coming up, the easing of power, instinctively I moved my hands and feet. The Skymaster broke out of her glide, flared above the runway, settled like a feather. That wonderful, gentle touch of rubber against macadam, the nose wheel settling, our speed falling off. *We were home!*

Every move of that airplane, every creak of the gear as we taxied, the squeal of brakes, and bare rumble of the flaps moving back into the wings—it was music. I felt the final dipping of the nose on its gear leg as the brakes locked, the tired sound of engines dying and propellers slowing in their revolutions. Then the ship was quiet, the only sounds and movement from her passengers and crew. And the one final sound of the door opening, the inrush of moist and wonderful air. I breathed deeply, enjoying to the full the wonder of it all.

On the steps I looked for Barbara. I couldn't see her; perhaps she was waiting inside for me. I asked the ground attendant; he didn't know a thing. Two Air Force majors came up to me and asked, "Are you Bob Johnson?" I nodded. "Where's my wife?"

"Oh, you can't see her now," one spoke. "In fact, you can't call anyone. We have orders directly from General Arnold. You're to transfer to another airplane immediately and fly to Washington. We have the plane all ready for you." My wonder at being home quickly dissolved into anger. "I'm not going anywhere for a while, mister," I snapped. "I haven't seen my wife in more than eighteen months, and I'm not leaving this field until I do see her." Barbara, I knew, was only several miles away, and I had no intention of dashing off to Washington when she was so close. The two majors seemed to be on the verge of apoplexy; I demanded a telephone. It took ten minutes to get the call through, but finally I spoke directly to the general. I explained the situation, and almost shouted with joy as he laughed, "Why, Lord, boy, bring her along!" I felt like a new man.

I called Barbara. She was sleeping when the phone rang. I started to say something to her when she recognized my voice and shrieked, "Bob!" In between our strangled conversation of happiness and half crying I managed to tell her to get to the airport just as fast as she could. And she made it in record time. When she stepped out of the cab . . .

It was almost like starting to live all over again. That night in Washington I hung out our hotel window for two hours, drinking in the marvel of all the lights and cars and people. What a sight! Lights everywhere! I closed my eyes and expected that when I opened them the dream would vanish, that there would be a blackout, the streets in darkness, the sounds of the night filtering through the deep and oppressive sightlessness. But no—there they were, all gleaming and shining. Wonderful!

The Air Force dragged us all through the Pentagon. We met generals and colonels and important civilians by the dozen. They took our pictures and did everything possible to make us feel that we truly were special. Every now and then I'd see a familiar face, and *then* I'd feel a bit at home in this incredible world of high brass. In a whirlwind of visits I walked around, up, down, through the Pentagon. Congressman Jed Johnson (another Johnson!) from my home state, a close friend of our families, brought Barbara and me to the Senate. It was almost too much to accept in so short a time—Major and Mrs. Robert S. Johnson being introduced to the entire Senate of the United States.

Later that day I was taken to visit the President. When I walked into his office, the very air seemed to be hushed; I was filled with an overwhelming sense of the responsibilities carried and fulfilled within this single room. He looked up and smiled at me as I stood before his desk. "You're kind of young to be a major, aren't you, son?" The Congressman spoke for several minutes, relating briefly my tour in Europe. President Roosevelt looked at me steadily. "No," he mused, "I suppose you're not so very young after all."

When we returned to the Pentagon I was introduced to Dick Bong, one of the hottest pilots in the Air Force. Flying a twin-engine Lightning fighter with the 5th Air Force, Dick had shot down twenty-seven Japanese aircraft, the first AAF pilot to do so. Against his protests, he was yanked out of combat and sent back to the States. When we met, he stared at me for several moments, and then smiled. "Well," he sighed, "I'm glad to see that you're a little guy, too." We managed to find an office where we could be alone for a while, where we discussed our future plans. Dick had been dragged around the country to make speeches for war-bond rallies. "I've got this coming out of my ears," he complained in disgust. "Johnson, I'm sure glad to see you. You can sort of help me to bear up under this nonsense." He laughed. "It's worse than having a Zero on your tail!"

Dick and I were ushered into the office of General Henry "Hap" Arnold, the Commanding General of the Army Air Forces. We discussed our combat and spent perhaps a half hour together with the Old Man. When I was alone with Arnold, he asked, "Where's your wife, Bob?" I told him she was waiting for me downstairs. "Well, don't just stand there," he barked. "Go get her!" For several minutes the general fired questions at Barbara about me and then, without warning, interrupted her replies.

"Barbara, how would you two like to fly home?" There was

only one answer to *that,* and Arnold grinned like a school-
boy as he punched a button on the wall. In came General
Giles. "General," Arnold said, "give this boy and his wife
an airplane and a pilot, and let them go anyplace in the
country they want to go. That's official." What a man!

At our disposal was a twin-engined Lockheed Hudson
bomber. Personal transportation home, and we were eter-
nally grateful to the "Old Man." On the morning of June
eleventh we took off from New York and settled down for
the long flight to Oklahoma. Over Tennessee a storm front
covered the ground, but finally the clouds broke and a
brilliant sun cast its golden warmth over the land. Little by
little the landscape grew familiar until, across the Oklahoma border and nearing Lawton, every inch of the countryside fitted into place, as familiar to me at the moment
as it had been those many years before. Only . . . the boy
pilot was history, and the dreams had all come true.

Our landing at Post Field was like closing the pages on a
long and eventful book. How very long ago was it that I
stared from my father's shoulders at the three little pursuits
as they wove their enchanting spell in the sky! Sixteen years
earlier the dream had been created, and subsequently had
been pursued, shaped and lived. And now the story was
full circle, a return sixteen years later to those moments
when I had resolved to be the *best* Army flier ever.

I came home as my country's leading fighter pilot, bask-
ing in acclaim and in new and rich friendships. Now that
I had reached the pinnacle sought so eagerly and for so
long, I knew that the "best" was a misleading description,
indeed. There is not, and never will be, a singular "best"
among any of us who fly and fight together.

I had learned far more in those wild and lethal battles
high over Germany than merely to outthink and outfight

any German opponents. I learned that each fighter pilot who flies, wildly free and more independent than any other man can be, is, strangely, never "alone." I would have been dead several times over in the substratosphere war over Germany without the concern, the skill, and courage of the men with whom I flew.

My final tally showed twenty-eight German fighter planes shot down in aerial combat, a figure of which I am proud.* The victories were not mine alone. Behind me were a long succession of men who loved flying, who were imbued with skill and courage and a belief in what they were doing. The line goes back to my youth, when the skill of others was first passed on to me. It ran all the way through my instruction as a cadet, to my first introduction to that tremendous weapon, the Thunderbolt. My strength came from my squadron and group commanders who burned the midnight oil devising the tactics to bring us victory, to return as many of us as possible to our home airbase after each struggle. I fought no war alone over Germany.

There was what I must accept as my own extraordinary good fortune. Jerry Johnson and Bud Mahurin were superb pilots, tremendously skilled and courageous. No German pilot sent them crashing to earth. The 56th Group carried the blazing guns of their Thunderbolts with increasing devastation to the Germans after my departure. No greater pilot ever flew than Gabreski, who went on to surpass my own record of twenty-eight kills, to become the leading fighter pilot of our forces in Europe with thirty-one German planes shot down in battle. The day before he was to fly

---

* I recently learned that Dick Bong at that time also had a probable which was later confirmed for his twenty-eighth victory. I am proud to say that at one time I was tied with Major Bong, who returned to combat to bring his total to forty aerial victories. He remains our leading ace.

his last mission, racing low over the German field at Coblenz, Gabby's propeller smashed into a mound on the field. Not a bullet brought him down, but he had no alternative except to crash his plane deliberately at nearly 250 miles per hour, an incredible maneuver from which he escaped without a scratch. Gabby ended the war in a prison camp. Who knows how high his tally would have reached except for that twist of misfortune that grasped his whirling propeller in the midst of an enemy airfield?

Fate often took strange turns with our fighter pilots, and so bizarre were the deaths that befell several of our outstanding fliers that each time I reflect on these events I can only give thanks for my own return home. No single case can better illustrate my point than the disaster that brought our own troops to cause the death of Major George E. Preddy, a brilliant Mustang pilot. In August of 1944 Preddy in a wild six minutes over Hamburg shot down six enemy planes. On Christmas Day of that same year he shot down two Messerschmitts to bring his score to twenty-six enemy planes destroyed in the air. He then pursued a Focke-Wulf; anxious American flak gunners, who tried to trap the German fighter, hurled a stream of explosive shells into the air. They missed the German, but tore Preddy's fighter apart, sending it spinning into the ground.

I have never permitted my own accomplishments to blind me to the intricate events which brought me safely back to the United States, and which claimed the lives of my closest friends through circumstances utterly beyond their control.

I regret having had to miss flying wing with the 56th Fighter Group during some of its most violent combat actions. Less than four months after my departure from England the Group went on the deck in a flak-busting mission, an assignment which is perhaps the most vicious and dangerous for a fighter pilot. Every flier dreads the moments when he sweeps at minimum altitude over nests of flak batteries, waiting until the guns actually fire so that he can determine their locations by the muzzle blasts. Then he must return to shoot it out. On September eighteenth, the mission ended with sixteen Thunderbolts shot down, and half of the returning fighters badly mauled. Sixteen planes down—and not a single Thunderbolt lost to a German pilot!

By the end of the war, the 56th Fighter Group had compiled a tremendous record. During the two years of fighting we lost 128 Thunderbolts in combat operations. At this grievous cost, the pilots of the 56th destroyed one thousand and six German aircraft, a ratio of eight to one against the toughest opposition which any American pilots have ever met.

Those battles in the sky high over Europe and Germany belong now to an era which has become history. The moments of the fighting, of the courage and skill, the exultation of victory and the despair over close friends lost, remain alive and clear only in the minds of us who flew during those years so long ago.

I shall not forget those moments, either now, or in the years to come. They were the proudest of my life.

EPILOGUE

Following the war I resigned my active duty air corps commission and continued flying in the reserve as Deputy Commanding Officer of the 26th Air Division protecting the Atlantic Coast from Maine to Florida. The 26th was based at Mitchel Field on Long Island. Later on, I was employed by Republic Aviation (builder of the P-47) as a test pilot with additional efforts in the Republic sales department.

As a Republic test pilot, I was able to convince the USAF that flight instruments should be located in the center of the cockpit instrument panel – directly in front of the pilots vision line of sight where they ought to be. This suggestion resulted in the standard location of instruments on all aircraft panels worldwide.

I remained with Republic until they were absorbed by Fairchild. An opportunity to go with another aviation company was presented to me but I decided to venture into the insurance business as an agent. My new career turned out to be a good decision for Barbara and me and is why we ended up where we decided to settle down – on a beautiful lake in South Carolina.

Barbara, the love of my life, is gone now, and I sorely miss her. I enjoy visiting with old friends and talking about the old days, now many years ago. I continue to fly – now and then – in anything available, and will do so as long as our good Father above will allow me!

Robert S. Johnson
August, 1997

Robert S. Johnson died December 27, 1998 after a short illness. He was on a Christmas family visit to Tulsa, Oklahoma. His ashes were buried January 2, 1999 in Lake Wiley, South Carolina with full military honors, including a "Missing Plane" Flyby formation of F-16's flown into the teeth of an approaching massive ice storm just closing into the Lake Wiley area. The storm struck the Memorial Service just as the thunder of the Flyby faded away into the distance – as if Mother Nature had held off her storm fury until after Colonel Johnson had been honored.

Ed. Y. Hall
Honoribus Press